3|03

WITHDRAWN

❖ **SACRED DOORWAYS**

A BEGINNER'S GUIDE TO ICONS

SACRED DOORWAYS

A BEGINNER'S GUIDE TO ICONS

LINETTE MARTIN

PARACLETE PRESS

BREWSTER, MASSACHUSETTS

All Scripture quotations, unless otherwise indicated, are taken from the Holy Bible, New International Version, NIV, © 1973, 1978, 1984 by International Bible Society. Used by permission of Zondervan Publishing House. All rights reserved.

Scripture quotations designated (RSV) are from the Revised Standard Version of the Bible, © 1946, 1952, 1971 by the Division of Christian Education of the National Council of the Churches of Christ in the USA. Used by permission.

Scripture quotations designated (KJV) are from the King James Version of the Bible.

Portions of the chapter "Icons and Prayer" have been used and adapted from *Practical Praying,* © 1997 Linette Martin, William B. Eerdmans Publishing Co. Used by permission.

Library of Congress Cataloging-in-Publication Data

Martin, Linette.
  Sacred doorways : a beginner's guide to icons / Linette Martin.
    p. cm.
Includes bibliographical references.
  ISBN 1-55725-307-2
1. Icons—History. 2. Icon painting—Themes, motives. 3. Christianity and art—Orthodox Eastern Church. 4. Christian art and symbolism. I. Title.
N8187 .M37 2002
704.9'482—dc21   2002011555

10 9 8 7 6 5 4 3 2 1

© 2002 by Joe Walton Martin

ISBN 1-55725-307-2

Published by Paraclete Press
Brewster, Massachusetts
www.paracletepress.com

Printed in the United States of America.

CONTENTS

List of Illustrations   viii

Preface   ix

Bouquets   xiii

Publisher's Acknowledgment   xiv

Introduction   xv
     Living Doors • Time to Look

ONE *What Are Icons?*   1
     Any Materials, Any Size, and Not Only Religious

TWO *Their History*   6
     When Were Icons First Made? • Periods of Byzantine
     Art • Russia and Icons • Changing Styles and
     Subjects

THREE *The Icon Makers*   30
     Alchemy • The Artist and His Assistants • Craftsmen
     Known by Name • Donors • Guilds

FOUR *Materials and Techniques*   40
     Introduction: The Limitations of Raw Materials •
     Colors and Pigments • Drawing the Design • Egg
     Tempera • "Frames"/Panels • Gesso • Gilding • Icon
     Covers • Jewels and Gems • Manuals and
     Patternbooks • Measurements • Mechanical
     Reproduction • Metalwork • Mordants • Painting the
     Icon • Panel Preparation • Repainting and Copying •
     Restoration • Stencils and Templates • Tones and
     Highlights • Various Media for Icons • Varnishing

FIVE *Portable Icons and Painted Panel Icons*   64
Icons Made to be Worn • Folding Icons • Miniature
Icons • Processional Icons • Relic Boxes

SIX *Several Pictures Together*   72
Calendar Icons • Family Icons • Hagiographical
Icons • Iconostasis • Icons in Icons • Six-Day Icons

SEVEN *Visual Language*   78
Introduction: Iconography • Hiring a Craftsman to
Follow Iconography • Animals • Arc of Heaven •
Arms, Very Thin • Arrested Movement • Body
Language • Buildings in Icons • Classical Details •
Clothes • Colors • Craggy Rocks • Drapery •
Enlarging and Reducing • Evangelists' Symbols •
Furniture • Haloes • Handheld Objects • Hands,
Divine and Human • Inscriptions • Landscape •
Mandorla • Nails in the Cross • Narrative Details •
Numbers • Optical Correction • Outer Darkness •
Particularity • Personification • Perspective • Picture
Space • Praying Figures • Profile • Proportions •
"Provincial" Style • Regional Schools • Scale,
Hierarchy of • Side of Blessing/Side of Judgment •
Simultaneous Narration • Skull • Stars on the
Virgin's Veil

EIGHT *God, Angels, and People*   146
Rublev's *Trinity* Icon • God the Father • God the Son
• God the Holy Spirit • Christ Pantocrator • The
Holy Face • Orders of Angels • Virgin Mary • How
to Recognize Saints • Hermits, Abbots, Monks, and
Nuns • Holy Fools • Bishops • Priests and Deacons
• Children • Satan and His Angels

NINE *New Testament Scenes in Icons:*
The Festal Cycle — 182
Introduction: Twelve Feasts • Annunciation •
Nativity • Presentation in the Temple • Baptism of
Christ • Transformation • Raising of Lazarus • Entry
into Jerusalem • Communion of the Apostles •
Crucifixion • Spice-Bearing Women • Anastasis •
Ascension • Pentecost • Life and Death of the Virgin
• Last Judgment

TEN *The Special Qualities of Icons* 204
Direct Communication • Observing Faces in Icons •
The Quality of Light in Icons • Time and Place •
Respecting Icons • The True Context of an Icon •
Getting to Know an Icon

ELEVEN *Icons and Prayer* 215
Looking at Icons in Silence and Stillness • What Is
Prayer? • The Terrain of Icons, the Terrain of Prayer
• Prayer Is Not Safe Because God Is Not Safe •
Fearful Love • Looking at God in Icons • Time and
Place • Praying Without Words • The Sense of Sight
• Praying with Icons • A Reflection

TWELVE *Windows of Eternity:*
The Theology of Icons
Nicholas Gendle 229

Appendix: Where Do You Go from Here?
Icon Collections Worldwide 239

Notes 243

Bibliography 246

ILLUSTRATIONS

Plates following page 158

1. *The Holy Trinity*
2. *Christ Pantocrator*
3. *The Holy Face*
4. *The Virgin of the Great Panagia*
5. *Virgin and Child*
6. *Virgin of Vladimir*
7. *The Archangel Michael*
8. *St. John the Baptist*
9. *St. George and the Dragon*
10. *St. Nicholas*
11. *The Angel of Milesevo*
12. *Baptism of Christ*
13. *Transfiguration from Pereslav*
14. *Christ's Entry into Jerusalem*
15. *Crucifixion*
16. *Anastasis*

PREFACE

Some eight years ago, one of my students, Linette Martin, came up to me after class and asked whether there was a good beginners' guide in print to the making and meaning of icons. I mentioned one or two titles, but none apparently quite addressed what she had in mind. Imagine my astonishment when, some eighteen months later, she told me she was writing an icon book herself and showed me the preliminary draft.

Linette was always a surprising, original, and very gifted person. She had been a dancer, a journalist, a biographer; and during the years I knew her, she was busy creating a medieval garden and keeping open house for the dozens of overseas students who came her way in the course of her husband's pastoral work. She was also a committed student of the History of Art. She was certainly one of the best students I have ever taught: enthusiastic and well read with perceptive questions and observations. Her class presentations often had a down-to-earth, practical quality. She produced samples of minerals and dye-stuffs, showed textiles she had spun and dyed herself, and once even amazed us by knitting an icon of the Virgin and Child. How, from what, and why things were made fascinated her, and to read about it was never enough—she had to have a go herself.

Her premature death, in her sixty-second year, was a great blow to her family and friends, including myself. After the funeral, I told her widower that I would be happy to do what I could to prepare the manuscript for publication. Work still needed to be done by way of correction, focusing of ideas, and augmentation (in places, the historical section was a bit thin, and the theological and iconographic elements needed filling out). My main contributions are in chapters 2, 7, 8, and 9; and I have also added chapter 12 "The Theology of Icons." I hope there are not too many outstanding errors of fact or interpretation and would be grateful if readers could alert us to these, as we hope to incorporate further corrections in any second printing.

I trust that my editorial efforts have in no way altered the basic character of the author's work. Her particular "voice"—with her brilliant down-to-earth metaphors and illustrations, her humor, and her keenness to communicate clearly and vividly—had to be preserved. Also, there is the spiritual dimension: Linette not only had studied icons and made stalwart efforts to visit collections, exhibitions, and monuments, she lived with icons and prayed with icons. No one meeting her could be unaware that she was a woman of prayer, and I think that comes across in her writing, too.

Finally, a word about what this book aims to be and what it is not. It is first and foremost a practical book, by a student for students, not a technical work for scholars, professional art historians, and theologians. We hope it will appeal to people new to the subject, those who have been intrigued by seeing icons in collections or churches, who have perhaps encountered Byzantine frescoes and mosaics on their travels and would like to know more. Basically, this is a book about how works of art were made, about materials (Linette's special enthusiasm), and a guide to the most important subjects found in Orthodox iconography, and what they mean. This last necessarily involves understanding something about the beliefs of Orthodox Christians, which the icons celebrate and express, and we hope there is a sufficient theological dimension provided. The chapter on prayer is very much a personal statement deriving from Linette's own living experience; she was not Orthodox herself, but had a warm appreciation of Orthodoxy, and what we have here is consonant with Orthodox faith and practice.

Conversely, this does not set out to be an art history book, one offering a fully illustrated account of the development of Byzantine and Slav religious art in a chronological sequence. Many such books are available, including some excellent introductory ones, and these are included in the bibliography. Here, we have provided only summary indications of historical context and the evolution of style.

I express some reservations about the inclusion of the section on alchemy in chapter 3. This tendency to read arcane meanings into color is not germane to Orthodox tradition. Linette had an interest in the influence of alchemy, though, and her knowledge was derived mainly from Western sources. Yet Linette's interest in materials may be seen as an additional—if speculative—perspective.

This book provides only a few illustrations, a starting point. I recommend that readers obtain from libraries or bookshops some of the illustrated albums and monographs on icons published in the twentieth century. These will enable them to see examples of all the different icon subjects that we have labored to describe and interpret, but have been unable to illustrate. I also regret that considerations of time precluded providing the sources of all the nonbiblical quotations and providing references to examples of all the types of icons discussed. Nonetheless, I hope enough has been provided to enable readers to "unpack" the meaning of the icons they see, and so appreciate them at a deeper level. Byzantine artists used to speak of "writing" an icon (the literal meaning of the word "iconography"): the icon as visual equivalent of the *word* of Scripture and Tradition. This books aims to help you *read* them.

Oxford 2002   *Dr. Nicholas Gendle, Editor*

BOUQUETS

My thanks to librarians in Oxford and elsewhere who were imaginative and helpful. My thanks also to Dr. Paul Binski (University of Manchester) and Corina Bos (Vrije Universiteit, Amsterdam), to Fr. Alexander Fostiropoulos for explaining haloes and the hand icon, to Prince Sergei Urievitch for telling me how to memorize pictures, and to the educator Charlotte Mason for simplifying the technique.

Above all, my thanks to Dr. Nicholas Gendle for patiently dealing with my questions in class, for inspiring me to love icons, and for giving hours of his valuable time to read and correct the manuscript. If there are still mistakes in it, they are mine, not his.

Oxford 1995   *Linette Martin*

PUBLISHER'S ACKNOWLEDGMENT

Our acknowledgment and deep thanks to Dr. Nicholas Gendle for his fine hand in editing and introducing this book. Not only did he provide needed information on the theology and history of icons, he also filled in gaps and corrected errors. His scholarly attention to this book is exactly what Linette Martin would have appreciated, making this beginner's guide to icons a strong foundation for anyone interested in the symbols, materials, history, and theology of icons.

INTRODUCTION

The other day someone said to me, "People recognize that a picture is an icon, but they don't know what it means so they just switch off." I remember what that experience was like: Icons seemed to speak to me in a foreign language, and I suspected I was missing something interesting.

Sacred Doorways is a first alphabet that will help you to read the language of icons. With a subject as complex as a thousand years of art history, one has to start somewhere. If you are a professional art historian, you already know much that is in this book, but if you are someone who simply is intrigued by icons, this is the place to begin.

Among Orthodox Christians, icons are described as being "written" rather than painted or carved; that is because they are designed to communicate. This book will help you to discover what they are saying.

LIVING DOORS

The art of icons is not dead; icons are still being made and still being used in Christian worship. Television news stories from Russia or Eastern Europe sometimes give a glimpse of the Orthodox Liturgy. The images leave us with an impression of darkness and brightness, incense and candles, deep voices chanting, and icons. The pictures are not there just to be looked at as though the worshipers were in an art museum: They are designed to be doors between this world and another world, between people and the Incarnate God, his Mother, or his friends, the saints.

If a door is to do its job, it must have throughput in two directions. As we move toward an icon, it moves toward us with a warm and precise Christian content—if we understand the language that it speaks. The primary purpose of an icon is to enable a face-to-face encounter with a holy person or make present a sacred event, but icons are also "theology in color."

The trouble is that the pictorial language of the Orthodox Church is unknown to many people in the West. They realize that something is being communicated but they do not know what it is.

Icons communicate precisely. They stand in opposition to deconstructionist art theories in which everyone who looks at a picture is free to make up their own ideas about what it means. Icons communicate Christian truth in a visual form. Narrative icons are complementary to the written Bible. Portrait icons mediate something of the living presence and power of the holy person(s) depicted.

TIME TO LOOK

Today we are more aware of visual communication than at any time since the Middle Ages. Five hundred years ago, Johann Gutenberg developed movable type, and people learned to get information from printed pages instead of from pictures. Now visual communication is becoming more important again. Early in the twentieth century there was mass advertising, then there were movies, and then television; today, videos and interactive media are a normal part of people's lives. It is time to acknowledge the power of visual communication: It is time to look at icons.

This book allows us to appreciate an icon's symbols, themes, and physical components without feeling that we must first plunge into Orthodox theology. For some, an appreciation of icons may lead further. For many, the enrichment that we have from understanding more about these beautiful pictures will be enough. Whenever possible I have avoided writing in art-historical language: Here you will find a saint described as "having a halo," rather than "a nimbed figure."

Research for this book has been fascinating: It took me from medieval lapidaries, optical correction, East Asian trade routes, and Byzantine guilds, to experiments with egg tempera and rabbit-skin glue. How a lifelong Anglican like me got hooked on the art of the Eastern Orthodox Church is, as they say, another story.

ONE

What Are Icons?

Computers have icons. Each one is a simple sign with a specific meaning that evokes a response. There is one that means "wastebasket," another "page," another "document." When we know what each one is (most are easy enough to recognize), we know what to do with it. The icon points us to something beyond itself. Highways have icons. They are signs simple enough to recognize at speed, like "hump-back bridge" or "double hairpin bend." When we recognize the sign, we do something, or if we are bad drivers we do nothing.

A religious icon is the same as a computer icon and a highway sign. It is graphic art: information concentrated in visual iconography. A Christian of the Orthodox Church would protest that a holy icon is far more; as a Western Christian I would say it is not less. The icon points us to something beyond itself; we recognize it and are expected to respond. That response may be belief, or disbelief, or praise, or wonder, or prayer, or encouragement, or terror about the Last Judgment or questions about Christian doctrine. The icon insists that we respond as much with the mind as with the emotions. Icons are not directed only to the gut; they are the thinking man's art.

That is what makes an icon different in motive and in effect from some other religious pictures, and that is why some people dislike icons: They prefer Christian art to be decorative and undemanding. The Orthodox Church teaches that an icon is a two-way door of communication that not only shows us a person or an event but makes it present. When we stand in front of an icon we are in touch with that person and we take part in that event. The historical event of the Nativity is here and now to us, when we look at a *Nativity* icon. What we call "our world" and what we call "the spiritual world" are opened to each other.

According to the ancient teaching of the Christian, and Eastern Orthodox, Church an icon is a door. If you cannot believe that it is a door, never mind. For you, I hope that icons come to be seen as beautiful and rich pictures, showing God and his work in a visual language that can be understood.

ANY MATERIALS, ANY SIZE, AND NOT ONLY RELIGIOUS

Today, we think icons portray only religious subjects, but one and a half thousand years ago the subject was not always religious. If a picture was of an emperor or an important official, the craftsman who made it would call it an icon, and in that broad definition (icon = image) he was right. The picture of the emperor announced that the authority of the emperor was present. A national icon in the present day from any monarchy in the world is the picture of the monarch on a postage stamp.

In the New Testament, the Greek word εἰκών is translated "image," "likeness," "portrait." The Old and New Testaments use the word "image" to describe all of us being in the image of the God who made us (Gen. 1:26; Matt. 22:20; Col. 1:15). In that sense an icon has written this book and an icon is now reading it. There is a Jewish saying that thousands of angels go before every human being, crying, "Make way, make way for the image of God."

A religious icon can be of Christ, the Virgin Mary, an angel, or a saint; it can be of an event from the Old or New Testament, or of a saint's life. It is painted on a wooden panel that is small enough to be portable, and placed on a shelf in someone's home for domestic devotion. Icons like that were made by the thousand and were an enriching focus of devotion for countless thousands of Christians, from famous theologians to the so-called "simple faithful." Icons were not only painted on a wooden panel. They were also made in mosaic, textile, enamel, fresco, ceramic, ivory or bone, silver or gold, bronze, and various semiprecious stones. They could be large and built into a wall-to-wall icon screen across the inside of an Orthodox Church or they could be as small as 2 inches (5 cm) square and hung around someone's neck.

The size made no difference and the materials made no difference. They were all icons as long as they were made in the canonical visual language of the Eastern Orthodox Church.

The visual language is not changeless and rigid, as though someone decided, a thousand years ago, that a picture of Christ or the Virgin should be done according to a precise recipe that generations of craftsmen just followed without thinking. The visual language of icons has developed over centuries because it is a language. Just as a spoken language develops but remains itself, so does that of icons. Most people in Britain and the United States speak English. Though it is not exactly like the English spoken by Geoffrey Chaucer in the fourteenth century, it is recognizably the same language. It has developed but it is still English, and with a little help, modern English speakers can learn to read Chaucer. In the same way, the visual language of icons has developed over one and a half thousand years (and still is developing), but it is still recognizably itself. With only a little help Western people can learn to read it. The word for visual language is *iconography*. To an art historian an icon is a picture made in the visual language, the iconography, of the Orthodox Church.

To an Orthodox Christian a holy icon is an image that is made according to the iconography of the Orthodox Church and that has been blessed by an Orthodox priest with the proper prayers. When you see an icon in an art gallery, can you tell? Perhaps. A picture that has been blessed does not glow with holy light; its status is hidden. Orthodox Christians will tell you that a holy icon is a picture made by a believing craftsman. When you see an icon, can you tell the painter was a sincere believer? Sometimes. There have been thousands of craftsmen working in and beyond the Byzantine Empire since the fourth century. If their personal faith flickered low they could still have followed the proper iconography and produced good, or at least adequate, work. On the other hand, an icon infused with prayer will have an indefinable "plus" quality that may come across even to a not particularly spiritual beholder.

❖ TWO
Their History

A useful starting date to remember is A.D. 330. That was when the Roman Emperor Constantine moved his court from Rome to a fishing town on the shores of the Black Sea. The little town had been there since the seventh century B.C. and was called *Byzantion*. The Emperor enlarged it to be a suitably imperial city and renamed it New Rome. Then it was named after him, Constantinople.

At its greatest extent, the Byzantine Empire stretched from the Euphrates to the Straits of Gibraltar. Over the centuries its fortunes and boundaries ebbed and flowed. The city was captured by Turks in 1453 and renamed *Constantiniya*. It was not until the twentieth century, with the modernization by Kamil Ataturk, that the Turks took the Greek words *eis ten polin*, meaning "toward the town" and bent them into the name "Istanbul." From the date 1453, hear in your mind's ear the cry of a muezzin from a minaret, "*Alla . a . a . . hhh akh-ba . a . a . h. . . .*" Constantinople had become what it is today: a Muslim town between Europe and the Middle East.

The visual language—the iconography—of icons began to develop even before Constantine and was established in the Byzantine Empire between 330 and 1453, the period of time that art historians call Late Antique and Medieval. After 1453, it was affected by the Western Renaissance to some extent, but its special qualities survived. In the West, icons were largely unappreciated until the twentieth century. In the mid-nineteenth century Byzantine items owned by the British Museum were stowed away in the basement with folk artifacts from Peru and Mexico. As recently as the 1920s a writer dismissed "Byzantine Madonnas and saints, conventionally featured, conventionally clad, conventionally colored, which are so definitely characteristic of western art in its cradle." Now people are discovering that Orthodox Christian art is not an outdated style whose only purpose was to inspire Duccio, but is something beautiful in its own right. There was no precise date when the visual language began because it grew out of Roman art; there was no date when it ended because it is still a living art.

WHEN WERE ICONS FIRST MADE?

The earliest surviving icons are to be dated to the sixth and seventh centuries, and are almost all now preserved in the monastery of St. Catherine of Sinai. The remoteness of this outpost of the Empire preserved them from the systematic destruction of sacred art ordered by the iconoclast emperors after 720. All are in a technique and medium called "encaustic wax," in which powdered mineral colors were blended in hot wax, laid on with glass rods. By the time of the restoration of the icons in 843, this technique had been lost, and we are only now beginning to learn some idea of how it was done.

However, literary sources make it clear that icons were being made from the late fourth century. For example, St. John Chrysostom speaks of having a portrait of St. Paul on his desk to inspire him when writing homilies on the Epistles. Already at that time, there was a small minority of churchmen (e.g., Eusebius of Caesarea, Epiphanius of Salamis) who had reservations concerning the legitimacy of images. Antipathy to Christian art did not begin with iconoclasm, though the fact that there was no controversy till the eighth century shows that the overwhelming majority of believers had no objections. By the late sixth century, indeed, icons were the principal focus of popular devotion among all classes throughout the eastern Roman world.

PERIODS OF BYZANTINE ART

The history of Byzantium from Constantine to minarets is a large swath of time and is difficult to perceive unless it is subdivided. Visualize it in time-blocks set end to end like a row of rectangles. The first is Early Byzantine, 330 to 726. If you find it difficult to memorize dates, think of them as the times of a train that you need to catch.

The time-blocks are: Early Byzantine, the Age of Iconoclasm, Middle Byzantine, the Latin Usurpation, Late Byzantine, Postbyzantine.

Early Byzantine Period

The dates are 330 to 726. People living in Constantinople called themselves *Romaioi* (Romans) rather than Byzantines, and for the first generations the official class continued to wear togas and speak Latin. The move to the new town brought a change of address, but kept a continuity of culture. The art of Christian Constantinople showed continuity with the art of pagan Rome because it was made *by* the same people and *for* the same people. The same patrons employed the same craftsmen who designed things in the same pictorial language that their grandfathers and great-grandfathers had used.

Many Christian motifs were adapted from the art of ancient Rome. Pagan *genii* had been shown with wings, so angels were shown with wings; pagan figures of divine power had been shown with haloes, so Christ was shown with a halo. As the Good Shepherd, he looked like a young Apollo or Hermes; enthroned as the Pantocrator, like Jupiter, the Ruler of the Universe, mature and bearded; in triumph he was like the sun-god in his chariot. Angels were dressed like court officials and the Virgin Mary like a Roman matron. Christian artists simply took the art of the day and injected it with new, specifically Christian meanings.

Gradually, Christian art began to develop a distinctive style. At first it had been a new religion shown in the old visual language; then it was a new religion that slowly evolved its own language. If you could flip through a series of pictures dated every twenty-five years beginning at the fourth century, when Christianity became the official religion, you would see a distinct style shift in the seventh century. Figures become tall, thin, and flat; the folds of clothing are a pattern of lines with no attempt at making you think you are looking at real fabric flowing around a real body. The faces are masks as stylized as the makeup of Japanese Kabuki theater. A picture like that was not just a reminder of a saint or an angel: it was intended to show that the saint or that angel was a present spiritual reality. The style-shift showed a shift in the Church's understanding of what an icon was and what it could do.

The new understanding enriched worshipers' spiritual lives as they prayed in front of panel icons in their homes, as well as their churches, where they saw the same iconography in large frescoes and mosaics. But to teach that an icon was a door between this world and the world of the spirit was potentially dangerous. There were cases of superstitious practices, for example, in which paint was scraped from a household icon to be given as medicine to a sick member of the family. It should not be surprising that some people got the Church's teaching so terribly wrong: Wherever God works, the devil works, and there is no aspect of Christian truth that has not been distorted sometime, somewhere, by someone.

Just at the time when the cult of the icons was at its height came a dramatic new addition to the religions of the world: It was Islam, a religion that began when Christianity was some six hundred years old.

The Age of Iconoclasm

The dates are 726 to 843. After their being an accepted part of Christian devotion for more than four hundred years, a shadow fell across the art of icons. For Muslims, to make a realistic picture of animals or people was wrong because the craftsman was behaving as though he were God, and God is the only image maker. To make an image of Christ was wrong to Muslims because they did not believe in the Incarnation, though Jesus was honored as one of God's prophets. Islam spread rapidly.

In response to the new religion, the Christian emperors might have carefully reinforced the Church's teaching about icons; they might have made a clear distinction between the Christian acceptance of an icon of the Incarnate Christ, and a Muslim's denial of the Incarnation; they might have encouraged their right use. Instead, Emperor Leo III ordered icons to be banned and his son enforced the decree more viciously. Yet, by standing *against* icons, they were standing *with* people who denied the reality of the Incarnation.

In defining the proper position, John of Damascus, an eighth-century monk, wrote:

> I boldly draw an image of the invisible God, not as invisible, but as having become visible for our sakes by partaking of flesh and blood. I do not draw an image of the immortal Godhead, but I paint an image of God who became visible in the flesh.

Causes of Iconoclasm

Why did the emperors ban the icons? It was a time of grave military crisis and domestic (especially economic) instability. The Empire was threatened by Persia, by steppe nomads, and by the final blow, the new power of Islam. The spectacular expansion of the new religion in the Middle East began with the flight of the prophet Muhammad in 622; by 722, a new empire, the Caliphate, was established in Damascus, and all the Byzantine provinces in the Levant and North Africa had been permanently lost.

A totally unexpected disaster of this magnitude was bound to have religious as well as political and military repercussions. If Christianity was the true faith, and the

Byzantines God's chosen people, why was he apparently abandoning them? For what sins were they being punished? Leo III's answer was clear: idolatry. He contrasted what he had seen as icon worship of the Christians with the image-free practice of the victorious Muslims.

There can be no doubt it was the imperial decision alone that began and carried through the destruction of sacred art.

The shock of the ban caused many tears. Though there had been ongoing debate about idolatry for generations, legal proscription of icons was new. Making or owning an icon was forbidden for over a century. There was a respite after a Church council talked through the issues and decided in favor of the icon lovers; then the ax fell again for another twenty-six years. Churches decorated between 726 and 843 had theologically neutral pictures of trees, animals, and birds, or a plain cross, one of the few religious symbols of which the iconoclasts approved.

Because the icon-cult had penetrated the home, the ban was not enforceable the length and breadth of the Empire. In some households and monasteries icons were hidden, handed down in secret, and honored. The few icons we have today that were made before and during the Age of Iconoclasm are ours to enjoy because people broke the law or lived too far from Constantinople to worry the imperial officials. The great majority of surviving pre-iconoclastic icons are preserved in the remote monastery of St. Catherine at Sinai in Egypt.

Visual communication is powerful; art can rouse people to rage. Neither secular nor religious iconoclasts say, "It's only a picture." They understand the power of visual communication and destroy what they fear.

Icon lovers liked to repeat the apocryphal story of the conversion of Bulgaria in the ninth century. According to the story, Boris of Bulgaria asked a Greek painter to make a fresco to impress his hunting guests. "I don't care what the picture is," he is reputed to have said, "as long as it is memorable and terrifying." The painter Methodius made a *Last Judgment* fresco; Boris looked and was converted. Christian doctrine, presented visually, can have a profound and lasting effect.

It is not necessary to be an Orthodox Christian (or even a Christian) to appreciate icons, but it helps to be able to understand the belief of the Orthodox Church. Icons show us people and events of sacred history as people and events that leap out of the past into the present. Above all, icons show us the Incarnate God, the materials of the image becoming a channel between two worlds. The images are

> an essential medium through which the holy may be approached and grace channeled, like a two-way mirror. . . . The icon is the real equivalent to, and venerated with the same honor as, the Gospel. The one communicates religious truth through words, the other through visible forms and symbols. Both equally are modes of revelation. (Nicholas Gendle, *Catalogue: Icons in Oxford*)

In the eighth and ninth centuries, pictures of Church councils establishing right doctrine were replaced with pictures of imperial chariot races in the Hippodrome. Mosaics and wall paintings of Christ and the Virgin, prophets and saints were whitewashed, hacked down, or literally defaced. Panel paintings and textile icons were burnt. Say the dates 726 to 843 and hear in your mind's ear the splintering of painted panels and the knock of hammer on chisel, obliterating mosaics and painted plaster.

It was only religious art that was forbidden. Secular art continued to be made in classical style while churches were stripped and whitewashed. A nonreligious picture in classical style did not frighten the iconoclasts because it carried no risk of idolatrous abuse and did not claim to be a bridge to the heavenly world. When icons were finally and officially accepted, Byzantines called it the Triumph of Orthodoxy. Orthodox Christians still celebrate the event every year.

After the Age of Iconoclasm it took some time for icon workshops and art techniques to revive. There was little significant production till the last quarter of the ninth century—then, a great revival in the tenth.

Middle Byzantine Period

The dates are 844 to 1204. In art history books the three and a half centuries are named for the dynasties of emperors; you will read of icons described as being in Macedonian style, or Comnene style. To keep it simple, think of the Middle Byzantine period as one long time-block that stretches between two crises of Byzantine history, from the end of Iconoclasm to the invasion of Western Crusaders.

By the end of the ninth century, the two superpowers of the Middle East, the Byzantine Empire and the Islamic Caliphate, had fought themselves to something of a stalemate. Sporadic battles continued along the eastern frontiers, but during the period of the Macedonian Dynasty (887–1035), the emperors were able to consolidate their dominions in Asia Minor and the Balkans, reform the administration and the legal and financial system, and once again encourage the arts of peace. By about 1000—the reign of the ferocious Basil II, known as "the Bulgarian Slayer" for his savage reconquest of Bulgaria—the Byzantine state was at its medieval apogee, stretching from the Adriatic to the Euphrates.

The late ninth and tenth centuries are sometimes called by cultural historians the "Macedonian Renaissance": There was a great renewal of literature, philosophy, and art. The enormous resources of the state were put to great programs of church-building, creating schools of higher studies, and commissioning vastly expensive mosaic programs. Ironically, the continuity of secular art during the Iconoclast centuries had led to a revival of classicism (partly because nonreligious art was not subject to the transcendental pressures that had led to a gradual sea change in the style of sacred art). The classical revival (based on the surviving illuminated books of Late Antiquity) led to the creation of exquisite ivories and lavish illustrated manuscripts (e.g., the Paris Psalter, the Paris *Nazianzen,* the Bible of Leo the Patrician in the Vatican). All these reflect the taste of the court: From now on, Constantinople sets the standards and taste to which the whole Empire aspires. However, one sees a more severe style in art in the *public* sphere (especially the apse mosaics of the cathedrals of St. Sophia in Constantinople and Salonica). The mosaics of Osios Loukas in Greece, a major mosaic program from around 1000, express an austerity and force that is not at all like the classical humanism so popular at court. Not many icons survive from this period, but some of the best (e.g., a famous *St. Nicholas* from Sinai) do show the new stylistic traits: modeling that shows figures as three dimensional, a return to idealized proportions of the human form, elegant flowing draperies, benign facial expression with a sense of inner life.

❖

The so-called Comnene[1] Period (1055–1204) was one of slow political and economic decline. Great aristocratic families competed for the control of the Empire, which lacked the central control of a powerful autocrat. Expansion of local aristocratic estates proceeded apace, the treasury was depleted, and it became necessary to give large trading concessions to Venice. The incursions of

Normans and other Western adventurers, hungry for land, were less of a threat than the rise of the Seljuq Turks in the East. Their victory at Manzikert (1071) robbed the Empire at a stroke of much of eastern Anatolia, with all that implied of loss of manpower, resources, and tax revenue.

The eleventh and twelfth centuries in art represented a return to a more graphic, expressionistic style in which classical form gradually gave way to a rather flat, stylized manner: The figures are again tall and thin (but with more animation and expression than the ghostly figures in seventh- and eighth-century art), and landscapes are reduced to juxtaposed planes and angular outlines. By the second half of the twelfth century, we have an extremely mannered version of this style, with convoluted, bunched draperies, serpentine hemlines, agitated gestures, compartmentalized features, and in general, much stronger expression of emotion (evident in some frescoes—e.g., Nerezi and Kurbinovo in Macedonia, Lagoudhera in Cyprus—but also in icons). This is the first period for which a significant body of icons survives: the collection at St. Catherine's at Sinai offers an excellent cross-section of examples.

The mosaics at Dafni and the wonderful icon of the *Virgin of Vladimir* (about 1120) are harbingers of a humanistic revival. This was nipped in the bud in the capital by the catastrophe of the Sack of Constantinople by the Crusaders (1204). Byzantine metropolitan artists, lacking patronage from the Latin usurpers, moved into Orthodox successor states looking for patronage. The thirteenth-century kings of Serbia and Bulgaria were happy to oblige; at Mileseva, Sopoćani, and Boyana, for example, we see the art of Constantinople in exile producing grand, monumental frescoes of an unparalleled sculptural quality, devoid of the fussy mannerisms and agitated emotionalism of the late Comnene style.

The Latin Usurpation

The dates are 1204 to 1261. As Constantinople was the link between Asia and Europe, Venice was the link between Western Europe and Byzantium. In 1201, over 30,000 Western knights, squires, and infantry were encamped in and around Venice, on their way to Jerusalem. The Venetians demanded 85,000 silver marks to ship them down the Adriatic to Constantinople. The Crusaders made a bargain: They would fight for Venice in Dalmatia and would pay off the remaining debt with relics and other valuables.

Anyone who has been taught to think that Crusaders were all noble, brave, Christian knights has to think again. With the date 1204, hear in your mind's ear the sound of wagon wheels, splintering wood, the screams of massacre. Crusaders in Constantinople behaved like ram-raiders in a jewelry store, trundling away everything portable. Because they were thieves, they wanted gold and gems; because they were medieval thieves, they also wanted relics of saints. When they landed in Constantinople to "refuel," a series of misunderstandings with the Emperor Alexius led to diplomatic impasse, and soon they resorted to arms.

> Constantinople can be considered the heart of the economic life of the Empire. It was there that for the most part the portable wealth and the principal branches of industry and commerce were concentrated; hundreds of thousands of working people lived within its walls. Of all this, after several days of pillage, massacre, and conflagration, hardly anything remained. (André M. Andreades, *Byzantium*)

The imperial center was scattered and relatives of the imperial family set up courts wherever they could:

Trebizond, Epirus, Nicaea. It was from Nicaea that Michael Paleologus recaptured Constantinople in 1261 and tried to revive the old glories.

The Late Byzantine Period

The dates are 1261 to 1453. In history books it is called the Palaeologan Period, named after the reigning dynasty, the Paleologus family. In 1261 a Byzantine, rather than a Western, emperor was reestablished in Constantinople, but the Empire was much depleted, both in territory and resources. In 1453 the last Paleologan emperor died defending his city against the Turkish army of Mehmet the Conquerer that was attacking the fortifications (by then all that remained of the Empire was Constantinople, the Peloponnese, and a few Greek islands). A contemporary historian writes how the emperor was identified only by his shoes and leg armor:

> When all resistance had ceased, the Sultan entered our city. His immediate concern was the fate of the emperor, as he was extremely anxious to discover whether he was still alive. Some individuals came and declared that the emperor had escaped, some that he had gone into hiding, and others that he had perished in the defense of the city. An immediate search was ordered to locate the emperor's body among the heaps of the slain. They washed the heads of many corpses, but the emperor could not be identified. His body was finally spotted by means of the golden imperial eagles traditionally imprinted on the greaves and shoes of our emperors. (George Sphrantzes)

According to legend, the last priest was interrupted partway through the Liturgy; he disappeared into the walls of St. Sophia and will reemerge one day to continue it.

Initially, the courage and diplomacy of Michael VIII and his immediate successors enabled the Byzantines to hold the Latins at bay and retain a sizable lump of territory in northwest Asia Minor. But the advance of the Ottoman Turks was inexorable, and the ongoing crisis was exacerbated by weak government in Constantinople in the fourteenth century, and by dynastic and religious disputes. It seems amazing the end did not come sooner! Fortunately for the Byzantines, the capture of the Sultan Bayazit by Tamerlane in 1402 brought half a century's respite.

But despite the extreme political and military situation, the fourteenth century is the last golden age of Byzantine culture, with lively theological, philosophical, and literary activity. In art, we have the final "renaissance" of the native Byzantine classical tradition. In all forms of art, a renewed delicacy, refinement, and spirituality is evident, not least in fourteenth-century icons, some of the most beautiful ever produced. Elegant modeling of idealized faces and bodies, elaborated landscapes and (often fantastic) architectural backgrounds combine with a tendency toward miniaturization. There wasn't enough money in the imperial treasury for ambitious mosaics now, but a very rich, disgraced civil servant commissioned the swan song of the genre, the Chora Church in Constantinople (1320s). All in all, the cultural achievement of the Palaeologan Renaissance was a triumph of the human spirit over adversity.

The Sixth Period: Post-Byzantine

Even though Constantinople was finished as the cultural and artistic center of Orthodox Christianity, icons continued. The Turkish sultans were tolerant, allowing the Orthodox Church many privileges, including the making of icons. Since the tenth century, craftsmen had been traveling north to Russia where they were continuing to make icons according to the proper iconography. The art lived on there officially from 988 to 1917, after which date many icons were destroyed in the Communist era. Even under Communism, Russian icons were still venerated, restored, and secretly painted. After seventy years of Communism—how short a time it seems now that it is over—a nation raised on atheistic materialism is openly returning to its icons.

Icon painters also worked in Venetian-owned Crete, the Ionian Islands, and other parts of Greece, the Balkans, Cyprus, and Asia Minor, where they painted for dispersed Greeks and even sometimes Western Christians. Cretan icons were popular in Northern Europe in the sixteenth century and were produced by the score. A century later there was little demand for them because Western taste had changed. Byzantine icons of the Paleologan period are as beautiful as late summer roses and, like late roses, they could not last. The cultural gateway between Eastern and Western Europe had been opened wider than it had ever been by centuries of east-west trade and through that gateway came the influences of the Italian Renaissance.

There is more to the changing styles of Byzantine history than this brief overview can indicate, but when we can see history in large time-blocks, we can place the details somewhere. Even if we never find out more of the details, we now have the thousand years or so of Byzantine history blocked out in a memorable shape. As for Byzantine art, it moves with history: not static, but developing as a spoken language develops—in essence constant, but in style, greatly varying.

RUSSIA AND ICONS

The wide influence of Christianity in Russia began in 989. In that year Vladimir Sviatoslavovich, Prince of Kiev, received Christian baptism. The story of what led him to take this step may be poetic truth rather than literal truth, but it bears repeating because of the point that it makes.

According to the story, Vladimir sent envoys to investigate the religion of the Jews, the Muslims, and the Christians. They returned and reported what they had found. They described the worship in a Catholic Church, in a synagogue, and in a mosque. Of the Orthodox Liturgy in St. Sophia in Constantinople they said,

> We only know that God dwells there among men and that their service is fairer than the ceremonies of other nations. We did not know whether we were in heaven or earth. We cannot forget such beauty.

The point of the story in the *Russian Chronicle* is that Christian doctrine, when expressed with beauty of sight and sound, will convert people.

It was not Russia's first contact with the gospel: Vladimir's grandmother Olga had converted over thirty years before, and some Christians existed in the upper levels of society. As for "Vladimir the Bright Sun," he had practiced human sacrifice and the worship of the pagan gods. Olga's prayers were answered in 989 when he received Christian baptism and proclaimed that his people should do likewise. From a modern perspective such a proclamation sounds like spiritual dictatorship, but it was the normal direction in medieval society: The king leads, the people follow. The first followers were among the aristocracy; after that the gospel filtered slowly out to pagan villages and small towns all the way to Novgorod, the fur-trading town far to the northwest. The common people held on for a long time to their familiar beliefs: the spirits of rocks and birch trees; *Dazhdbog,* the sun god; *Chernobog,* the black god; and *Perun*, the god of thunder. For people close to woods and the soil, paganism is a long time a-dying.

In Russian towns, icon painting became a growth industry. Since icons were an integral part of Orthodox

Christian worship, every new church had to have some. Enterprising craftsmen from Constantinople packed their equipment and moved north by the trade route up the River Dnieper that linked the Black Sea and Scandinavian Novgorod. By the early eleventh century there were forty churches in Kiev. The Metropolitan (Archbishop) of Kiev described it as "a city glistening with the light of holy icons, fragrant with incense, ringing with praise and holy, heavenly songs."

There was a widespread belief that the world would end at the year 1000; Greek Christians believed that Russia had turned to God just in time. For aristocratic Russian Christians, Constantinople was "Tsargrad," the emperor's city and the cultural and spiritual center of the world.

In the thirteenth century the Mongol armies thundered over the steppes, crossed the Ural Mountains, and flung themselves against the wooden palisades of Kiev. When they entered a town, the khan's army had a simple order: Kill everyone. Neither defense nor surrender made any difference. Across Russia they imposed taxation and travelers' tolls; one traveler who had to pay was Marco Polo. Novgorod, at the northern end of the Russian trade route, remained independent because it was surrounded by marshes and forests; where a cart or flat-bottomed boat could get through with tallow and furs, enamels and icons, an army could not. In 1240 young Alexander Nevski defeated the Teutonic Knights who tried to snatch Novgorod for the Latin Church, so Novgorod remained free and Russian.

Moscow Crusade Against Mongols

The Mongols were beaten in Russia in 1380 when Prince Dmitri Donskoi of Moscow won a battle that proved to be a psychological turning point for the people. Because Russia had not been a unified state but an aggregation of principalities, the Mongols had been able to conquer each area, plucking victories one by one like apples from a tree. After the battle, the cultural center of Russia moved north from Vladimir to Moscow. The Islamic military depredations and tribute, which were bleeding Russia to death, led the energetic Moscow princes to strive to unify the disparate principalities under their leadership, and launch a crusade to push the Mongols back into Asia. By the end of the fifteenth-century, they had achieved these goals, and with the fall of Byzantium (1453), the Grand Prince Ivan the Great was able to assume the imperial title and rule as undisputed "autocrat of all the Russias."

It was Russia above all that continued to make icons after 1453 when Constantinople had become a Muslim city and the widespread Byzantine Empire had crumbled. The fifteenth and sixteenth centuries, when the Western Renaissance was influencing Byzantine iconography, is considered the golden age of Russian icons. At that time, Moscow was proud to call herself the Third Rome, continuing the role of Constantinople as political and cultural leader of the Orthodox world. In the late fifteenth century Ivan the Great was the first Russian ruler to call himself Tsar, the Russian version of Caesar. In 1523 Philotheus, an Elder of Pskov Monastery, wrote:

> The Church of old Rome fell because of its heresy; the gates of the second Rome, Constantinople, were hewn down by the axes of the infidel Turks; but the Church of Moscow, the new Rome, shines brighter than the sun over the whole universe. . . . Two Romes have fallen but the third stands fast; a fourth there cannot be.

When Western people today think of a "typical icon," they think of a panel painting of figures with stylized features and intense eyes gazing from the painted surface in direct communication. That style lived on in Russia till the seventeenth century when Western influence on Russian icons first became apparent.

In 1551, the Council of the Hundred Chapters, in Moscow, warned:

> Let great care be and caution be taken that skillful icon painters and their pupils paint from ancient models, but let them not depict the divinity from their own fancy, by their own conjectures. . . .

Iconographers continued to paint traditional icons, but in country districts the style was slipping into folk art. Though Ivan the Great had brought Italian architects to Moscow in the late fifteenth century to design cathedrals, the big break with the past was made by Peter the Great (1682—1725), who made the Church into an arm of the State. Under him, Russia's cultural center moved northwest. He had the new capital of St. Petersburg constructed on a virgin site near the Gulf of Finland, at the cost, it was said, of the lives of 100,000 serfs brought in to drain the marshes.

Under Western influence, Russian icons were painted with more anatomical details, and the figures floated on cotton-wool clouds or sat on elaborate Baroque thrones. By the nineteenth century, metal icons were mass-produced by contemporary technology. Russian soldiers in the Crimean war carried small metal icons around their necks, objects of curiosity to English soldiers searching the dead. For panel pictures, metal icon covers were heat-stamped into a mold, the faces and hands sometimes being the only parts of the panel that had paint on them. In homes, icons were placed in "the beautiful corner," a shelf on the east wall of the main room, and over every bed. Old ones were handed down through families, their surface pickled like a meerschaum pipe by decades of exposure to the smoke of oil lamps and the smoke from domestic hearths. Some were so dark that the figures could no longer be identified; they were called "black things."

Academic Revival of Old Russian Icon Painting

In nineteenth-century Russia, the first to amass large quantities of old Russian sacred art—grimy icons, textiles, and liturgical metalwork—were Old Believers (members of ultra-conservataive schismatic sects), reacting against the westernization of the national religious culture by the educated upper classes. At the end of the last century, rich discriminating enthusiasts like the industrialists Tretiakov and Ostroukhov laid the foundations of the serious study and collection of icons. This in turn led to an academic revival of icon painting: Craftsmen felt they must studiously emulate examples from the golden age of the fifteenth and sixteenth centuries in order to recover the genuine Orthodox theological aesthetic, if sacred art were to recover its true identity and renew itself.

Though there were times when the use of icons was marred by superstition, and the style was degraded by Western sentiment and mass production, the iconography of Byzantium lived on in Russia and Eastern Europe. Icons continued to be made even in the dark but passing shadow of the Communist era, a severely testing time for Russian Christians; it is estimated that in the 1930s Soviet Russia had only a hundred and fifty working churches. How many household icons survived as small centers of devotion, only God knows.

In the mercy of God, times change. In the 1990s, churches were restored. In Zagorsk, Moscow, and other centers for making icons, spectroscopic analysis of medieval pictures is helping painters to make copies using authentic traditional materials and techniques. A new generation is making the same discovery as the envoys of Vladimir in 988: "We cannot forget such beauty."

CHANGING STYLES AND SUBJECTS

Through the centuries of Byzantine art history, the style changes. Solid classical figures give way to immensely tall formal creatures with stylized faces. At one time saints are pictured standing in a row as on a shallow shelf; at another time they move in a landscape. Clothes hang in damp-looking folds, or flutter as in a breeze, or are as stiff as the robes worn by a figure on a playing card. Seen in retrospect in the grand perspective of one thousand years of Byzantine art, we may detect an alternation roughly every two hundred years between a classicizing style (Christian humanism) and a more schematic, linear, and expressionistic manner (the abstract tendency). Far from being a static and petrified tradition, Orthodox art shows a remarkable creative energy, especially in the Middle Ages, so that (on internal stylistic evidence alone) a competent art historian can now date an icon to roughly within half a century.

The Influence of Church Councils

The heading seems strange today: We find it hard to imagine how theological debate could influence art. In Byzantine art it could and it did. While secular pieces (such as serving dishes for a rich man's table) continued to be made in a classical style with dryads and bacchantes, nymphs and shepherds, religious art was affected by Church councils.

Negatively, it was affected by iconoclasts. Positively, it was affected by, for example, the Council of Ephesus in 431 that proclaimed the Virgin Mary to be *Theotokos,* the Bearer of God. After that, she was shown with more dignity, enthroned and robed as an empress. Visual communication had a didactic and corrective role; icon craftsmen knew that making their pictures conform to the teaching of the Church was important. Unlike many Western Christians today, who hang religious pictures as gently inspiring decoration, Byzantines believed that icons were quasi-sacramental objects, doors to the spiritual world. Because God had become man, the permanent saving efficacy of the Incarnation could—and must—be celebrated and communicated in and through the icon of Christ.

The Influences of Technology, Geography, and Politics

The development of gem cutting (rather than gem polishing) meant that jewels had a new sparkle and could be used in more decorative ways. Previously, a jewel or gem was put on an icon as much for its intrinsic value as for its gleaming beauty, whereas cut stones might be chosen more for their visual effect. Improved methods of coloring glass influenced the colors of mosaics. When cinnabar could be man-made, rather than panned from a Spanish river, craftsmen used more of its distinctive vermilion. Think of how art would be influenced by something as prosaic as improved access to gold mines or a greater supply of slave workers to work in them. The availability of a pigment or dye was not incidental information to the icon painter, so it should be taken into account in our understanding of what colors he used. The political alteration of a trade route made the difference between his working with one color or with another. It made the difference between carving elephant ivory or steatite. We are used to ready-made paints from an art shop, so when we see the range of colors in icons change from one generation to the next we assume it was a change of fashion. Colors may have changed because a different administration had taken over in another country and the caravan of raw materials could not get through.

The light and bright colors, the vermilions and deep green of Novgorod paintings may have been influenced as much by availability of raw materials as by spirituality or psychology. When the Aegean port of Phocea was captured by the Genoese in 1264 it would have made a difference to the dyers of Constantinople because Phocea was where alum was mined, and alum was the principle mordant used by dyers. In various ways new styles were influenced by the availability of raw materials.

New Subjects

Within the iconography of Byzantine art, the possibility of new subjects allows the art of icons to remain alive. Byzantine iconography was supple enough to include new subjects. New details in icons appear from time to time, just as new words appear in a spoken language because they are needed.

Orthodox iconography from its beginnings well into the early modern period has been in a continuous state of development. Churchmen and artists had to devise new compositions to celebrate newly instituted feasts (e.g., the Dormition, sixth century; the Exaltation of the Holy Cross, eighth century) and to make iconic portraits of newly canonized saints (e.g., St. Gregory Palamas, fourteenth century; St. Seraphim of Sarov, nineteenth century). The fourteenth to fifteenth century was a period of remarkable innovation, especially in the creation of new liturgical themes: for example, the Celestial Liturgy (see chapter 9) and the illustration of the great Akathistos Hymn to the Mother of God (a hymn in honor of the Mother of God during the singing of which the congregation stands; the title Akathistos literally means "not-seated.") In the sixteenth to seventeenth century, the Russian Church devised new icon-types of the Virgin (e.g., *Joy of Those Who*

Grieve), of St. Nicholas (the *Mozhaisk* icon), and of Christ (as *Sophia,* or *Angel of Great Counsel).*

The addition of new iconic subjects to the canon is to be distinguished from the iconographic elaboration of existing basic themes, for which see chapter 7.

In spite of charming traditions about the origin of some icons as "simply manifesting," each one was made by someone and for someone and expressed a particular point of view. It was as true in the medieval period as it is now that how people think affects what they make. So how did they think? The next chapter is about the people who made icons and the people for whom they were made.

❖ THREE
The Icon Makers

ALCHEMY
Alchemy was a way of explaining the physical world that predated modern chemistry. Go just a little further back than the seventeenth century and we are in the period in which in the West, at least, alchemy was a normal way of looking at the world. People believed that things could change into other things; they could be transmuted. If the alchemist could find the essential ingredient of life, called

the Philosopher's Stone, he could use it as the universal medicine, a means of becoming spiritually perfect and immortal. It was not a stone as we think of a small rock; it was a substance like yeast that could transform and multiply everything into which it was put. It was a tincture that could color everything without the dyestuff ever becoming exhausted.

Whether or not *we* could believe in alchemy is irrelevant when we look at medieval art: Medieval people believed it, and some of the ideas of alchemy were shown in visual form.

The earliest alchemical writing that we know is from China, in the fifth century B.C. Since then, from China to Egypt, men and women had engaged in what they called the "Great Work," searching for a spiritual medicine for humanity as well as for precious metals. They believed that, given the proper circumstances, metals could be changed into gold, so they tried to find the proper circumstances that would effect that change. After the Middle Ages the attempt to make physical gold became the alchemists' chief preoccupation—ironically, just at the time that travelers to the New World were bringing it home in shiploads.

To an alchemist the whole world was vibrant with life. They added to the four elements of earth, air, fire and water a fifth essence (quint-essence), the life-quality that is in everything made by the living God. There was no inanimate matter; things were not just *things* (the medieval world was more interesting).

When the alchemist tried to find the Philosopher's Stone, he was on a spiritual as well as a chemical quest. Unlike people in our century, he would not have made any distinction between the two: His world was more integrated. He believed that everything was connected: minerals, stars, plants, planets, shapes, numbers, and symbols, words, musical notes, and the passions of the mind.

In alchemists' books the Philosopher's Stone was pictured as a small child or newborn baby; he was the Royal Child born of Mother Mercury who was of the Moon. Such associative thoughts were stirred when medievals looked at an icon of the Virgin and Child. The historical fact of the Incarnation did not need to be jettisoned; instead, their minds expanded to include alchemical symbolism as well as the Gospels. A *mandorla* surrounding Christ could be the radiance of his light, or it could be an alchemical symbol, the closed vessel in which the Great Work was accomplished.

Those ideas may have flowed naturally and unexamined into the minds of a Western medieval craftsman, just as diffused ideas of Darwin or Freud flow into ours. Alchemy was so taken for granted that it colored everything, as tinted spectacles color everything the wearer sees. Though it is an esoteric, occult subject today, it was not that to medievals.

Alchemists believed that God's work in a man can transform not only the personality but also the physical body, working through it as yeast leavens dough, as indigo dyes silk, or as the Stone makes gold. Like the alchemist, the icon maker was involved in a spiritual activity when he took raw materials and turned them into a bridge between the saint in the picture and the worshiper who prayed before it. Making an icon was an awesome responsibility: It was important to get it right.

THE ARTIST AND HIS ASSISTANTS

The medieval artist was not a solitary operative, like some nineteenth- and twentieth- century artists. He worked in a team, his role and status depending on his place within the hierarchy of the workshop (*atelier*). At the head of the shop was the master, who dealt with patrons, made the designs, and oversaw the whole process of production of the art work, perhaps intervening with his own brush only in the final, most delicate stages. He was at once the controlling mind behind artistic production and the boss.

Aspiring artists in the Middle Ages didn't go to art school. They learned by hands-on experience within the workplace. In an icon shop, the new boys would be set to prepare the boards and make the gesso; only after some months might they be taught to grind and mix colors, and to gild. Gradually, they would learn to paint—starting with undercoats, then draperies, then backgrounds, finally figures and faces. All the different stages of production would progress simultaneously under the eagle eye of the master; it was coordinated division of labor. At each stage in the hierarchy, assistants could learn by emulating colleagues a little more experienced than themselves.

By running a large, diversified workshop a master could undertake a large number of commissions. And, as the controlling figure who "conceived" the icon, all products could be ascribed to him.

Craftsmen Known by Name

Throughout this book I refer to the makers of medieval icons as *he* and crafts*men* because it is a fact of history that the vast majority of them were men. Women spun silk, linen, cotton, and wool, silk spinning being a prestige craft done within the walls of the palace precinct. It was men who traded dyestuffs from other countries, manipulated skeins of spun fibers in and out of huge dyepots, set up looms, and wove fabric. In the medieval period and for long beyond, the word craftsmen really does refer to crafts-*men*.

There is a romantic idea that medieval craftsmen did not sign their name because they offered everything to God and wanted to remain humble and anonymous. The truth is more down-to-earth. The medieval craftsman did not think of himself as a divinely inspired artist but as a well-trained artisan doing a necessary job. An icon painter prepared himself for his work by praying, and the importance of his work was recognized by the Church, but his social status was not high; he was regarded as an artisan rather than an artist or independent virtuoso. Icons were useful objects that were needed for the Liturgy and for people's devotions at home: He had been trained to make those objects. Why should he sign his name? It would have been as pretentious as a plumber signing his name on a new washbasin when he installs it on your wall.

Some medieval secular objects that were signed show the name of the patron who paid for the work rather than of the craftsman who made it. The object spoke, announcing the name of the patron. When a piece was signed with the name of the master of the workshop, it meant that it was from his workshop team, his name being a guarantee of good workmanship and good design.

Though signed icons became more common in the fifteenth century, we know several names from before that. There was Tydor Gvasavaisdze who made an icon of *Christ Enthroned* at Mestiya, Georgia, in the eleventh century; Philip the Goldsmith who worked at Tiflis; and Theodore Apseudos who painted the walls of St. Neophytos' cave in 1183. There was Theophan the Greek, painting in Novgorod in the fourteenth century, a craftsman a long way from Constantinople, where he had previously worked, and probably bearing his nickname with pride as a guarantee of excellence. There was his colleague, St. Andrei Rublev, whose *Trinity* icon is the standard by which all other Russian *Trinity* icons have since been measured.

Those craftsmen would be amazed that their work is so highly valued centuries after they cleaned their brushes. They would be disturbed to see so many pieces hung in museums, far from the devotional atmosphere for which they were made. For every craftsman that we know by name, there were scores of others who are nameless to us; they made their own brushes, ground their own pigments, hammered goldleaf, chiseled ivory, painted frescoes, spun, dyed, and embroidered wool and silk, and set mosaic tesserae in plaster or wax. We do not need to know their names: We have their work.

DONORS

To the other people in the town, the man who paid for an icon to be made was a donor; to the craftsman he employed, he was a patron. Depictions of donors are more common in icons made under Western influence than purely Byzantine ones. They stand or kneel on the sides of the icon, facing or turning toward the main figure. Their hands are extended in prayer or hold a model of a building that they have commissioned. Sometimes the donor is prostrate before Christ the way someone would bow himself to the ground in the presence of the emperor. Some imperial figures stand in the presence of Christ, showing that the emperor was God's representative on earth and his court was a showing-forth of the court of heaven in which the Divine Liturgy continues forever. Donors might be aristocrats (or their wives—female patronage was very important); bishops, abbots, or whole monastic communities; small landowners or merchants. The patron of a church building was often a different person from the person who commissioned the mosaics or wall-paintings after the building was complete. Thereafter, many different local donors could contribute icons for the iconostasis and other sites in the church.

Donor-portraits are rare in icons until the late Middle Ages, but are more common in post-Byzantine icons. They are more often found as frontispieces to illuminated manuscripts and in frescoes, especially in Cyprus after about 1300.

The donor may be half-scale to the main figure, showing the difference of status between them. A different spatial logic had to prevail. The difference between donor and saint was that the saint wore classical robes and the donor wore contemporary clothes. It was the clothes and the relative scale that showed the difference of status.

Often all that we know about a donor is that he lived and prayed. An art historian suggests why donor pictures were popular for so many centuries:

> Perhaps something of the ancient magical attitude toward the image still survives in the custom. . . . Who can tell whether the donor did not feel somehow reassured in the rough and tumble of life, in which his own part was perhaps not always very saintly, to know that in some quiet church or chapel there was something of himself—a likeness fixed there through the artist's skill, which always kept company with the saints and angels and never ceased praying? (E.H. Gombrich)

In many cases the patron was a monastery, a local church, or a charitable institution such as an orphanage or hospital. In the Byzantine Empire, the most sought-after patron was the emperor, a member of his family, or someone in the imperial court and in the various layers of bureaucracy that surrounded it. Whether the patron was a banker or the emperor's minister, he was the driving force behind the icon.

The patronage system worked in an age that painted according to iconographic rules: A client could order a *Virgin of Mercy,* or a *Baptism,* or a half-length *St. Theodore* and have a reasonably good idea of what it would look like. He specified the size, medium, and subject and dealt directly with the craftsman, leafing through his pattern-book and manual to see what the iconographic possibilities were. The patron didn't just put limits to expense (specifying the size or materials of the artwork), but would also express preferences about subject matter. If he was a cleric or monk, he would probably have the religious education to devise his own iconographic program. However, lay patrons would have required here the assistance of a theologian, especially in the case of a complicated schema of church mosaics or frescoes.

Of course, the painter would be very much part of the discussion: After all, he had to execute the project, and from experience gained in carrying out earlier commissions, he knew what could feasibly be done in what situations and in what detail. So making a medieval fresco-cycle or icon was the result of a cooperation between a triumvirate: patron, religious advisor, and artist.

Within the limits of the iconography, there would be decisions about style or the position of the figures. If the patron visited the workshop he could see finished icons and say, "Make it like that one with a bit more blue," or "Can you do this in the new style from Thessalonica?" It was the craftsman's job to please the patron within the parameters of an iconography that had been decided generations before. We are so used to thinking of a painter as a specially inspired and gifted individual that the idea of employing one to paint in obedience to iconographic rules requires a conscious mental shift. Why did such a system of patronage not produce boring and badly made work, as an analogous system today might from someone paid by the hour to design cheap wrapping paper?

The system produced magnificent pieces because of its underlying idea: that an icon was a living bridge between saint and worshiper. Though some craftsmen were out-standingly good and others were not very good, they approached their work with, at least, some degree of faith and with deep respect because of what society and their Church told them an icon was. More fundamentally than the iconographic rules, a deep respect controlled their hand. They were not just painting a figure on a piece of wood: They were making a door to the spiritual world.

GUILDS

In the West, craft guilds were economic in origin and in motive: They protected the members from exploitation (though increased numbers of middlemen made internal exploitation easier than when a maker dealt directly with his patron). In Byzantium, craft guilds were needed to prevent icon makers from producing pictures made according to their own ideas and not according to the norms fixed by Church authority. By the tenth century, guild membership was not always hereditary. To join a guild the assistant had to be recommended by five members; he appeared before the notaries and answered questions about himself and his craft. If the answers were satisfactory, he became part of an organization that ultimately was controlled by the imperial government.

Every city in the Empire had a guilds department headed by the city prefect who represented the State and controlled the making, importing, exporting, buying, and selling of all goods from bread to silk. Living in a later millenium, we perceive such control as claustrophobic, but the Byzantines did not see it that way. *The Book of the Prefect*, a tenth-century outline of the rules, explains the purpose of control:

> God, after having created all things that are and given order and harmony to the universe, with his own finger engraved the Law on the tablets of stone and published it openly so that men, being well directed thereby, should not shamelessly trample upon one another and

the stronger should not do violence to the weaker but that all things should be appointed with just measure. Therefore it has seemed good for Our Serenity also to lay down the following ordinances based on the statutes in order that the human race may be governed fittingly and no person may injure his fellow.

Order, justice, and accurate measurements were not just politically expedient ideas to medievals: They were a showing-forth of the character of God, who was, in himself, order, justice, harmony, and righteousness. If the craftsman failed to keep guild rules he was guilty of something akin to blasphemy, and it was perfectly reasonable to flog him or confiscate his workshop equipment. The Orthodox Church laid down the iconography of the art of making an icon, and the guild enforced those rules. Whether it was a painted panel, a small brass pendant, an embroidery, or a mosaic, it was a channel linking the worshiper and God. The guild was responsible for seeing that it was made the right way because sooner or later everyone, from prefect to painter, would have to answer to God for what he had done. To be an icon maker carried spiritual responsibilities.

They were making those sacred images with physical materials. The next chapter is about the media and techniques that they used.

❖ FOUR
Materials and Techniques

INTRODUCTION : THE LIMITATIONS OF RAW MATERIALS

To know how medieval icons were made can give us an awareness of the detailed craftsmanship involved and so enhance our appreciation of them. Such knowledge can bring a sense of wonder that physical substances can be manipulated to make an object of spiritual power.

A medieval craftsman began his work with the preparation of raw materials and learned, through years of apprenticeship, how to gouge, grind, sieve, stir, chip, chisel, and pound them. He was in close touch with what he made from first to last, and from that hands-on knowledge of his materials he learned their inbuilt limitations. He understood that it was part of the way that things had been made: God had designed an elephant tusk in one way and steatite, the spotless soapstone, in another way; therefore they could not be carved the same way because they had not been created the same. The craftsman could do nothing to change these facts because he was part of the same created order.

His challenge was to take the raw material to the edge of its potential. Far from being a source of frustration, the limitation of raw materials became his inspiration. A mosaic could be made with tesserae forty-one to the inch or it could be made in larger pieces to cover the dome of a Church. Gold could be formed into granules that were teased into a line like beads. Egg yolk, powdered minerals, and vinegar could be mixed to paint a cloud, or a piece of metal like the diaphanous feather of an angel's wing. The craftsman understood that he was a creator in the image of God, the primordial artist—not that he could create from nothing, but he manipulated raw materials to make something that had not existed before in that form.

The following materials and techniques are listed in alphabetical order.

COLORS AND PIGMENTS

An icon painter's pigments came from various sources, and he took care to select which ones were most appropriate to use. The right pigment was whatever gave him the color he wanted, whether it was blue from lapis lazuli, or red from cinnabar.

A master craftsman had personal contacts for buying the minerals and dyestuffs, which were traded across the

Middle East and the continent of Europe. The best colors for icons are always mineral, not vegetable.

The craftsman who worked with paints had an explorative mind; the world was his art shop and he could draw color from many sources. As he worked with raw materials he observed the processes by which animal, plant, or mineral substances are changed into a pigment with which he could paint. He saw things change into other things: The alchemists had told him amazing change was possible, and it happened in his workshop in many ways.

Among the colors taken from animals or insects were the scarlet and crimson of medieval icons. These may have been from *Kermococcus vermilio*, which is the small pregnant beetle that clings to the holm oak in Greece, North Africa, and Spain. The colors were obtained after beetles were steamed in the fumes of boiling vinegar. Another source of color, this time of yellow pigment, was the pulverized gall bladder of a tortoise or large fish. And colors were often lightened with powdered ivory, bone, or cuttlefish. Ivory had special value because the Bestiaries (even though these are primarily Western sources) taught that anything from an elephant had power to protect from evil. When the craftsman wanted black to outline figures in a painting, he took bones or wood and had his assistants burn them, then grind them with pestle and mortar.

But for the most part, vegetal and other organic colors are not suitable for panel-painting in egg tempera. Ground-up minerals always produce the strongest "fast" colors, made from salts of, for example, iron, copper, and manganese. These details should not scandalize our twentieth-century minds but increase our appreciation of medieval paintings. Their beauty shines through the craftsmanship as ordinary materials have been manipulated into icons with transcendent power. Some colors were hard to obtain and came from various distant countries, such as the expensive lapis lazuli (ultramarine) from remote Afghanistan. Because they were expensive these were often used for the smaller touches of color.

Reds and blues often are the predominant color in icons, but yellows and greens are also common. Sources for this yellow pigment were salts of copper and chrome.

Blacks? The dense black of Satan and his angels was a pigment made from shoots of grapevines or sticks of hardwood burnt to charcoal, ground, and mixed with gum arabic. Another source of black was lamp soot, readily available in a society that used oil lamps.

Browns? There are deep, rich browns in medieval icons, saints' robes of velvety depth, the color (made from colored earth and minerals) standing clear from the gold background.

The people who painted animals on the walls of the Lascaux caves used some of the mineral colors that Byzantine icon painters were to use seventeen thousand years later: manganese, red ochre, hematite, yellow ochre, burnt ochre, charcoal. The prehistoric painters mixed their colors in shells, too, as painters continued to do till the modern era. Colored earth was dried and sifted, then stirred in water and allowed to settle till the impurities rose to the top and the grit sank to the bottom. This technique produced the cheaper red and yellow ochres, used in wallpainting. Not only soils, but ground rocks and minerals, from malachite to lapis lazuli, provided various colors to icon workshops.

That distinctive "purple" of Byzantine icons? It is Byzantine purple, a deeply saturated red-brown, the color of porphyry marble. From about the sixth century it was the preferred color for the Virgin Mary's veil, dyed with the color associated with the imperial court, and the highest in the color hierarchy of alchemy.

These are only some of the colors and sources of colors and pigments that we see in icons. Medieval colors can still be seen in egg tempera paintings that have been carefully cleaned, in textile icons that have spent most of their life folded from light, and in illuminated books whose closed pages have preserved the colors for hundreds of years. Knowing the sources of pigments will not detract from our appreciation of the pictures but will enhance our understanding. For all their spiritual impact, icons did not drop from the sky ready-made; craftsmen transformed the ordinary materials of animals, plants, and minerals to create them.

DRAWING THE DESIGN

While assistants were preparing boards and mixing gesso, the master of the atelier would be getting on with the most important job—drawing the design for the icon. Doubtless, there were many preparatory sketches, but the finished drawing (or "cartoon") on thin parchment would contain all the fundamental outlines of the image, and would of course be the exact size of the panel. Using a sharp stylus, he could incise the design onto the surface of the gessoed board, and then pencil the incised marks so the drawing showed up clearly. These blueprints could, of course, be reused or adapted in the future. As painting an icon proceeds, the drawing tends to get painted over, so it may be necessary to press through parts of the design from the parchment onto the panel again.

EGG TEMPERA

Egg tempera is the medium with which most pictures were painted. The powdered pigment is mixed with egg yolk, then diluted with a little water or vinegar. It was known in the early years of Christian art and for about a thousand years was the most common means of applying color to a panel. Flemish painters continued to paint with egg until the fifteenth century and most icon painters still do. Most

Orthodox icon painters believe a "real" icon can be painted only with egg, applying the conservatism of an ancient style to the materials with which the picture is made.

When mixing egg tempera, some painters prefer wine vinegar as a dilutant because it acts as a preservative for the egg. Craftsmen's descriptions use the term "laid on," which describes the action of application well. Short strokes are necessary for a quick-drying medium on a smooth surface: an example of how raw materials determine technique, which, in turn, affects the style of the picture. Layers of progressively lighter hue are laid on within each color-zone, and shading and highlights are made by thin, parallel strokes called hatching and cross-hatching.

The medieval craftsman mixed the prepared paint in an oyster shell cradled in the palm of his hand. For small amounts of paint, he used a mussel shell, light in the fingers and easy to wipe clean. He noticed that eggs from country hens had rich yellow yolks that were best for painting the flesh tones of men's faces. Eggs from town hens, kept in a courtyard and fed on scraps, were paler and better for painting the faces of maidens. Because his colors came from raw materials rather than from readymade pots and tubes, he was aware of subtle differences and bought his eggs accordingly. Egg tempera dries fast and must be used with precision, so the artistic decisions must be made in the mind rather than on the panel and new ideas worked out on a spare piece of gesso-covered board. It is a medium that imposes order and forethought on the process and is well suited to iconography. One can, however, make quick corrections by overpainting inadequate passages once their paint is dry.

"FRAMES"/PANELS

Figures in many icons are painted as though close to the picture surface, ready to step out into the room; the absence of a separate frame and glass enhances that sense of communicating with the viewer. A picture with a protruding frame pushes the picture back into the wall whereas one with no frame comes forward to meet the viewer.

Panel icons are made with built-in frames that extend the plane of the picture flatly on four sides. In this case, the "bed" or surface for painting is chiseled out of the solid block. There was a practical reason for this method: With the picture painted on gesso there had to be something to prevent the edges from becoming chipped. Often a detail of the icon, such as a halo or foot or the tip of a lance, extends into the frame, increasing the impression that the figure is floating forward from the picture surface. The built-in frame, originally designed to protect the gesso, was copied in icons of metalwork and enamel, and sometimes (especially in Russia) strips of stamped silver, or silver-gilt, were pinned onto the frames of painted wooden icons.

Icons sometimes also had simple frames nailed on the panel after they were painted. The frame's wood strips were gessoed and painted with egg tempera to harmonize with the colors of the icon. Sometimes the corners were mitered. The frame was still a narrow extension of the picture plane rather than being a strong feature that modified the viewer's relationship to the picture space.

Traditionally, the "frame" is an integral part of the panel: The image was painted on the plastered surface of a bed, chiseled out from the block, leaving the edge (about 1 inch [2½ cm] wide "framing" the composition. Frames in the modern sense (least of all with glass) were *never* used; in post-Byzantine practice, strips of wood might be glued around the picture space, but these could easily become detached in time.

To eyes tuned to Renaissance Western art, an unframed picture looks unfinished, as though it has just been lifted from an easel in the artist's studio. We have grown used to pictures contained within a frame of four neat walls, so an unframed painting gives a feeling of insecurity. We prefer art to be tame. But icons are not tame art: They are designed to float forward from the wall into the space in which we live.

GESSO

Gesso (*jess*-so) is the Italian word for gypsum, the layers of plaster put on a wooden panel or wall before the picture was painted. The chalky material was ground to a fine powder and mixed into a solution of 5 percent fish glue and 95 percent water. It is warmed and carefully stirred so as to dissolve all lumps, while avoiding the creation of bubbles (these appear as small craters on the final surface, when dry, and necessitate the tedious work of prolonged sanding down). Usually, several layers of gesso are laid onto the board with a spatula, allowing each to dry before applying the next. The solution looks like gray thick porridge, but when dried and sanded smooth, it is pure white and takes a fine polish. Gesso is a necessary and a lasting base for an icon's paint layers, providing a smooth and consistent surface on which to work. Getting a smooth, perfect gesso surface on a panel was the principal task of the painter's assistant. But gesso has an advantage over wood as a painting surface because it has no grain, so is equally absorbent in every part. Also, painting directly onto a wooden panel is impossible; the paint would soon flake off.

At every stage the craftsman's aim was to make a surface for the paint that was not only even but was white and shining, to enhance the brightness of the paint. Every stage in panel preparation was directed to the final result: an icon that would glow with inner light.

GILDING

In icons, gold was used where it could best express the eternal light of God; it gleams from haloes, from the robes of the glorified Christ, and from the backgrounds, indicating a radiance of uncreated light. Of course, not all patrons could afford gilded icons; in this case, yellow paint can be used for highlights, and a neutral tone (often ochre or green) used for the background.

Gold Paint

The paint was called shell gold because it was held in an oyster shell or mussel shell, cupped safely in the craftsman's hand. It uses about three times as much gold as goldleaf but fine lines can be drawn with it. Cennini, a fifteenth-century writer recommends mixing gold powder with green pigment "if you want to make a tree look like one of the trees of paradise." Rays of fine gold lines flaring on the robe of Christ spoke to the medieval eye of the uncreated light of God beaming through his body. Gold on the clothes of the Virgin and the saints spoke of their holiness: that already in this life, the bodies of the saints are being transformed ("deified") by the immanent energy of God.

Rubbed Gold

Glass was ground to powder in a pestle and mortar, mixed with resin or white of egg, and painted on the areas of the panel to be gilded. When it was dry, a lump of gold was rubbed on it and minute flakes of the soft metal were abraded by the ground glass. It gave a gentle gleam, a surface minutely textured.

Gold Leaf

Give a medieval goldbeater one ounce of gold and he could hammer seven hundred and fifty sheets of gold leaf, each weighing between a half and a third troy grain (20–30 mg) and each 3½ inches (9 cm) square, which is still the most convenient size. He used a goldbeater's hammer, beating the lump first to foil, then layering the pieces of foil between squares of parchment.

To fix gold leaf to the panel, the craftsman used water gilding or mordant gilding, tree resin or white of egg that had gone bad, or the juice of rotten garlic (in both cases the rottenness increased the stickiness). A mordant had to retain enough stickiness during the painstaking process of placing the gold leaf, then it had to dry hard.

The leaves of gold were dropped gently onto the panel from a little shovel made of thin cardboard, and tapped into place with a square brush. The craftsman tried not to overlap the sheets because it would have been wasteful. Each leaf had to be handled, placed, and smoothed with extreme care, for a careless breath would send it sailing across the worktable to land in a folded heap. Finally, using a stylus, the affixed gold leaf had to be shaped to the exact contours of the painted areas (e.g., a halo round a head).

Tooled Gold Leaf

A gold halo had to be distinguished from its gold background. To accomplish this, the craftsman placed the point of a compass at the eye of the saint (for full-face, between the eyes) and swung the other point around to make a perfect circle, pressing the line into the layer of mordant. From the eleventh century, craftsmen developed a technique of drawing many concentric circles with a compass so the halo looked like a golden disc. When the icon was seen by the light of a gently swinging lamp, the reflected light made the gold-leaf halo seem to rotate.

For a glittering design, finely carved metal punches were placed on the surface and tapped down, the patterns imitating the work of goldsmiths. Usually, such raised passages of gesso would be stamped before gilding.

Gold was the ultimate metal for the craftsman to work with: malleable, rust proof, and expressing the light of God in a visible form.

Burnishing

When the underlying mordant was dry enough, the surface was burnished. The original meaning of burnish is not to make something shiny but to make it dark brown. When gold leaf is burnished, the surface draws the light down in a rich reflective gleam as a deep pool of water. Instead of being merely bright, burnished gold is dark-bright. The burnishing tool was the tooth of any carniverous animal, usually a dog's canine tooth, mounted on a small stick.

Chrysography

Any word with "graphy" at the end has something to do with writing, and "chrysography" (kris-*og*-graff-ee) means writing in gold. The word can mean the drawing of fine gold lines as well as writing inscriptions. To accomplish chrysography, the craftsman mixed powdered gold with paint, or laid a carefully cut strip of gold leaf along fine lines of mordant, then scraped the excess gold from either side of the line, or used a stylus to scrape off paint over gold leaf.

Chrysography in icons is not just a pretty decoration: It shows spiritual light shining through the robes and body of Christ as God Incarnate, especially in scenes of his glorification: the Transfiguration, Resurrection, Ascension, and Christ Enthroned in Heaven. In later icons the drapery-folds of the robes of the Virgin Mary and the saints were outlined with gold as a reminder that salvation is not only for the soul, but that matter also must be transformed by the power of God.

ICON COVERS

In addition to the use of gold leaf to provide a gold ground, stamped or engraved sheets of silver (often gilded) could be used to cover the neutral background on an icon; similarly, heavier strips of patterned precious metalwork could be used to enrich the surface of the borders. In both cases, the metal plates (often known as *oklad*) would be cut to measure, decorated by tooling for punching, and then pinned with tiny nails onto the woodwork. This practice goes back to the twelfth century, but did not become widespread until the sixteenth, and then mainly in Russia. In addition (especially in Russia), decorated silver haloes and collars (sometimes with gems, or enameled) could be fixed onto the painted figures of saints.

Until the early seventeenth century, the metalwork acted as an enriched surface to set off and complement the figural painting. But in seventeenth- to eighteenth-century Russia, gleaming metalwork, sometimes gemmed, pearled, or enameled, came to be what people most valued, usually at the expense of the painting.

By the eighteenth century, icon covers (or *rizas*) fashioned all in one piece and covering the entire board, might substitute not only for the background but for the figures too. By the end of the nineteenth century, with a riza covering so much of the painted area of the icon, sometimes all you can see of the paint surface are the faces and hands.

When one sees an all-over icon cover for the first time, the motive is difficult to understand. Why hide a picture? Seen in imagination from within Orthodoxy, it has its own logic. The icons that have covers are usually panel pictures with one or two figures that relate directly to the viewer.

An icon is believed to be a point of contact between the viewer and the subject. Given that belief, the most important parts of the icon are the hands and faces; the hands make gestures of intercession or blessing, or they hold something significant, or they point our attention to Christ. A riza focuses attention on the areas of greater importance and by being worked in precious metal, it endows the whole picture with greater splendor. When you see an icon cover, it is worth considering that the design may have something to say about the main figure.

Icon covers function not only to enhance a picture, but also to protect the surface of the paint. In cases where there is damage to the surface or an area of the icon is darkened, the riza covers the damage without drawing attention to it. We must remember that until the late nineteenth century, there were no effective ways of cleaning icons: They had to be either repainted or covered with a riza.

JEWELS AND GEMS

Some metalwork icons, book covers, and icon covers are set with precious and semiprecious stones chosen for their virtues.

Because of the color hierarchy of alchemy, red or purple stones were considered the best; there were rubies from India and red garnets from Eastern Europe. Blue garnets or sapphires from India were valued because they were the color of heaven; porphyry marble, a brooding, dusky purple, was the stone associated with the emperor; amber from the Baltic glowed like gold. Rock crystal and, in some late Russian icons, diamonds from India sparkled like solidified light.

In the Byzantine period, small portable icons were carved on polished gems such as emeralds and also on semiprecious hardstones such as chalcedony, jasper, or sardonyx.

A craftsman and his patron may have chosen a particular stone for an icon cover or a frame because it was available and balanced the color of the picture, or perhaps their reason was the virtues and powers that the stones were believed to have. To say that gems were chosen only for their beauty or display of wealth would be to interpret a medieval object through modern eyes, though sheer glitz had a special appeal for Russians!

MANUALS AND PATTERNBOOKS

Manuals listed the rules for painting: the hand positions of the Virgin and Child, the physical characteristics of an apostle, the colors of a saint's robe. Much of the iconography was known to the craftsman by heart and eye and by repetition over years of daily work. In the same way today, an experienced cook may need to follow a recipe the first two or three times and then uses the recipe book as a collection of ideas. If a patron asked for something that was outside the rules of iconography, the craftsman, backed by his guild, could appeal to the manual or consult a churchman. New styles and subjects developed within the framework of Orthodox tradition while the manual of instructions was an anchor against the tempting winds of novelty.

A *patternbook* held the craftsman's personal collection of designs. They were drawings copied from his own, his master's, or other craftsmen's work, in any medium. It is unfortunate that no patternbooks survive, and the earliest manual is by Dionysius of Fourna, written in the sixteenth century. It undoubtedly reflects earlier practice as enshrined in previous manuals no longer extant. We can only surmise the use of patternbooks from ongoing practice in Orthodox countries.

A patternbook was likely to contain pictures of heads and hands in various positions, patterns to stamp on gold haloes, an ox and ass for a *Nativity*, faces of various saints, and unusual devices to fit into difficult architectural surfaces (for icon painters could do wall paintings as well as panel pictures). There were patterns for borders and trees and tiled floors, a sheep with its head up, a sheep with its head down, a seraph's face, an angel's wing, gold vessels for the Wise Men to carry, and inscriptions for pictures of scrolls, held by prophets and saintly writers. Painters' apprentices in fifteenth-century Florence were recommended to practice drawing for a year; during that time they would have copied pictures from the patternbook. This may well also have been the practice in the Christian East.

The patternbook was as much for the patron's eyes as for those of the craftsman. The craftsman was visually fine-tuned; once he had mastered a design he could probably carry it in his head, but patterns were still useful for reference and for teaching apprentices. It was the patron who needed to have designs spread before him. Patternbook and manual would both be on the table when a piece of work was being discussed.

MEASUREMENTS

If you have ever pulled a length of string along your outstretched arm from fingers to nose, and called it a yard, you have used a medieval measurement. Icon craftsmen measured in simple units based on the width of nail, length of thumb, spread of fingers, length of foot, length of fingertip to elbow, to armpit, or to nose. They weighed valuable pigments in balance scales as carefully as pearl traders, and they weighed lower-priced pigments in homely measures: half an eggshell, or a walnut shell. Master craftsmen had exact measuring rules, checked by the representative of the city prefect, the Byzantine equivalent of a government inspector of weights and measures.

MECHANICAL REPRODUCTION

The Orthodox Church teaches that an icon is a privileged point of contact with the saint or Gospel scene. That teaching was formulated when all pictures were original pictures and the only way to copy an icon was to set up a prepared panel on an adjoining easel and paint another icon. When it was finished, there would be two "originals."

Today, a picture can be copied by mechanical means. An icon can be photographed (that is one copy) and the photograph scanned (a copy of a copy) and put onto the screen of a computer, or an image put onto the page of a book (a copy of a copy of a copy). The page of the book can further be xerographically reproduced by a copier in an office supply shop.

Some churches on the outskirts of Moscow, now reestablishing themselves after the Communist era, have paper pictures on the walls, blessed, venerated, and loved as though they are original panel icons even though the materials are ephemeral. Provided the original painting is made according to the proper iconography, a mechanical reproduction of it may be thought of as an icon. Some Orthodox churches sell selections of color reproductions of icons, often mounted on boards and varnished, for those who cannot afford original works.

METALWORK

Wherever metalworkers were, neighbors had to bear with the chink and tap of hammers on blocks, the grump-grump of animal-skin bellows, and the long roar of the furnace. The sounds of metals being crafted have not changed through millennia. Some workshops specialized in making metalwork for painted icons and portable icons of metal. Among the tools were specially cut punches for decorating the gold of a halo in imitation of hammered gold, and a collection of soldering bits, horn hammers, gravers, and burnishers familiar to metalworkers today. The workshop smelled of copper, borax, and pitch.

A goldsmith cooperated with an icon painter, for they worked together on icons that were gilded. The prepared panel, marked with the area where the haloes were to be, went to the goldsmith to be gilded, burnished, and sometimes decorated with (gilded) silver strips or grounds, then it went back to the painter to be painted. A silversmith cooperated with an icon painter for making an icon cover, or a silver frame. The surface of metal was decorated with chasing (fine lines engraved on the surface, for details of hair or draperies), punching (of mechanical repeat patterns using dies), or *repoussé* (patterns hammered into the metal from the back, making raised patterns on the front surface). For all techniques a heavy iron bowl was filled with warm pitch mixed with gesso and tallow, and set on a coil of rope so that it could be tipped at different angles without shifting. The surface of the pitch cushioned the blows on the piece of metal and held it steady.

Mordants

A mordant was used to fix colors into threads or fabric, and to fix gold leaf to a panel. Dyers' mordants were alum, copper, iron, stale urine, or tin. Mordants for fixing gold leaf to a gessoed panel were water, stale egg-white, animal glue, garlic juice, or the craftsman's breath.

Painting the Icon

Once gilding was complete, the artist could finally turn to the business of painting. The outlines of the design already would be drawn on the gesso surface of the panel. Then the artist would start with undercoat, then move always from dark hues to lighter, often finishing one section or figure at a time.

When a craftsman paints a given color-zone (e.g., the red-brown of the Virgin's veil), it is essential to make a good reservoir of the dark base-tone. This forms the first layer, then the craftsman paints increasingly less extensive layers of lighter tone, always adding brighter color to paint from the reservoir (this ensures tonal harmony). White by itself is *never* used to lighten the tone within a given hue; great experience is required to know what complementary color is needed to brighten up a darker tone.

PANEL PREPARATION

A panel picture is one that has been painted on a board rather than on stretched canvas. To make a panel icon the craftsman began with a piece of wood. That sounds obvious until we remember that a medieval craftsman did not have ready-made things from an art shop; he worked with raw materials from their most basic state.

The wood was seasoned hardwood, preferably poplar or limewood, which was hard and not too resinous. A panel riven from the center of a log had an easier grain to work with than one nearer the periphery.

But even if the slice had come from the middle of the log, the panel would tend to bow outwards on the painted side as the unpainted side swelled and contracted differently with changes in humidity and temperature. Red bole and gesso and paint on the back all helped to keep it flat to a small extent, but bowing was inevitable if the board was not first thoroughly seasoned.

If pieces of wood were joined to make a large icon, they were butt-jointed with a glue of quicklime and a cheese similar to ricotta. For very large and heavy pictures, there was a variety of dovetail or butterfly grafts, with struts and pegs. The back was either finished as smooth as the front or left somewhat rough, depending on the workshop and what the patron was willing to pay. Sometimes wooden slats were let into the back to counteract bowing, but unless these were well seasoned and physically compatible, they could accelerate the cracking of the paint surface.

A recessed panel was prepared differently. It was marked in a rectangle, then cut out with an adze to make a recess with a depth of ⅓ inch (1 cm) or less, depending on the thickness of the wood. The recess was called the ark or shrine because the holy picture would rest there. The depth of the recess was half-filled with gesso, the edges of the panel around it making an integral frame. To strengthen the panel, the back might be braced with thin struts of the same wood. Nails were sometimes hammered in from front or back (workshop practice varied) and the rectangular nail-heads were countersunk. At this stage the carpentry was over. Then, the whole panel was painted with several applications of a gelatinous adhesive.

A large panel had a piece of loose-woven linen or coarse hessian (burlap) soaked in glue and smoothed over it to prevent the picture coming apart if the wood should split or to serve as a binder for the gesso. Next, the panel was covered with layers of gesso.

Every stage in the process of preparing a panel had a practical purpose. The built-in frame protected the icon from chipping at the edges. The first brushings of glue filled up the porous structure of the wood. The linen strengthened the panel against cracking and provided something for the first layer of gesso to bite on, after which each layer would fuse to the one beneath. The depth of the panel recess allowed several layers of gesso to be brushed on without its rising up above the frame. A wood surface would be of varying density because of the grain and knots; a thoroughly smoothed gesso had a surface as even as polished ivory, and prevented wood grain from showing through the paint layers.

Repainting and Copying

An icon was believed to be a privileged point of contact between the viewer and the subject of the picture, so logic demanded that the picture be clear: You had to know who you were looking at and who was looking at you.

In homes and churches, lamps were lighted near the icon so it could be seen and to draw attention to its presence. The fumes of oily carbon floated invisibly upwards and settled on the panel while dust floated invisibly down, and after several generations, the icon would gradually become illegible. If the paint needed to be freshened, an icon painter would also repaint the picture, partly or completely. Provided a craftsman worked within the proper iconography, he could change details or indeed style, brighten or alter a color, or add gilded highlights to the robe of the figure.

The motive for the changes was not the same as with a present-day picture restorer who claims to make as few additions as possible and will make no change that is irreversible. A craftsman repainted an icon to make the picture clear to its contemporary owners because as a sacred image, it had to communicate. He knew that, in turn, others in the long future might repaint his work. The work, the craftsman reasoned, did not belong to him or to his own artistic expression, but to believers within the Church—which was a thing far greater.

Sometimes a craftsman made a new icon by copying an old one as closely as he could, or he might repaint it in the current style of his period.

Restoration

From the moment an icon is made, it begins to degenerate. Changes of humidity, temperature, and light affect the materials; the wood panel swells and contracts, making layers of paint crack or flake off; the wood develops a curve like a shield so the icon no longer rests flat against the wall. With the wood in movement, an icon cover pulls against its tiny nails, lifting at the corners. Lamp and incense smoke and dust settle on the painted surface. As well as the inevitable changes caused by the passing of time, an icon may even need to be restored because of deliberate violence or (more often) accidental damage from a fall or a fire, or because it has been put away in a shed for over a century, as with an icon that is now identified as by Rublev.

The first thing restorers recognize is that they cannot turn the clock back. To try to make any ancient picture exactly as it was originally is not technically feasible, given the inevitable changes wrought by time. A restorer stabilizes the situation without trying to recreate the original condition. The grime of ages is very carefully removed by people who know what they are doing. Flakes of paint can be fixed, or bent icon covers can be eased back to their place if they are not so brittle that bending would crack them. There was a time when restorers tried to flatten curved panels, often with disastrous results. Also colors can change with time: In some textile greens made of blue overdyed with yellow, the yellow is so faded that the balance of colors has shifted, the picture showing blue grass and blue trees. A small, computer-enhanced photograph could be displayed beside the original to show gallery goers what it might have looked like originally, but for the icon itself, the color must be corrected by imagination. If mosaic tesserae have fallen from walls or ceilings, our skill can replace or stabilize them, but if they have been dashed from the walls and thrown away, our imagination must replace them. With the shifting of a wood panel, pieces of painted gesso fall off: Our imagination must put them back and cover the paint with some neutral shade. Not all modern restorers would agree—some insist on repainting, but in our view one should respect the integrity of an ancient work of art: Conserve, not remake.

But a cracked and mellowed icon has much to communicate; prayers have been said before it for centuries, and it may have lost its youth, but it has gained what only time can give.

STENCILS AND TEMPLATES

For drawing a repeated shape, such as a border, the craftsman used a stencil of cut parchment or stiffened linen, then tidied the edges and added details in freehand. For a row of figures in very similar shape and position, such as the sixth-century *Procession of Martyrs* in St. Apollinare Nuovo, Ravenna, he might have used a template or mold made of thin wood or stiffened canvas like those used by quarry workers for cutting pieces of building stone. Other examples that were probably made with the help of templates are icons showing figures in brocade robes. A seventeenth-century Romanian icon of *Sts. Constantine and Helen*, and another of *St. Nicolas*, show them wearing robes decorated with precisely repeated patterns as though they had been cut out of wallpaper.

TONES AND HIGHLIGHTS:
THESE SPEAK OF THE LIGHT OF GOD

Some icon figures painted in the fourteenth century shine as though there is light inside them. The effect is achieved by altering the relationship between the tones; a greater difference between the light-middle shade and the highlight makes the drapery folds and faces shimmer as though with spiritual light. Some robes are painted with a dark line down the middle of each thick white highlight. Seen in bright daylight or gallery light the effect is startling; seen as the icon painter intended, in gently moving lamplight, the figures seem to be wearing clothes of thick silk. You can almost hear them rustle. The highlights may not be a paler shade of the robe but a different color; an icon of the Prophet Haggai shows him in a purple robe with turquoise highlights, opposite colors of the spectrum.

Tones and colors may be blended into one another by thin washes of egg tempera. A luminescent effect is achieved by mixing more water with the egg tempera so it will not dry so quickly. When one color is brushed thinly over another the one underneath glows through, looking like veils of different colored silk floating in front of a gentle light.

Highlights are always the final touches to be added to an icon, together with inscriptions, which identify the person or scene depicted.

VARIOUS MEDIA FOR ICONS

Icons have been made in different ways through the centuries. There are many media for icons that deserve a mention—mosaics, textile icons (tapestries, etc.), lacquer icons, wall paintings (frescoes), and tablet icons. In order to keep to basics, however, this book focuses on the most traditional portable medium—the panel painting.

VARNISHING

The final touch to a painting was a varnish of resin, heated and mixed with two parts of linseed (flaxseed) or walnut oil. By the time the craftsman had reached that stage he would have had a feeling of friendship with the icon. He and his assistants had made it grow from a rough section of wood through all the stages from cutting the panel to painting the figure. Now it had dried and was ready for the varnish.

Assistants heated the resin and filtered the linseed oil to clear it of impurities that might scratch the gold. With the icon flat on the worktable the varnish was painted onto the panel and left to dry completely. Varnish deepened the colors and prevented the egg tempera from cracking with changes of temperature and humidity. The varnish would, however, trap dust and lamp carbon, and also darken with time, problems with which future craftsmen would have to cope.

Medieval Orthodox Christians valued icons so much that they not only had them in their churches and in their homes, they also made small ones to take with them on journeys and to hang around their necks. The next chapter is about portable icons.

❖ FIVE
Portable Icons and Painted Panel Icons

ICONS MADE TO BE WORN
A citizen of pagan Rome wore an amulet around his neck; Christians often wore crosses or portable icons. They could be as small as 2 inches (5 cm) square with a ring at the top for a waxed string to go through. They were carved in wood, bone, steatite, ivory, and semiprecious hardstones, and cast in brass, copper, bronze, silver, or gold.

Bronze or brass amulets were popular because they were easy to mass-reproduce by casting. Cheaper icons could be reproduced from a metal prototype. And final detail could be incised on the surface (when hard-set) with an engraving tool (a technique called "chasing"). The icon was sometimes enhanced with enamel or gilding. Other portable icons were cast as *ampullae,* which were tiny bottles for holy oils or water (especially from pilgrimage sites). The pictures followed the iconography of larger painted icons of Christ, the Virgin, saints, and scenes from the Old and New Testaments. By the nineteenth century they were made by sandcasting with or without chased or engraved details, and later were sometimes electrotyped on thin metal. They were unfamiliar in the West; an early nineteenth-century writer, quoted below, described a portable diptych as a "little brass book." Small portable icons taken from soldiers who died in the Crimean War were brought to England as "curiosities of Russia."

When a peasant is about to send his son to serve in the army, he often takes from his neck the icon that he and his forefathers have worn and places it, with his benediction, on the young soldier's breast. . . . he carries it suspended round his neck, through the vicissitudes of a campaign; and when, his labours ended, he returns to his native parish, he often hangs this cherished possession upon the iconostasis of his village church, as a votive offering to commemorate his preservation. (Rev. W. S. Simpson)

Such portable icons had been worn in Russia since the tenth century; a man's icon might be buried with him or be nailed to the wooden tomb marker set up at the foot of the grave. Portable wooden icons were made with a narrow frame nailed on after the picture was painted. Grooves in the vertical strips of the frame allowed a lid to be slid down to protect the picture when its owner was traveling; or the icon might be made as a triptych, in which the wings could fold over to protect the painted surfaces. (Portable metal icons of this type also exist, often enameled.) Triptychs could serve as traveling altarpieces, to be set up on a bedside table for prayer.

FOLDING ICONS: DIPTYCHS, TRIPTYCHS, AND POLYPTYCHS

Icons were sometimes made in two or more panels hinged to unfold. When a picture is sometimes open and sometimes hidden behind its little door, we have a different relationship with it than with a picture that is open to sight all the time. There is a subtle sense of meeting and greeting when we open the door. The nearest that Westerners come to that experience is the medieval or Renaissance multi-paneled altarpiece, or the opening of a door on an Advent calendar.

Early icons made in separate leaves were joined by having strips of wood nailed along the top and bottom edges, extending about ½ inch (1¼ cm) beyond the width of the wood panel on either side. A hole was bored in the extensions, which were held together with wooden pegs or brass rings. Later the leaves were joined with pintle hinges.

Diptych

Businessmen and scribes traveling in the Roman world wrote on tablets of beeswax set into wooden panels. To protect the writing, two wax tablets were hinged to fold together and the outside was decorated with pictures. The structure of the Roman bureaucrat's notepad was a *diptych* (*dip*-tick), literally "two-fold." The hinges were metal or leather rings. A traveler in the Christian world had an object the same size and structure as the writing tablets with pictures on the inside painted on a gesso ground. It opened to provide a devotional focus, similar to the twofold photo frame that a modern traveler would put on the bedside table in his hotel, to provide familiar faces in a strange room.

A Roman consul (chief magistrate) was appointed to serve each year from January 1. The official announcement was placed between two decorated ivory or bronze rectangles hinged like a book and with a message in wax. Some of the ivories now in museums are panels from such consular diptychs. Others originally may have been part of a relic box or a box for jewels, or may have decorated a piece of furniture or a book-cover.

Triptych

The logical development from the two-fold was the *triptych* (*trip*-tick), or "three-fold." It stood up more steadily than the diptych. The center icon was often a *Crucifixion,* the side panels could be the Virgin and St. John or the two praying figures of the traveler's patron saints. From about the eleventh century the top of the triptych was often shaped in a lobed semicircle like the top of the Royal Doors of an icon screen, though rectilinear shapes were more common.

Polyptych

The *polyptych* (*pol*-ip-tick), meaning "many-fold," developed from the triptych, with additional leaves to unfold. There could be as many as seven tall narrow panels on either side of the center picture; the icon would fold zigzag to form a solid block. Unfolded, such a polyptych resembled a small icon screen and was taken to wars by Orthodox priests to celebrate the Divine Liturgy near the field of battle. Some of the icons that we now admire were originally parts of di-, tri-, or polyptychs that later owners (or thieves) have sawn apart to sell as separate pieces. An icon of one figure looking and gesturing to the side of the panel may be part of such a dismembered group. Very often such groups form a *Deisis* (Greek for "intercession") group, in which *Christ Enthroned* occupies the central panel, flanked by interceding saints with raised hands, standing in pairs.

MINIATURE ICONS

They include the small icons to be worn around the neck, as well as calendar icons, family icons, and icons of a saint and his life. Whether they are of high quality or provincial style, they are often examples of careful, dedicated craftsmanship.

The most daring examples of miniaturization are the tiny mosaic icons made in the late Byzantine period. A full-sized mosaic set on the dome of a church was designed to be seen from a distance, so the colors merged as though they had been painted, but the colors of a mosaic designed to be held in the hand would only work the same way if the tesserae (or cubes of semiprecious stones) were very small. Miniature mosaics were made with all the details of a full-size mosaic in a picture sometimes smaller than a postcard— examples of virtuosic workmanship in an age of affluence. To be a usable object for devotion, it did not have to be that detailed; to be portable, it did not have to be that small. One may wonder whether the agonizingly slow and minute facture was worth the effort and expense, when miniature painting could have produced an equally exquisite result.

To make a miniature mosaic a craftsman had to cut hundreds of square tesserae, smaller than a pinhead. The skill was that of a jeweler except that no jeweler would need to cut so many tiny pieces for a single piece of work. The glass tesserae, called *smalti*, had to be well made so it cut clean rather than splintering. Without a well-ground magnifying lens, the cutter would have been able to work for only very limited periods of time, and the hours taken to finish one icon would have made the job very expensive. But such tiny objects were clearly valued by the Byzantines for the skill of the workmanship and the preciousness of the materials.

What a mosaic cutter needed was a single magnifying glass held in a frame above the work surface so he had both hands free. He cut the glass or marble tesserae with a *hardie* (a chisel mounted in such a way that the glass or stone could be tapped with a hammer and "cut" against the sharp edge of the chisel). The icon panel with its recess would be cut and prepared as for a panel picture.

We seldom see a miniature icon in its true size; usually it is enlarged to fit the page of an art book or a screen in a lecture room. In a museum case it looks too small to be real, like something seen through the wrong end of binoculars. It looks as though it was designed larger with every detail, then miniaturized, but in fact, the models were probably painted miniatures from manuscripts.

PROCESSIONAL ICONS

Some icon panels were taken from their church for the procession and returned to their place on the wall or the icon screen. The ones described here are banners, made especially for carrying and painted on fabric rather than wooden panels, though wooden processional icons, painted on both sides, were also common. A processional icon of fabric was stretched on a wooden frame or suspended from a crosspiece on top of a carrying pole, similar to trade-union banners today.

If it was to be embroidered, the fabric was silk or silk brocade backed with canvas, linen, or hessian. If it was to be painted, the fabric was primed like a tablet icon with two generous coats of animal glue, beeswax, thick honey, and gypsum in roughly equal quantities. The mixture had to be sufficiently pliable when dry so as not to crack with the soft movement of the fabric in air. When it was dry it was burnished with a bone or pumice; the result was a smooth, pliable surface that could take egg tempera or the limewater pigments used for wall paintings.

The back of the canvas was also primed to prevent moisture getting through to the picture and to make sure both surfaces of the canvas expanded and contracted at the same rate. A processional icon usually had an image painted on both sides. The painting had to be bold in style, like stage scenery, so people at the back of the crowd could see it clearly.

RELIC BOXES

The relic box, or reliquary (*rel*-i-kwer-ee), was a small container, richly decorated, containing parts of what was claimed to be the body of a saint, or something he had worn or owned. Relics make some Western Christians uncomfortable and prevent them from appreciating relic boxes as the beautiful objects that they are. The belief behind the veneration of relics is that God redeems the physical world, including our bodies, and that his power can reach us through material objects. A reliquary is an object of magnificent workmanship, jeweled, gilded, and carved to the highest standards that the craftsman could attain.

Reliquaries were made in the form of a small box with an arched lid, a similar shape to an early twentieth-century steamer trunk or a treasure chest in a children's story about pirates. Some reliquaries have a pitched roof in order to make it look like a shrine or chapel. Images on reliquaries may be painted or made of ivory, metalwork, or enamel, and follow the same iconography as panel paintings.

Some painted icons of saints held what was described as "sacred dust": A physical part of the saint or his clothing, or dust from his tomb, was incorporated into the painting materials used to prepare the wood panel. An icon made like that was, in itself, a relic. Another type of a relic-icon is *St. John the Baptist and Saints,* sixteenth century, Walachia. Blocks of wax are built into the panel, one beneath each saint and fifteen small ones surrounding the Baptist. There is a relic inside each one. When Crusaders looted Constantinople they took away not only gold and jewels, but also many relics. To the medieval mind, hallowed bones were even more precious than jewels.

In the early development of the icon-cult, there is a close connection between image, relic, and pilgrimage. Images which incorporated "sacred dust" or enshrined bones, or decorated reliquaries, gradually became charged with spiritual power believed to be immanent in the relics of saints. There was a lively trade in relics in Late Antiquity and the Middle Ages, closely associated with pilgrimage to the Holy Places in Palestine and to the shrines of saints.

The creation of prototypes at the pilgrimage site—be it of scenes of the life of Christ stamped on ampullae (metal flasks) from the Holy Land, or commemorative icons of a wonder-working saint, mass-produced at his shrine as sacred souvenirs for pilgrims—all served to standardize the iconography.

Some of the icons brought to the West were sawn apart, because they were composed of several different scenes or saints' portraits. The next chapter is about such icons.

❖ SIX

Several Pictures Together

CALENDAR ICONS

Calendar icons are icons with several saints, painted in miniature and arranged in rows. Today we have dictionaries of saints, a list of saints for every day of the year with a short biography. The Eastern Orthodox Church had *menologia,* which were collections of saints' lives, each connected with the day of the month that was the saint's feast day. A calendar icon is a visible menology in which the saints of a given month stand in rows facing us directly, or in a scene of martyrdom, or with their hands raised in prayer. Each is identified by a written name. The inscription is essential to an icon, because (unlike in the medieval West), very few saints in art carry personal attributes (the keys of St. Peter are an exception). Often, however, generic attributes attach to types; for example, martyrs usually hold palms. A church that could not afford to have a separate icon made for each saint could have several on one panel. It was an opportunity for a painter of miniatures to display his skill. The background is plain and the saints stand on a narrow stage like a shelf, often against a gold ground.

FAMILY ICONS

A family icon is a domestic icon designed for a household in which everyone has their own patron saint. The main picture is in the middle, and several smaller pictures of different saints or scenes form the border. Depending on the size of the household, the icon's outer border may consist of many smaller pictures, each of a different saint. If the craftsman was trained as a miniaturist, the border pictures are exquisitely painted. After several generations the center could have been sawn free of its borders to lead a separate existence.

HAGIOGRAPHICAL ICONS·

The word "hagiographical" (ha-gee-oh-*graff*-ickle) means something written about a saint, a saint's biography, except that a biography is meant to be factual, whereas a *hagiography* (ha-gee-*ogg*-graf-fee) may contain traditional stories (some the products of pious imagination) designed to inspire the reader in his own Christian life. (Of course the painter and the beholder would have believed them to be factual.) A hagiographical icon has a large central picture of a saint surrounded by incidents from his life. A calendar icon or a family icon shows several saints; a hagiographical icon is about the life of just one. Byzantine icons of the saints focus on victory rather than violence. In the case of martyrs, the main figure stands in the middle, calm and victorious, giving the whole icon a strong sense of the centrality of peace. Details of how he was chopped, sawn, pressed, flayed, wheeled, spiked, and hanged form smaller pictures in the border. The direction in which you are supposed to read the incidents varies, but it is usually left to right, from top to bottom. You need to know about the life of the saint to know in which order to look at the pictures.

A hagiographical icon invites reflection on one incident at a time, while the main figure looks back at us from the center like a friendly adult watching a small child.

It is that flexibility in iconography that makes icons fascinating. Each one may have variations that were decided by the patron's personal choice or that reveal a theological issue being debated at the time. You look at the basic format, then look at the variations and consider why they are what they are. Looking at icons is never boring: One can always discover more.

ICONOSTASIS

An *iconostasis* (eye-kon-oh-*sta*-sis) is a screen of icons in an Orthodox church that divides the main body of the church from the sanctuary, where the altar is. The icon screen developed slowly as a line of demarcation that defined the sanctuary in which holy things happened. In Early Byzantine churches the first step toward an icon screen was a *templon,* a low marble wall with pillars topped by a marble beam. After the fifth century, curtains were hung between the pillars; later the curtains were replaced with a row of icons at eye level.

It is understandable that Western Christians should think an iconostasis is an Eastern version of the rood screen, but it is a development of the altar rail. The idea of a separate sanctuary or holy space may horrify modern Christians who have never worshiped in an Orthodox church, though the experience of those who have is that priests, deacons, and laity take part in a unified act of praise because "God is holy and loves all mankind." On the other hand, it is true that the iconostasis makes it impossible for the laity to see much of the service. Orthodox Christians think this adds to the sense of mystery.

It was the Russian Church that developed the iconostasis in its present form. By the sixteenth century the arrangement of icons on the dividing wall had settled to a logical pattern. Read from the top down and from the center outwards, an iconostasis shows God's work in history from Abraham and Moses to the Christian period. The center doors, called the Royal Doors, are opened during the Liturgy for the sacrament to be brought out to the people. Painted on the Doors are the *Annunciation* and the four Evangelists because the Virgin Mary bore Christ for the world—he is the "way in" to salvation—and the four Evangelists told us about him. The bottom row of figures are of local saints, with Christ, the Virgin, and the patron saint (or feast) of the church nearest to the central Royal Doors. On the beam above are icons of the Festal Cycle; on the next register is the Deisis, showing the intercession of the Virgin and the Baptist and pairs of different categories of saints (archangels, apostles, bishops) converging inward from both sides. Christ is the axis, the center point of the composition, and the Christ figure is presented frontally. (These figures may be half-length or full-length.) There may be even higher tiers of prophets, and of patriarchs, especially in later Russian churches—often surmounted by a crucifix, dragons, and ornamental crestwork.

Such towering Late Medieval/Early Modern iconostases completely block off the sanctuary from the nave. Instead of witnessing the action of the Liturgy, the worshipers are confronted with the hierarchy of heaven and the history of salvation in iconic form.

When you see a complete iconostasis, first look at the Royal Doors, then identify the figures to the right and left of them. Then look up to see what is happening above the doors and who is looking at you.

ICONS IN ICONS

It is easy to miss them but they repay deliberate looking. In a panel painting, an icon *in* an icon is sometimes very small and is painted with as much attention to detail and iconography as the main figures. It is not there merely to fill the space: The figure in the roundel, or segment of the heavenly sphere, is an integral part of the icon.

Here are some examples. In an icon of the saints Prokopios, Demetrius, and Nestor from the eleventh century, Christ looks out at us from the top of the picture over the heads of the saints. He is there as the source of their sanctity, as the one who awards them the crown of martyrdom. In the *Virgin Paraclesis and George of Antioch,* 1143–51, Christ is in a segment of a circle at the top corner of the picture; he holds a scroll and leans toward the Virgin, giving her his blessing and receiving her prayer of intercession. In the *Virgin of the Sign,* twelfth century, from the Spaski Monastery, Christ is in an icon in an icon on the Virgin Mary's breast, his hands spread in blessing. This is an icon of the Incarnation, showing the Virgin as God-bearer (*Theotokos*).

Occasionally you see an icon *of* an icon: One example is the *Triumph of Orthodoxy* (celebrating the Restoration of the Icons, which occurred in A.D. 843), painted about 1400, in which two angel-deacons hold the miraculous icon of the *Virgin Hodegitria.* They look at us and point to the icon, as with the same gesture, the Virgin looks at us and points us to Christ. On either side of the angels stand the imperial rulers of the ninth century who restored the icons to veneration, while the lower register shows various saints who participated in the struggle against Iconoclasm. The icon is shown with a stepped wooden base and has red curtains behind it and a gold embroidered curtain hung below. Also, the Orthodox heroes of the Iconoclast Crisis are often shown holding icons—for example, St. Stephen the Younger, an iconodule martyr, is shown holding an icon in the twelfth-century monastery of St. Neophytus on Cyprus (he's the originator of the definition of an icon as a two-way door).

SIX-DAY ICONS

This format is a Russian development; a six-day icon may have more than six pictures but it includes one specifically for each day of the week. Sunday is the *Anastasis* (Resurrection, shown as Christ's descent into Hades). He is shown plucking Adam and Eve from their tombs. Monday's picture is the *Assembly of the Archangels*; he is the Christ child as an icon in an icon, held by archangels. Tuesday is a Russian subject, the *Assembly of the Baptized*. It shows St. John the Baptist on the banks of the Jordan baptizing several people, while others on the opposite shore take off their clothes ready to step into the water. Wednesday's icon is the *Annunciation*. Thursday is the *Washing of the Disciple's Feet*. Friday is *All Saints' Day,* the icon showing several groups of men and women standing in clouds of glory; there may be a child martyr among them. Saturday's picture is the *Entry into Jerusalem.*

Whether an icon was large or small, a wall painting or an amulet, mosaic or embroidery, it had to be made according to the iconography that reflects the mind of the Church rather than the whim of the craftsman. The next chapter is about that language.

❖ SEVEN
Visual Language

This chapter has been arranged alphabetically according to the visual and thematic details one might find in an icon.

INTRODUCTION: ICONOGRAPHY
Orthodox Christians believe that an icon is a window into the heavenly world, a privileged point of contact between the viewer and the subject of the picture that communicates a living, power-filled presence. Its purpose is to convey or

mediate spiritual realities rather than merely to show a saint or to describe a scene from the historical Gospels. That is why icons are made according to an iconography that develops from generation to generation but remains recognizably itself.

In the same way the spoken and written language is an iconography that changes little and slowly. We do not re-invent our language for every new generation of babies but speak to them with a collection of words and grammatical structure that we were taught. A language can communicate only when speaker and listener both understand the words. Icons are a visual language; they are made according to iconography that develops but that remains rooted in tradition.

When we see styles of icons slowly changing from century to century, it is easy to think triumphantly, "Ah, good—in spite of being chained down by a rigid system, an artist's individuality could still force its way through!" That is a modern reaction, a historically limited and con-ditioned attempt to make the past conform to our ideas so that we can feel more at home with it. The average Byzantine icon craftsman did not feel manacled by the sys-tem within which he worked: on the contrary, it gave him security and focused his creative efforts in a disciplined way. Such changes as there were in icons came almost without being noticed and were sometimes at the instigation of the patron. There was a tendency here, a flourish there, figures a little more (or a little less) elongated than they had been in the craftsman's father's time. The guild with its rules was the ground on which the craftsman stood.

Anyone who has grown up with the Anglican *Book of Common Prayer* or the Latin Mass can understand a little of the Orthodox Christians' love of icons. Those who are cradle Orthodox have grown up with them; they cannot remember the first time they saw one, kissed one, or had one explained to them. The iconography has sunk deep into their hearts and minds. It is an art that has taken them to God, consistently, year in, year out. If they have studied the history of that art, they know that the style has been changing continually and subtly over the generations, and they also know that there is a continuity that has been able to absorb the changes without a wrenching sense of shock. The pictures speak to them and for them; the familiarity of the iconography allows a depth of relationship.

Hiring a Craftsman to Follow Iconography

Somewhere behind every icon there was a craftsman working at a commission for his patron; the impulse for a new icon was from the patron who paid for the work, rather than from a painter or carver or metalworker who wanted to express himself. The patrons expected the craftsman to follow iconography rather than giving his imagination free range. If the patron was not himself a churchman, the importance of theological advisors to select and control the iconographic program was key.

A prosaic parallel from present-day life is of someone hiring a plumber to put in a washbasin. The householder is the patron, hiring the craftsman for a particular job. He chooses the design and color and tells the plumber which wall it is to go on and how high off the floor, but technical details of pipes and washers are for the plumber to work on. If he belongs to a union, it stands behind him, telling him what he can and cannot do. The parties agree on a price, and the craftsman does the job. When it is finished, the washbasin must be steady on the wall, the taps must turn on and off, and all the pipe joints must be properly sealed. To earn his money, the plumber must leave the householder with a functioning object.

So it was for a patron and a maker of icons as for any other object, sacred or secular, that a medieval craftsman was commissioned to make. They discussed details and agreed on money. Finally the craftsman presented the patron with an object that was primarily purposeful, rather than decorative: It was to communicate Christian truth and to be a bridge to the transcendent world of reality. Since an icon of a saint, was a privileged point of contact with that saint; the face, figure, attributes (if any), and inscriptions had to be recognizable according to the accepted language of Christian art.

To parallel an icon maker with a modern plumber will be shocking to Orthodox Christians, but I am writing to Western readers. In the West we have absorbed the romantic idea that an artist is a specially gifted and sometimes eccentric individual who paints whatever he likes. Medieval craftsmen were not thought of, and they did not think of themselves in this way. They were highly skilled craftworkers undertaking a spiritually important job, and they were guided by the tradition of the Church rather than their own whims and emotions.

Though styles shifted over the course of generations, we can look at two icons painted several hundred years apart and know them both to be the *Annunciation,* or it might be, *St. John the Baptist.* It is because icons teach facts of revelation or unchangeable Christian doctrine or portray a unique sacred individual that they cannot change their fundamental iconography. The iconography is not limiting: it is like the disciplines of classical ballet or music, pan-cultural and pan-generational, capable of development and capable of expressing everything in human experience.

Think of the iconography as like the structures of a written language, and think of the different styles as like language written in different typefaces, or interpreted, creatively used, by different native speakers, especially poets. When you can read a language, the difference of typeface or emphasis or interpretation does not confuse you.

Throughout this book I have referred to the men who made icons as craftsmen because that is how they thought of themselves. If we had applied the word "creative" to them, they would have been shocked: they would have reminded us that only God can create. In their own perception they were craftsmen or artisans, and their place of work was a workshop where they made icons within the accepted tradition handed down to them. The beauty and variety of icons shows that the iconographic canons (rules) are not a limitation.

The following details of iconography are in alphabetical order.

ANIMALS

As with other details in an icon, an animal is not just a meaningless space-filler but is part of the message of the whole picture. To medieval people, animals and birds were more useful than decorative. They had been created to be eaten, ridden, worn, loaded with burdens, or harvested for quills, fleece, or leather. Animals were living bundles of usefulness.

Since medievals were not materialists, they could not think of animals as only useful objects, so they gave them spiritual value as well. Animals in icons either make a spiritual point as symbols, or they help to identify one of the human figures. For example, camels are usually in the picture to identify the saint such as St. Menas, an Egyptian martyr, who is usually portrayed praying between two kneeling camels. In a *Nativity* icon in the later medieval period, camels identify the men with them as the Magi.

Lambs are often featured in icons. A lamb on a throne in Early Byzantine art is the *Agnus Dei* (anyus *day*-ee), the Lamb of God. It is visual code for Christ from John the Baptist's recognition of him: "John saw Jesus coming toward him and said, 'Look, the Lamb of God, who takes away the sin of the world!'" (John 1:29). The book of Revelation also refers to Christ as the Lamb of God, once slain, and also as the victorious Ram.

Interpreting the spiritual symbols of an animal can be tricky because medievals had no trouble in giving *different* symbolic values to one creature. For instance, the serpent slain by St. Michael or by St. George represents defeated evil. But a serpent is not always a symbol of evil, for Jesus told his disciples to be "wise as serpents" (Matt. 10:16 RSV).

Not every animal in an icon is a symbol: Sheep in an icon of the *Nativity* represent sheep. They are in the icon to show that the men near them are shepherds. A nice touch in a fifteenth-century icon by Nicolous Ritzos is that the four sheep are looking up at the angelic host, showing that the sight and sound of the angels are objective realities. They are not religious ideas inside the shepherd's heads because the sheep can see the angels, too. In other *Nativity* icons, it is the shepherd's dog who is looking up.

Any given animal can mean different things in an icon; it is important, then, to interpret it by its context.

ARC OF HEAVEN

The arc of heaven is the segment of a circle at the top of the icon. It is shown in icons by a half-circle at the top, or a quarter-circle at one of the top corners. In an icon, heaven is represented spatially, as though it were a defined place: as though heaven were "there" while we live "here." Medieval people were not uninformed; they understood that God is transcendent and ineffable, yet also that his presence and influence are everywhere throughout his creation, that he is not really peering over the edge of a heavenly window at a world down below. The half-circle is visual shorthand.

The arc of heaven is usually blue and there may be stars in it. Divine intervention (or the presence of the undepictable Father) may be indicated by a ray or a hand. Sometimes Christ is shown as the head and shoulders of a figure with a cruciform halo. He leans over the edge of the arc, his attention focused on the saint or the scene, conferring blessing or receiving prayer, or witnessing a martyrdom or a miracle. The shaft of power in an *Annunciation* icon comes from the arc of heaven, with the dove representing God the Holy Spirit. A similar shaft of light (containing often the star of Bethlehem) descends from heaven onto the head of Christ in the manger in a *Nativity* icon, and also on Christ at his Baptism and at his Transfiguration.

ARMS, VERY THIN

Some figures in icons have sunken cheeks and extremely thin arms and legs. They look like someone dying from AIDS. Craftsmen knew that a man in that condition would hardly be able to stand, but they were painting spiritual rather than physical suffering. *Christ on the Cross*, in the Middle Byzantine period, is shown with thin arms and legs when the image shows him drooping in pain. St. John the Baptist and hermits are painted with sunken cheeks and emaciated limbs. Icon art communicates spiritual reality; what something looks like, as though seen through a camera, is of minor importance—though, of course, in the case of ascetic saints, the emaciation may have been literally true. But in general, there may be a tendency toward dematerialization to heighten the spirituality of the icon, though such an expressionistic tendency is more evident in certain periods—in the seventh to eighth or the eleventh to twelfth centuries.

ARRESTED MOVEMENT

Icons have a quality of stillness that is presented in one of two ways. Compare an icon of *Christ Pantocrator* or a *Virgin Hodegitria* with, for example, an icon of the *Raising of Lazarus*. Looking at the *Pantocrator*, we are confronted with the changeless reality of Christ as Judge and Savior, or the *Virgin and Child* as presenting the fact of the Incarnation; looking at an icon of the *Raising of Lazarus*, we see the same Jesus Christ acting in a moment of human, historical time, but yet also a moment of eternal significance.

The *Lazarus* icon shows that moment as arrested movement: Christ's hand is raised in authority, the once-dead man shuffles from the tomb, two members of the crowd carry away the door of the grave, a man claps his hand to his nose, saying, in effect: "Lord, he's going to stink." If we had been there with a camera, the figures might have been arranged differently showing the moment in arrested movement, a decisive moment of time when the clock ticked and something unrepeatable happened. But iconography makes it possible to show a moment of history, and to point to its spiritual significance. It shows us timelessness in time.

There are many other examples of arrested movement in icons. Elijah is swept up to heaven in a fiery chariot, his cloak drops to the ground toward his successor Elisha. The archangel runs in to tell the Virgin Mary that she has been chosen to bear the Messiah. The archangel's wings are half spread and his feet barely touch the floor. At her surprise, the spindle in her hand drops. In a *Dormition* icon Christ lifts up the Virgin Mary's soul and holds her for us all to see: Death is not a process but a decisive moment of time. In an Early Byzantine *Annunciation* mosaic (St. Maria Maggiore, Rome, fifth century), an archangel stands, and turns, and turns again from facing the Virgin to facing St.

Joseph. As we run our eyes over the picture from left to right, we almost have the experience of watching a figure in movement. A hagiographical icon has the saint in the center, confronting us in great stillness, while the surrounding pictures show him in moments of arrested movement.

BODY LANGUAGE

People express their feelings all the time without words, and the stronger their feelings the clearer the body language; instead of their words being shouted, their body speaks. Think of a silent film directed by Eisenstein or Chaplin, or think of an advertising billboard: We understand the body language so clearly that spoken words are not needed. Reading the body language of people in icons is no different from reading it in real life or in silent films because all people express themselves choreographically. It is a language more basic than sound or speech. Here are some examples in icons:

Christ and St. Menas (sixth-century panel painting, now in the Louvre): Christ has his arm around the saint's shoulder and is looking at us, introducing us to his friend. *The Angel with Joachim* (about 1100, mosaic at Daphni, near Athens): The angel is blessing him with quiet authority while Joachim sits, his hand held forward as if to ask a question. *The Forty Martyrs* (ivory, twelfth century, now in Berlin): Forty soldiers, stripped of their warm clothes, are huddled together on a freezing lake at Sabaste, visibly shivering, awaiting death. *The Virgin of Vladimir* (a panel painted in Constantinople about 1125, now in Moscow): Christ's tiny hand is curled around her neck. They are actively embracing. Looking at the icon, we can feel the softness of the child's cheek against our face. *Rachel Weeping for Her Children* (a fourteenth-century painting at the Markov Monastery, Serbia): Rachel, representing all the mothers of Israel, mourns the killing of the first-born.

We see TV news footage of some disaster in which a woman in the crowd is flinging her arms about like Rachel in the icon. The choreography of personal grief is universal and unchanging through time. *The Anastasis* (a fourteenth-century wall painting in St. Saviour in Chora, Constantinople): Jesus has gone down to hell to lift up Adam and Eve, who represent the whole human race. He pulls them out of their coffins like a mother plucking children out of a snake pit. You can almost hear him say, "Come *on!*"

Sometimes the figure of a donor is shown in the position Orthodox Christians call "proskynesis" (pross-*kin*-ee-sis), a posture of deep humility and supplication. It is a prostration, kneeling with the body and arms stretched forward and the head and forearms touching the ground. That deepest bow had been the position taken by someone who had been granted an audience by an emperor; how much more appropriate when in the presence of the King of Kings?

BUILDINGS IN ICONS

One building that was intended to be identifiable in icons is Solomon's (or Herod's) Temple. It is the craftsman's way of telling us that the scene of the icon is taking place in Jerusalem. The Temple has pillars and towers and may be taller than the other buildings. The houses are shown with clustered walls, roofs, and windows.

To eyes tuned to Western art, the perspective looks wrong: Doors and windows are out of scale with themselves, and the group of buildings is out of scale with the figures. The icon painter is not concerned with drawing a precise architectural elevation. Instead, he creates an impression of a town and lets us concentrate on the event that is taking place in it. The event is more important than the setting. The setting is there to show us whether the historical event took place inside or outside, in a man-made environment or in a landscape.

The buildings are not specific. The event really happened, but it has a spiritually timeless quality, having occurred in a particular time, and yet being for everyone always. Icon buildings cast no shadows, which is another indication of their timelessness; shadows show the depiction of time by the passing of the sun across the sky. The event similarly has a spiritually placeless quality, having happened in a particular place, but being valid for all people everywhere. The fantastic character of the architecture (often surreal in color as well as literally unbuildable) points to the significance of the event as a moment in salvation history, the intersection of the timeless moment. Eyes tuned to Western art flicker across the oddly shaped buildings searching for a horizon line or a perspective vanishing point. It isn't there, so we return to the figures because they are the center and purpose of the picture.

Sometimes a *Crucifixion* icon has a turreted wall behind the cross in a straight line from frame to frame. It is visual shorthand that means Christ was crucified outside the gates of the city. An icon of the *Incredulity of St.Thomas* has the risen Christ in the center of the picture, showing his wounds to the doubting apostle. Immediately behind him is a shut door, a reference to the Gospel of John (20:26), when he came to the apostles even though the door was shut. Though unusual for medieval icons, the door is natural scale to the figures rather than being shown half-size. That is because the door is a feature of the story.

Icons of a pillar saint (or *stylite*: an ascetic who spent his life on top of a column, like *St. Symeon Stylites)* show a figure in a waist-deep box set on a pillar. To Western eyes the proportions are ludicrous, but the picture is not meant to be realistic in the Western sense. These saints built platforms on their pillars, like a treehouse without the tree.

Most were several feet square with room to walk and lie down and make prostrations in prayer. What the icon says in visual shorthand is "Saint on a pillar." A drawing goes straight to the heart of the subject by showing what it *is*, rather than only what it *looks* like.

As we try to sort out some logic in the buildings in icons, it is like walking through the architecture of memory or dream. It shows someone's subjective perception of a town. Think of a familiar town: In the first split-second of memory before your inner eye settles on a particular scene, you see a composite picture; you may see both ends of a street at once, or two elevations of the same building. What you see in your imagination is what it feels like to be there: In memory you see all of it at once. It was centuries before Western artists painted buildings like those we see in icons. When they did, they were called Expressionists, or Surrealists.

CLASSICAL DETAILS

The term "classical art" refers to the art of ancient Greece or Rome. Christian art was established in the Roman Empire, and it returns to its classical roots from time to time. After generations in which figures were painted in an elongated two-dimensional style like tall, cardboard cutouts, a change of style brought figures modeled "in the round," with shadows on cheeks and limbs. Clothes cover and reveal the three-dimensional shape of real bodies, fingers are a believable length, feet stand solidly on the ground. In such cases, the proportions also change: Figures become average human height, more solid, and rounded. From time to time Christian art feels its classical roots twitch.

Details from the art of ancient Rome (or more precisely, of Late Antiquity) persist in icons no matter what the style. One example is the clothes of supernatural figures.

In Byzantine art, angels are generally shown with classical heads. Curly hair follows the line of the head with some curls trailing down the neck; a narrow fillet or ribbon is around the head just back from the browline, often with a jewel in the middle and with two ends flying at the back. Angels wear the clothes of the Roman Empire or the Byzantine court. Look at a late-twentieth-century Christmas card with angels; it is likely that they are still wearing a Roman *dalmatic* and classical hairstyle. It is as though they got dressed to accompany the first Christian martyrs to the Coliseum, and never had time to change!

Roman art included figures that were not historical individuals but *personifications,* and icons use the same visual language. Some icons of the *Baptism of Christ* show the figure of a man, reclining in or near the river Jordan. He is the river-god Jordan, who was vanquished when the Incarnate God stepped down into his wet kingdom. "The sea looked and fled," says the Psalmist (114:3), "the Jordan turned back." Often, too, we see the (female) personification of the Sea, holding a ship. By being baptized, Christ claimed—and purified—the element of water for his kingdom, just as he was to claim earth by being born in a cave and being buried in one, and, Hades, by descending into the abyss to rescue the lost souls, and he claimed air by being lifted up on the Cross and by ascending through the air to heaven. Such icons emphasize the cosmic dimension of the Incarnation.

A miniature of Isaiah in prayer shows the prophet standing beside a haloed figure who has a burning taper held upside down and a dark veil swirling over her head; she is the personification of Night. An icon of the *Anastasis* sometimes has a figure lying under Christ's feet, fettered and powerless; he is not Satan but a personification of Death, the last enemy to be destroyed (1 Cor. 15:26).

Whenever the art of the icon swings from classical to transcendental or abstract style, personifications are abandoned and the immensely tall, thin, formal figures represent historical individuals from the Old or New Testament, or saints from Church history. Making them look "real"—that is, as though seen through a camera—is not important because icons show more than material reality; they focus on the inner spiritual person. Then, as time rolls on, Christian art's classical roots twitch yet again. In fact, there was a classicizing renaissance in Byzantine art roughly every 150 years, centuries before what we think of as *the* Renaissance in Italy, which (except in Tuscany) generally began after the fall of Constantinople in 1453. In Byzantium (unlike in the West) the humanistic classical tradition never died, but was periodically renewed.

(See also *Personifications*.)

CLOTHES

Some of the clothes in icons are a reminder of the classical roots of Christian art. Because they are pictures that show us eternal realities, they are not concerned with being up-to-date. And because they are not up-to-date, they never look out-of-date. The clothes are free from what the fashion historian James Laver called "the tyranny of time."

Christ

Early pictures of the *Crucifixion* show Christ in a *colobium*, an ankle-length, T-shaped tunic similar to a liturgical dalmatic with short sleeves. The crucified figure in a loincloth began to be seen in icons only in the ninth century. He now looks more vulnerable than in a robe, his wounds and emaciation can be shown clearly, and there is a greater emphasis on suffering than on victory.

In icons other than the *Crucifixion*, Christ is usually shown wearing classical, rather than Jewish, clothes. The main garment was a T-shaped tunic (*chiton*) with wide sleeves from a dropped shoulderline and with two broad purple or gold bands, called *clavi*, running down the seam lines from shoulder to hem. They were originally part of the structure of a robe that was once woven in separate pieces, though first-century weavers with a wide loom could make a robe without seam from top to bottom; it would have been a T-shaped garment made of one piece of fabric about 45 inches (1.14 m) wide with a hole cut for the head. Over the tunic is a mantle or cloak (*himation*), an ample garment, usually painted blue. Christ's robes shine from inner spiritual light, revealing to us the divinity of the Eternal Son hidden beneath his human nature. Although in Byzantine art he never wears royal robes or a crown, he is often enthroned as *Pantocrator* (Ruler of All). A sixth-century poem describes the earthly emperor as an icon of Christ, "The earthly lord is the image [icon] of the Omnipotent." Conversely, the imperial court and its solemn ceremonies is often used (especially in the fifth to sixth centuries) as a model of the glorious court of heaven.

The Virgin Mary

In icons she wears a *maphorion* (mah-*for*-ee-on), an ample veil, imperial (red-brown) purple in color, which covers her head and upper body, over a simple ankle-length dress. A striped coif binds her hair; you can see the edge of it (but not her hair) under her veil. However, like Christ in Byzantine art, she is humble, never wearing crown or regalia, even when enthroned.

The craftsmen who made icons could not bear to portray her in anything less than regal dignity because in their eyes she was the Queen of Heaven. They knew the Gospels, and understood that Mary of Galilee had never worn such fine clothes, nor was she attended by heavenly courtiers. In icons they showed her status, rather than merely what she would have looked like in history.

Apostles

At first the court who moved to Constantinople dressed as though they were still in fourth-century Rome. As their society evolved away from the western part of the Empire, the plain classical tunic was replaced with a more luxurious one of elaborately patterned silk brocade, the style imported from the Far East along with the silk fabric. For military or civil officials, a large trapezoid of a different color, a *tabellum*, was sewn on the edge of the cloak to identify the wearer's status.

The Apostles are pictured in court robes rather than as fishermen and tax collectors, because Church tradition respected them as the twelve men chosen by Jesus Christ to be leaders of the Church. For centuries of Christian art, they were pictured as patricians, men of the imperial court rather than of the lakeside.

Angels

An angel of God's imperial guard may wear parade-armor and carry a sword or spear, or he may wear a white tunic and *chlamys* (cloak broached at the shoulder) as did a court chamberlain or eunuch. An archangel who rules one of the four continents as Vicegerent of God wears imperial vestments, a smooth-fitting tunic and *loros*, a long scarf (in fact, a stylized toga) set with neat rows of jewels and wound round the body, one end hanging over the left arm. It was originally worn by the Byzantine emperor on the first of January to celebrate his accession to the imperial throne, and later at Easter, to celebrate the Resurrection; the jeweled scarf was given the symbolism of a jeweled winding sheet expressing death and life. So when you see a figure in an icon wearing a *loros,* think of Easter, the chief festival of the Church. The clothes communicate the message that, for this figure in the icon, the archangel, it is always Easter Day.

The clothes are not chosen at the whim of the crafts-man, but indicate that angel's relationship to other figures in the icon or to us: he is a guardian, or a defending soldier, or an ambassador, a viceroy, or an official in the court of heaven. His clothes identify his role as clearly as though he had a label around his neck.

Saints

A female saint wears court dress, a long, brocaded tunic with a wide scarf stiff with gold and jewels, a jeweled collar as wide as her shoulders and large drop-pearl earrings. Most male and female saints are shown as inhabitants of the court of heaven, in their triumphant glorified life rather than their earthly state, which may have been miserable.

Female virgin saints and martyrs often wear white. Even when they are pictured during their moment of martydom, they wear formal robes to show the spiritual importance of their death. Among the exceptions (in developing iconography there are often exceptions) are St. John the Baptist, who wears a sheepskin tunic as he did in the desert, and St. Mary of Egypt, and sometimes St. Mary Magdalene, who is covered by her long hair.

Clergy

A bishop wears an *omophorium* (omm-o-*for*-ee-on), a wide stole around the neck and shoulders with Greek crosses on it, black on white; a Greek cross has four arms of equal length. His chasuble is shaped like an ample poncho or (later) he may wear a *sakkos*, a wide-sleeved dalmatic. It, too, may have an overall pattern of square crosses. A deacon wears a stole (*orarion* [or-*ahr*-ee-on]), a long, narrow strip of fabric that, in the case of deacons, is worn over the right shoulder. He carries a Gospel Book to show he is ready to read the Gospel in the Liturgy, his principal liturgical function.

Laity

Young men generally wear a belted, knee-length tunic and sandals; older men wear a long tunic. Women wear a long dress with a long, wide scarf over the head and around the body. One end of the scarf sometimes wraps around a baby, in the manner of mothers in Wales up to the first half of this century.

Foreigners

A man who comes from east of Byzantium wears tight Persian trousers, a short, belted tunic and a hat made of soft fabric with the point tipped forward (the "Phrygian cap"—popular much later in the French Revolution!). The Magi are an example of this style of dress—they were said to be astrologers from Persia.

Old Testament People: Prophets and Patriarchs

Old Testament people wear long robes and distinctive hats with a small, cone-shaped crown, often red, rising from a turban. It was the hat that Jews wore in the Middle Ages, and it identifies the individuals as living under the Old Covenant before Christ came. This is especially the way in which Old Testament patriarchs (like Abraham and Jacob) or prophets (like Isaiah) are shown. The latter often wave prophetic scrolls, with messianic texts.

Shoes

Figures painted in classical style have Roman sandals. Military angels and saints wear the laced *buskins* (soft calf boots) of the later Roman legions with *cuirass* (breastplate) and short tunic. Red slippers are for Byzantine royalty so they are worn by holy kings and queens (such as Constantine and his mother Helena) and by the Virgin Mary because she is the Queen of Heaven.

Figures in icons made in Russia, the Balkans, or anywhere much to the north of Greece have curious black threads running across the tops of their feet from toes to ankles. Craftsmen in colder countries were copying classical prototypes; they had never seen Roman sandals and misinterpreted the pictures that were in an iconography developed in Southern Europe.

COLORS

Color Meanings

A medieval craftsman was not completely free in his choice of colors for an icon: He had to observe details of iconography, some of which were based on Christian doctrine. He chose his colors for three reasons: harmony, symbolism, and availability. The wishes of his patron had to be subsumed into those three.

Harmony of Color

Often a color does not mean anything: It simply balances the colors in the rest of the picture. For example, the icon of *St. George and the Dragon* painted in Novgorod is almost all in red, white, and steely blues. Beneath the saddle there is a quilted cloth painted in shades of tawny yellow. When we cover that part of the picture, the other colors go a little flat without the small contrast. It does not dominate the icon, but without it something is lost.

Medieval craftsmen were not tied by realistic convention with every color they used: A male saint might wear a full length robe of pale pink or a house might be green or blue. To emphasize the splendor of a saint, a particular garment might have the main hue and its highlights in two very different colors, for example, turquoise and fuschia pink.

Craftsmen were adventurous with color, painting a group of horses red, blue, and tawny yellow. (Horses in the eleventh-century Bayeux *Tapestry* were equally bright.) When the Fauve painters of the early twentieth century played games with color, they were doing nothing new. Sometimes the colors in an icon simply express joy!

Symbolism of Color

Much symbolism is obvious. Red, the color of blood, turns the mind to thoughts of life and vibrancy, or in the case of a martyr, death. Less obvious to modern Western eyes is that deep, reddish-brown purple was the highest color in the spectrum in alchemy. It had connotations of sacred monarchy, so it was worn by the Virgin Mary and by emperors. Yellow is the color of the sun and of life. The background of a saint may be gold or yellow to show that the saint is living in eternal light. Angel faces in Western art are the color of Caucasian flesh; faces of icon angels are sometimes golden as though glowing with the light of God.

Green, the color of leaves in springtime, speaks naturally of life and growth. Blue is a reminder of heaven for all people: Even in cold northern countries the summer sky is blue. The Virgin Mary wears purple to emphasize her queenliness, or blue as a reminder of her heavenly home. The most expensive pigments were cinnabar red and ultramarine. Because they were rare, they were expensive; because they were expensive, they were associated with high status, whether human or divine. The Council of Ephesus in 431 established that Jesus had been God in the flesh from the moment of his conception when the Virgin Mary said yes to the angel's message. She was therefore not just the bearer of a human baby, but also the Mother or Bearer of God. The color of her clothes shows her status. The blue of the Mediterranean sky was appropriate for a picture of the Mother of God, the Queen of Heaven.

In a fifth-century mosaic in Santa Maria Maggiore, Rome, crafted shortly after the Council of Ephesus, the Virgin Mary's dress is cloth of gold like that of a Byzantine empress. Later, gold was used for haloes and backgrounds while the Virgin's dress was painted Byzantine purple. (In Western art, her tunic is usually red and her cloak blue, visual memories of the most expensive and highly regarded fabric dyes of a thousand years ago.)

Black is the color of darkness and separation from the glory of God. The unmodified color (really a noncolor, devoid of the vibrancy of light) draws the eye like dead black in stage clothes. Since it was the lowest in the color hierarchy, it was used for pictures of devils. White, the opposite of black, is the color of light; Christ and the saints wear white tunics.

Keep the basics of color symbolism in mind without getting too analytical. If we go to an icon saying, "That color always means that, and that color always means that . . ." our minds and perceptions will be constricted instead of deepened and enlarged. The craftsman wants us to open our eyes and heart to the whole icon. In fact, no absolute or rigid color symbolism can be derived from the Byzantine texts, but often art and common sense together give us the clue!

Availability of Color

If a local supply of natural pigment ran out, or if a patron wanted a blue textile but it was not the season to pick woad, or if the price of imported indigo rose very high, or if a crop of yellow/orange saffron failed, the craftsman could not use the color that he wanted. This is even more true of the vagaries of availability of rare imported mineral colors used for icons, such as cinnabar or lapis lazuli.

Because he worked from raw materials rather than ready-made paints, if he could not get a color, he could not paint with it. Though availability may not have been a constant or a large factor in a craftsman's choice of colors, it was one of the factors. Consider that colors in an icon may have been chosen to mean something, but hold that consideration lightly.

CRAGGY ROCKS

The landscape of some icons shows mountains thrusting into the air; perhaps volcanic rock formations in Cappadocia, in central Turkey, were their inspiration? Jagged rocks appear in icons of hermit saints in the wilderness, the *Transfiguration*, the *Nativity*, and *Lazarus*, dancing with life from the presence and power of God. Indeed, they may figure in any outdoor sacred scene.

A nineteenth-century icon of Elijah has rocks transformed into flames fluttering from the wind of the Prophet's chariot. In an *Anastasis* icon, they bow toward Christ. When he entered Jerusalem, some of the Pharisees objected to the joyful noise the disciples were making. "He answered, 'I tell you, if these were silent, the very stones would cry out'" (Luke 19:40 RSV). The dancing rocks show the icon painter's vision: the rejoicing of an all-redeemed creation and the life of God diffused throughout everything that he made.

"Let the rivers clap their hands, let them sing before the LORD, for he comes to judge the earth" (Ps. 98:8–9). "The mountains skipped like rams, the hills like lambs" (Ps. 114:4).

What would mountains look like if they burst into song and skipped like lambs? They would look like the dancing rocks in icons—but it takes the eye of the imagination to see it!

DRAPERY

Some icons show a curtain hooked along a wall or looped up; in others is a piece of fabric like a bright towel twirled around the angle of the roof. If it is in an *Annunciation* or *Presentation in the Temple* icon and is red, it is perhaps a reminder of the scarlet veil of the Temple for which the Virgin Mary spun the thread and which was torn in two when Christ died (Matt. 27:51). In other icons it is usually also red because this color has become traditional for a drape signifying "indoors." (In a sixteenth-century *Annunciation* icon from Moldova, the drapery over the roof is green but has the same visual function as the red cloth.)

In visual shorthand, the red drapery means the scene of that icon takes place inside a house, even though the figures look as though they were standing outside with buildings behind them and the open sky over their heads. Since icons avoid any kind of Renaissance illusionistic picture-box, this drapery is an important sign.

In Russian icons, if the drapery is stretched above the Virgin Mary's head by angels, or held like a long scarf over her outspread hands, it is her Protecting Veil, signifying her role as special patron and guardian of Holy Russia.

ENLARGING AND REDUCING

Today we would enlarge or reduce a picture by using grid lines, a method that seems obvious. It was not obvious to medieval craftsmen, though they used a grid to lay out a building. As a system for enlarging a drawing, a grid is mathematical and external to the picture. It depends on fixed mathematical units, for example, one inch gridded up to one foot (or 2½ up to 30 cm). It developed with the Renaissance interest in perspective. Medieval craftsmen enlarged and reduced images the same way they drew their drawings: by proportions and by the well-trained eye.

The craftsman would draw the picture on paper or parchment, fixing the proportions with a small pair of dividers; his basic measuring unit was not inch or meter but a part of the main figure, for example, the nose-length. Having decided that the length on the paper should be such-and-such on the wall, he fixed his large pair of dividers and walked them across the plaster, scratching points of reference. He joined the points with arcs, using a compass, and with lines using a set-square, and established his perpendiculars by a plumb line. For a long horizontal line he established the true horizontal with a plumb line set in a wooden triangle. When this was squarely set, he then had an assistant extend the line with string.

He did not need a grid system with a yardstick marked in mathematical units. Give him a pair of large and small compasses, a set-square, a plumb line, and a piece of string, and he could enlarge or reduce any of his pictures to any size.

EVANGELISTS' SYMBOLS

The four Evangelists, Matthew, Mark, Luke, and John, are shown symbolically by the four creatures mentioned in Ezekiel 1:5–14 and Revelation 4:6–9. St. Matthew is represented by a man, St. Luke by an ox or bull, initially St. Mark by an eagle, and St. John by a lion; later, and in art, the last two are the other way around. It took a while for the iconography to become fixed. The identification of the four living creatures of Ezekiel with the four apocalyptic beasts of Revelation first occurs in the exegesis of St. Jerome in the third century.

In Byzantine churches, the creatures sometimes accompany their evangelists on the four *pendentives*[1] that support a dome illustrated with *Christ Pantocrator*. Maybe it was the decoration of those pendentives that led painters of panel icons of *Christ in Majesty* to put the four creatures at the four corners of a pointed aureole.

The Evangelist symbols are challenging figures for the craftsman, and the visual image does not always work successfully. The whole body may be shown, or only head and shoulders; they are winged and often hold a Gospel in hands, hooves, paws, and claws. They often have haloes; they all may have human hands.

When an Evangelist in human form is shown writing, his symbol may be included in the picture or worked into the decoration of the frame. The Evangelist is seated at his writing desk with his feet on a footstool that has the skewed "perspective" of icon art, or sometimes he stands. There is a piece of drapery looped up behind him. He is holding a quill pen, and in some icons he is sharpening it with a short bladed pen-knife; in others he is holding the parchment flat against the desk with the knife in his left hand while he writes. Parchment does not lie absolutely flat on the desk so it must be held down by something lacking the natural grease of the human hand. The penknife was also used for scoring lines on the page and scraping out mistakes. There may be an ink pot on the sloping desk or an ink horn held in the Evangelist's left hand. (Such images of Evangelists, seated writing at their desks, are normative as author-portraits and are used as frontispieces to their respective Gospels in illuminated Gospel Books.)

Medieval scribes generally wrote on parchment that had been shaped and folded into "gatherings" for sets of pages for a codex. Sometimes the Evangelist has a spare pen propped on that universal pen-holder, the top of the ear. In some icons he is looking toward an angel of inspiration who spreads out a scroll toward him. The angel stands in front of the writing desk and a little above it, where a medieval scribe would have put his *exemplar* to copy.

FURNITURE

Icons contain very little furniture. What there is shows status rather than describing any particular room. Icon furniture is like an icon landscape: It tells us something about the event and the figure.

Beds

In icons of the *Nativity* and of the *Birth of the Virgin Mary*, the mother reclines on a kidney-shaped mattress, which is often drawn with criss-cross lines as though it has been quilted. Medieval mothers gave birth crouching on a birthing stool; icons show the mother resting after the event. In *Dormition* icons the Virgin is lying on a bier with fabric hanging to the ground in front. It is tipped slightly toward us like a stage bed, so we can see her properly.

Footstool

An important figure is separated from others in the icon by having their feet on a footstool or *podium*. It is a small platform decorated as though made of inlaid wood or marble, or a hard cushion brightly upholstered. The perspective tips the footstool toward the viewer.

An Evangelist writing his Gospel has his feet on a stool, and so often does the *Virgin Annunciate*. The regal figure of Christ, or the *Virgin and Child, Enthroned,* always rest their feet on a podium. (All this follows Late Antique secular practice: author-portraits of, for example, Virgil or Homer or official portraits of enthroned emperors or consuls.)

Altar

There is an altar in icons of the *Presentation of Christ and of the Virgin in the Temple* and in the *Communion of the Apostles*. It is a solid cube, usually draped with fabric, and recalls medieval liturgical practice, as do the altars in sixth-century Old Testament sacrifice scenes at St. Vitale, Ravenna.

Throne

In Byzantine art from the fifth century onwards, there is the *hetimasia* (etty-mass-*ee*-a), a prepared throne awaiting the Second Coming of Christ as King at the end of time (Rev. 4:2–5, 14). The throne is empty because Christ has not yet returned. His coming is confirmed by the dove of the Holy Spirit, who stands on the throne, hovers above it, or perches on its back. On or beside the throne may be the instruments of the Passion and usually the Gospel codex, or a scroll with seven seals (Rev. 4–5), and also a purple cushion that represents Christ's imperial status. Though we still await the End when Christ is to be enthroned as king of all creation, the Holy Spirit is already present in the Church, an earnest of the final consummation.

Christ or the Virgin Mary are shown on thrones that are carved and gilded. Before there was upholstered furniture, the only relief that people had from sitting on wood was a large, torpedo-shaped cushion. The two ends of such a cushion are visible on either side of seated figures in icons. It is usually red, a color associated with the imperial court.

The shape of the seat in an icon says something about the status of the person who sits on it. In some images, especially monumental ones (e.g., apse frescoes), Christ is on a so-called lyre-back throne, the curious curved outline of the back seen especially in sixth-century and tenth-century artworks. The original throne may have been made of a pair of large, perfectly matched ivory tusks from an elephant. Rather than cutting them up, which would destroy their rarity value, a way was perhaps found of displaying them fullsize. Such a throne would have been worth a king's ransom. Christ on a lyre-back throne is the heavenly Emperor.

A square throne is often shown in an *exedra* (ex-*ee*-drah), a semicircular architectural niche (e.g., the famous sixth-century Sinai icon of *Christ Pantocrator*). A tier of stepped semicircular stone benches is a *synthronon* (*sin*-thron-on), a place for the concelebrating clergy to sit in the apse of a Church. The synthronon is seen in some icons of Pentecost. A rounded seat with a back as though made from a cutaway barrel is the *cathedra* or professorial chair where a philosopher sat to teach. (Later, it becomes the bishop's throne in the center of the synthronon: hence our word "cathedral," the seat of a bishop.) It is in icons of *Christ in Majesty, Christ the Wisdom of God and the Power of God.* The fact that Jesus, the first-century rabbi, or Mary of Galilee never sat on such furniture was irrelevant to the icon makers: Icons communicate eternal truth, and a throne is a place of power (Christ as Emperor) or of the highest honor (the Mother of God).

HALOES

A halo or *nimbus* is the circle of light around the head of Christ, a prophet, saint, or angel. The word halo is from the Greek word *halein,* the circular path trodden by oxen around the threshing floor and the slow, circular movements of the stars. Though it is shown as a disc, it should be read as a globe of light pouring from the head in all directions. We are so used to seeing it as a disc that it requires a continuous mental shift to read it as a sphere of light. The halo was a word in the visual language that meant the figure was already sharing in the glory of Christ in heaven.

As a visual symbol, the halo was a detail of the visual language that identified the picture of a man or woman as a saint, rather than just a person in a robe, or of the Virgin and Child rather than just any mother and baby. More precisely, Christ alone is given a "cruciform nimbus," in other words, a halo containing a cross.

The craftsman drew the halo with a compass. For a full-face picture, the point of the compass was placed between the eyes; for a three-quarter face, it was in the outer corner of the eye nearest the viewer. According to a manual of iconography written in the eighteenth century the size of the halo was determined by the length of the nose. The craftsman measured five or seven nose lengths in diameter before he marked the circle. Haloes might be painted gold, or gold leaf, or embossed in gilded *stucco* (plaster), and stamped with patterns so they coruscated in the light of lamps and candles. They were also made of separate pieces of sheet gold or silver and applied to the picture after it was painted. In Early Byzantine mosaics, the tesserae of haloes were often set in concentric circles to enhance the roundness of the head. In the twelfth century, haloes in paintings were scored with close circular lines like golden discs and appear to revolve (many examples of this period are at St. Catherine's Monastery, Sinai).

Craftsmen making a two-dimensional picture had to compromise the original idea of the halo. Rather than being a globe of light, it was drawn as a solid object like a golden plate.

(See also *Mandorla.*)

HANDHELD OBJECTS

Because the art of the icon must communicate meaning, an object in the hand may have significance. When you first look at an icon, look at the faces and the hands, including the handheld objects: Much of the icon's message is in the faces and hands.

But beware of making your interpretation of an icon simplistic: In narrative details a handheld object may not mean anything more than what it is. For instance, in icons of the Nativity, one of the midwives preparing a bath for the newborn baby pours water from a water jug, which is simply a water jug. Interpreting icons is not like deciphering a code in which *everything* means something else. If they were like that, only clever people could understand them. Icons, like the written Gospels, are for all people and if anything in them needs to be explained, it can often be explained simply. A lot of things are obvious; we need look no further. However, some handheld objects have a significance that was understood by their original viewers but has to be explained today.

Bag (or Purse)

In some icons of a Byzantine emperor or high official, he is holding a sausage-shaped bag, similar to a Victorian coin purse. It was filled with dust and the emperor carried it during public functions as a reminder to himself and to the reverential crowd that he was not immortal. Dust he was and unto dust he would return. It also meant that the land of which he was emperor was held in his hand as the dust in the bag.

A bag of money, which an emperor or donor may carry, is the usual round money-bag shape, tied at the top like an old-fashioned steamed pudding, sometimes hanging from the belt.

Book

If a book is held by Christ the Judge, it is either closed as the Book of Judgment to be opened at the Last Judgment, or open with an inviting verse such as "Come unto me." The writing was on animal skin called *parchment* or *vellum* (the names were interchangeable). Rectangles of animal skin were folded and sewn into gatherings of eight or ten pages, then the gatherings were sewn to thongs, which you can sometimes see in the picture, and held between wooden boards covered with leather. The boards were necessary to keep the parchment from curling; such was the practical origin of the first hardback book. It was closed on three sides by thongs slipped over knobs on the opposite board, like knob-and-loop buttons. A medieval scholar owned only a few books so there was no need for a spine with the name on it, just front and back covers. We can see the edges of the sewn gatherings between the covers.

A medieval book was not stored on its edge like a modern book but flat and in a cupboard. Because it was not stored on edge the pages did not need to be much smaller than the covers, as in a modern hardback. That is why a book in an icon has a blocky look: The pages and cover are almost the same size. With covers made of pieces of wood, solid objects could be fixed on them: jewels or icons of ivory, steatite, enamel, or metalwork. The boards, originally a practical addition to keep the pages flat, were a solid base for decoration; that is one of many examples in which the structure of an object affects the design.

Censer

A censer is a container of hot coals on which spices are sprinkled; it is swung from a chain, so that fragrant smoke is tossed through the air.

> Another angel, who had a golden censer, came and stood at the altar. He was given much incense to offer, with the prayers of all the saints, on the golden altar before the throne. The smoke of the incense, together with the prayers of the saints, went up before God from the angel's hand. (Rev. 8:3–4)

A church that believes worship on earth is a reflection of the heavenly liturgy has incense. Sometimes, the censer is swung by an angel; in icons of the *Death of the Virgin* it is swung by an apostle.

Drop Spindle

In many icons of the Annunciation, the Virgin is shown spinning. Note that she is spinning, not weaving; weaving is a different craft. The tuft of fibers is held in her left hand and the spindle–which is a shaft with a weight at the bottom— hangs from her right. The scarlet spun thread is drawn out between them. (In a twelfth-century *Annunciation* at Sinai she is spinning left-handed, a curious variation.) In a fifth-century mosaic in St. Maria Maggiore in Rome, she is seated with a basket beside her and is drawing out a roving, in other words, forming a long, loose rope of scarlet wool before spinning it. Making a roving and spinning were actions as familiar in medieval society as knitting is in England today.

The drop spindle is a visual reference to the *Gospel of James*, a second-century writing not accepted as part of the inspired New Testament. According to the apocryphal story, thread was needed to make a veil for the Temple. It was to be spun and woven from gold, as well as fine linen and silk dyed in hyacinthine, scarlet, and purple. Lots were cast to see who was to spin the scarlet and purple, and it fell to Mary.

An icon of the *Annunciation* shows the moment of surprise when the archangel explains that the Holy Spirit is to be the "father" of her child. In sixteenth-century Russian icons, the drop spindle swings out as Mary jumps in surprise at the angel's greeting. It is an unusual and real-istic detail and well within acceptable iconography. Iconographic art lives and breathes by just such small touches of individuality.

Fan

Held by angels in icons of the *Communion of the Apostles*, liturgical fans are flat round objects on long sticks. They look like outsize versions of the fans that are held by worshipers in American churches that have no air-conditioning. In some icons the shape is an outline of a six-winged seraph. In the Byzantine Liturgy, fans were used by deacons to waft away flies from the communion bread and wine. In icons, angels act as deacons at the Celestial Liturgy and wear diaconal vestments. In the Orthodox Liturgy here below, deacons represent the angels because the Liturgy here is a temporal showing-forth of the eternal Liturgy there, celebrated by Christ, the great High Priest, assisted by angels.

Flask

Held by a doctor-saint, the flask is a *curcubit*, a gourd-shaped bottle that is almost all neck. It is the vessel used by doctors for a urine sample, which was once one of the chief methods of diagnosing illness. Today, the quickest way to identify a picture as that of a doctor would be to draw a stethoscope hanging from his neck; in the Middle Ages, he was identified by the distinctively shaped flask and by a spatula and medicine box (e.g., St. Panteleimon, Sts. Cosmas and Damian, all physicians).

Horn and Other Brass Musical Instruments

If a group of instruments is playing, brass loudly predominates, the sound flaring forward. For centuries, trumpets have been sounded for announcements, whether the arrival of a stage coach, royalty, or an angel.

> Then the LORD will appear over them; his arrow will flash like lightning. The Sovereign LORD will sound the trumpet; he will march in the storms of the south, and the LORD Almighty will shield them. (Zech. 9:14).

When the apostle John was on the island of Patmos he heard a voice saying,

> I am the First and the Last. I am the Living One; I was dead, and behold I am alive for ever and ever! And I hold the keys of death and Hades. (Rev. 1:17–18)

He described the voice as that of a trumpet (Rev. 1:10). An angel holding a trumpet means an announcement from God. As well as looking at icons, we can get a great deal out of "listening" to them. In Byzantine art, we occasionally see such instruments depicted, for example, in illustrated psalters, and where the psalmist calls on us to praise God with instruments of music, and in scenes of Christ mocked.

Instruments of the Passion
Instruments of the Passion are the cross, the crown of thorns, the nails, the spear that pierced Christ's side, and the lance with a sponge and the pot of vinegar that was offered to refresh him. In icons of the *Virgin of the Passion,* angels in the upper corners of the picture, fly toward the Christ Child, carrying the instruments in veiled hands. They also appear sometimes in the icon of the *Hetimasia. (See page 104).*

Lance and Sword
Carried by military saints, such as St. George, the lance was used for fighting on horseback; the sword was for closer combat. Mounted *St. George* icons usually show him wielding a lance that makes a strong diagonal across the picture. The Archangel Michael has a sword because he protects God's people from their enemies and slays Satan at the end of time. Western religious art tends to show angels as comforting and comfortable. Angels in icons are often well-armed soldiers ready to fight, or

formidable agents of divine justice. Byzantine angels are never cozy or sentimental (cf., the poet Rilke: "Jeder Engel ist schrecklich" [every angel is terrible, awe-inspiring]).

Model of a Building

The patron of a new church or monastery bows or kneels before Christ and holds up a model of the building. If the picture of the church is not idealized, it is useful to historians because it appears in its original form before it was altered by war, fire, or later architects.

Craftsmen sometimes made a wooden scale model of a building to test for construction methods and stress, which they presented to the patron. By presenting the model to Christ, the patron in the icon is acting as a humble servant offering his work to Christ, *his* heavenly patron. Such votive images of donors are often found in the narthexes (vestibules) of medieval Byzantine and (especially) Serbian and Romanian churches, often showing royal or aristocratic/episcopal donors introduced to Christ/the Virgin by their patron saints.

Orb and Scepter

Familiar in the hands of Western monarchs, the orb and the scepter represent, respectively, the world surmounted by the cross, and the staff of rule. The Archangel Michael carries an orb with the Greek initials of the words "Christ the Righteous Judge." In Early Byzantine icons he holds a roundel with the half-length figure of Christ, a *clipeus* portrait derived from classical art. In later icons he carries a translucent orb, the clipeus having become a sphere.

Scales

Weighing or balance scales have a short vertical shaft joined at the bottom to a longer horizontal one that can rock freely and that has a dish on either end. A small upright pointer on the horizontal aligns itself with the vertical when the weight in both dishes is equal. Balance scales are accurate when they are held in a steady hand. The head of a workshop had balance scales checked by the representative of the city prefect, the Byzantine equivalent of an inspector of weights and measures. The scale had to have the stamp of the prefect.

Balance scales are held by the Archangel Michael in icons of a soul being judged, a subject more popular in Western than in Byzantine pictures. Sometimes a soul, like a naked or white-robed child, kneels in one dish while a black demon tries to hook down the one on the other side, while other demons bring up bundles of carefully wrapped sins to put into the scales. Such images are often found in large frescoes of the *Last Judgment,* from the fourteenth to the seventeenth centuries.

Scalpel/Spatula

Medical saints such as Cosmas and Damian hold a scalpel or *spatula,* "spoon," in their right hand and a lidded container for medicines or medical instruments in the crook of their left arm. As saintly doctors they were healers of moral and spiritual ill as well as of physical pains, and they were ready to administer whatever was necessary: spiritual advice, medication, or the knife.

Scroll

When Christ holds a rolled-up scroll it refers to him as Divine Wisdom. Western Christians visiting the Church of Hagia Sophia in Istanbul are surprised to find a Church dedicated to Holy Wisdom rather than to St. Mary or some other saint.[2] The name is Christ's for he *is* the wisdom (*Sophia*) of God and the power of God (1 Cor. 1:24). He is the fulfillment of the wisdom of all the philosophers and prophets who came before him. When he is pictured on his mother's knee holding a scroll, it shows that since he is God Incarnate, his knowledge is not limited to that of a merely human baby.

In the ancient world, a *rotulus* (*rot*-you-luss) was a long parchment scroll stored in a tube with a lid, a form that is retained in the containers of the Torah scrolls in present-day synagogue worship. In icons (especially of Evangelists) we see several *rotuli* stored in a basket or a box with a lock. By the Early Christian period, writings were more often in the form of a codex (bound book) while the rotulus was retained for legal and liturgical documents. It remained in iconography long after it ceased to be used in real life. In icons, the rotulus held by Christ is closed, because Christ has knowledge of deeper mysteries than we can understand.

An unfurled scroll in the hand of a prophet has an inscription of a prophetic text pointing forward to fulfilment in Christ; for example, Isaiah's scroll has the prophecy of the virgin birth of Jesus (Is. 7:14), and the scroll held by St. John the Baptist has his words, "Repent for the kingdom of heaven is near" (Matt. 3:2). An imperial figure may hold a scroll that is a legal document relating to the foundation of a church, and monastic saints and Fathers of the Church may hold scrolls, (or books) with a quotation from their teaching visible to us.

Staff

When the Roman emperor rode at the head of his cavalry, a staff or *labarum* (lab-*ar*-um) was carried before him. It was topped with imperial insignia, looking like a small rigid flag or a small square on top of a pole. In Early

Byzantine art the labarum had a cross or the *Chi-Ro* (kye-row), the monogram of Christ, imprinted on it. An angel carries a labarum because he is a standard-bearer of God's army in heaven.

In later icons, the labarum is a long, thin staff topped by a small rectangle with an inscription (often "Holy, holy, holy" in Greek) or a cross. In some icons the thin staff has disappeared altogether, leaving the archangel's fingers curved in memory of what he once held.

White Cloth

In Early Byzantine icons the Virgin Mary holds a small, white cloth in her left hand, folded over her fingers. If she has both hands raised in prayer, the cloth is tucked into her girdle. It represents her purity, but in iconography, her perpetual virginity is symbolized by three stars on her veil (*maphorion*). She was a virgin before, during, and after her child-bearing.

Wreaths and Crowns

The laurel wreath of victory was given to successful athletes in the Games in pagan Rome. Wreaths of victory and their metal equivalent, jeweled crowns, appear in early Byzantine pictures of Christian martyrs, for example at St. Vitale, Ravenna (sixth century). The victorious cross in a laurel wreath appears in early Christian art as a symbol of Christ's victory over death and of the triumph of the Christian Church and empire under Constantine.

HANDS, DIVINE AND HUMAN

Hand of God

In the art of the Orthodox Church, God the Father is not shown. Instead, a hand appears from the segment of a circle at the center top, or top corner, of the picture. There may be a shaft of power, such as a ray of sunlight, coming from the circle and directed to the head of the main figure in the icon. The hand may be in a gesture of blessing or simply indicating the divine presence.

Hand Positions

In everyday life and in art, the position of the hands often tell us what the person is saying. In icons, people communicate with their hands as vividly as the deaf sign a conversation.

There are several distinctive hand positions that help us to read the picture. Except for the blessing hand, the hand positions in icons are the normal body language that people still see and use. Mind and body are so closely linked that if you make the gestures described below, you begin to understand how others feel when they make them.

Hands Blessing

In the Orthodox Church a priest blesses a congregation with a hand that is an icon: The fingers are held in a position that speak of something beyond themselves. What the fingers signal is the sacred name, Jesus Christ, written in Greek letters: IC XC (Ιησούζ Χργστόζ). The index finger is held straight as the letter I, the long finger is curved as the letter C, the thumb and ring finger cross each other to form the letter X and the little finger curves for the final letter C. (In the Western Church the position is ring finger and little finger held down by the thumb, a hand of a Roman emperor announcing his authority.)

The different hand positions in the Greek and the Latin parts of the Church were not fixed in iconography until the Middle Byzantine period. The position of the fingers shows whether the icon's patron was Catholic or Orthodox. Duccio, a fourteenth-century Western painter influenced by Greek style, painted an *Annunciation* with the archangel's hand in the blessing position of the Latin Church. An X-ray photograph shows that the little finger was originally extended and then painted over. Presumably Duccio's patron made him change it.

In icons of *Christ Pantocrator,* he has the blessing hand turned toward himself. His hand is saying, "I am Jesus Christ, Son of God, Savior." Similarly in icons of saints, the left hand is often turned toward the heart, saying, "Jesus Christ lives here," in the "place of the heart" so dear to Orthodox contemplatives. (The heart is not just the seat of the emotions; for the Greek Fathers, it is the deep center of the self, indwelt by the Holy Spirit.)

Hands Commanding

In icons of the *Raising of Lazarus,* Christ says, "Lazarus, come out!" He points with authority. The face stares straight forward, and the forearm is raised with the open hand at the level of the head. Made forcibly, an upraised, open hand is a confident affirmation, a gesture of power rather than an acknowledgment of equals: It derives from depictions of Roman emperors.

A single finger is a gesture of command or power: "Depart" or "Go there!" as, for example, in narrative scenes of Christ healing or casting out demons. By contrast, the fingers all extended is a gesture of courtesy and indication, still used when someone is making an introduction, as in "May I introduce . . . ?" or greeting/welcoming a friend.

Hands in Despair or Grief

A universal gesture of grief is a hand held to the face, often with a piece of clothing, veil, or handkerchief. The instinct to hold fabric to the face, to feel some small answer of texture, goes back to infancy when the crying child brushes its face against its mother's skin or clothes, or holds a cloth as a "comforter." It is also the beginning of the gesture of covering the whole head with a veil, protecting the raw and shrunken personal identity while the first storm of grieving spends itself.

To show interest or consideration, the hand goes to the chin or lower lip; in shock it covers the mouth; in despair it goes to the side of the face or over the eyes. The head tips sideways to be supported by the hand, as though the skull feels too heavy to stand the weight of thoughts and impressions at that time. The apostle John stands by the Cross like that, head supported on the side by right hand, finger extended along cheek, an ancient gesture of grief.

Praying Hands

In Rome, people prayed to the gods with their hands held up on either side of their head (the *orant* gesture, still used by priests at the altar).

The first Christians were Jews, who prayed with hands lifted up and spread out towards heaven, but orant figures (who were often female, representing the departed soul at prayer) appear in the earliest Christian art (in the Roman catacombs). An abbreviated version of this gesture, often used in icons where space is limited, is to bring both hands together in front of the chest, palms outward (especially common in icons of martyrs).

In icons of intercession (the *Deisis*, or the *Virgin Paraklisis),* the saint turns at three-quarters to the picture plane, and raises one or both hands to shoulder height in supplication to Christ.

Hands in Surprise

The universal gesture of surprise is a hand or hands brought sharply upwards, the palms open to the front, the body jerked slightly backward from the waist. In the first split-second the surprise is not perceived as either good or bad so the hand comes up to be ready for defense if it should be needed.

The Virgin Mary in an *Annunciation* icon shows surprise at the archangel's words. "Mary was greatly troubled at his words, and wondered what kind of greeting this might be. But the angel said to her, 'Do not be afraid, Mary. . . .'" (Luke 1:29–30). Similarly, in miracle scenes onlookers make such a gesture of surprise.

Teaching and Talking Hands

Someone teaching has the index finger touching the thumb, a gesture still used when the speaker is making a point with precision. (The position of the fingers distinguishes between a hand blessing and a hand teaching.) Someone talking with authority has a hand raised with the index and middle finger upright and the other two fingers flexed. The gesture was seen on Imperial Roman coins: "Listen! The Emperor speaks!"

Veiled Hands

Hands in an icon are veiled when the thing or person they hold, or are about to be given, is sacred. Angels in an icon of the *Virgin Mary Pelagonitissa* hold the instruments of the Passion in veiled hands, so does a donor offering a model of a church to Christ. In festal icons of the *Presentation of Christ in the Temple*, Simeon stands at the altar with veiled hands, waiting to receive the Child. Today, in a synagogue service, the Holy Book is touched with a pointer as the reader follows the words, or by a veiled hand. In the Catholic Church, the priest's hands are veiled during part of the service of Benediction, when holding the Blessed Sacrament in the monstrance.

Icons of an Evangelist, deacon, or bishop-saint holding a Gospel shows their left hands veiled. Angels in an icon of the *Baptism of Christ* stand on the bank of the Jordan, their hands apparently veiled ready to receive him when he rises from the water. In fact, they are waiting to hand him towels. Veiled hands denoting respect was a detail of the visual language of Roman art that continued in icons.

So when you first see an icon, look at the faces, and look at the hands; they will tell you a great deal about what is going on.

INSCRIPTIONS

If the icon is from Russia or Eastern Europe, the letters are usually in Cyrillic script. The script was devised in essence by St. Cyril when he and St. Methodius took the Gospel, translated from Greek into Slavonic, to the Moravian Slavs in the ninth century. Soon afterward, the same translations were used in the conversion of the Bulgarians, Serbs, and (later) Russians.

Names on icons are often abbreviated. We do the same in writing the title HM the Queen, or we sign a memo with the first letters of our name and say we have initialed it. In earlier centuries a name was sometimes abbreviated by writing the first and last letter: Written in such a way, George Washington would be GE WN. Words and names were shortened to save space on handwritten manuscripts or panel pictures; what had begun as clear identification of the figure became a necessary part of the iconography. They were felt to be so necessary a part that a rare example of Byzantine sculpture in the round, a tenth-century Virgin and Child *Hodegitria* (in the Victoria & Albert Museum, London), has the Greek initial letters of *Mother of God* carved on the figure. An ancient notion held that personal identity is somehow invested in the name, which embodies the essential character and power of the one signified.

Saints

Sometimes the name is written with the first and last letters of the title and the name. Letters of a name were not always arranged from left to right but in whatever pattern best fits the picture. One icon of St. Simeon has the six letters of his name arranged in three rows: SI, then ME, then ON. A name may run behind a halo with just enough showing on either side for us to know what that name is. In a largely illiterate society, the purpose was easy identification of the figure. In icon-art, which is a teaching and communicating art, figures are recognized as much by their iconography as by a written label.

Icons painted for Latin patrons sometimes had inscriptions written in Greek because it was traditional and sometimes in Latin. Modern icons painted for Western patrons may have inscriptions in English (St. George, or St. G.). What matters is that the iconography makes clear at whom we are looking. But the inscription is also very important because, for example, one bishop-saint or virgin-martyr looks much like another. The inscription clinches the identification.

The Four Evangelists

Their names are written with the title *Hagios* (saint). If there is not enough room on the panel, their names are abbreviated to the first and last letters.

Scrolls

Inscriptions on scrolls may be of the first few words of a biblical or patristic text, the words standing for the whole passage if there is not room to write the whole passage.

Inscriptions that Identify a Scene

Narrative icons are usually identified with the briefest inscription. Examples include *The Resurrection*, or *The Transfiguration*. Others may be longer, such as *The Entry of the Most Holy Mother of God into the Temple*.

LANDSCAPE

In Shakespearean theater, a branch in a bucket represented a forest. It was visual shorthand that the audience understood. The event taking place in the forest was more important.

The landscape background to an icon (denoting an outdoor scene) could sometimes be described as "the least you can get away with." A few simple lines mean a hillside; craggy rocks mean a range of mountains; and scattered trees mean arborial vegetation. Since a tree is not an identifiable species but a tree-symbol, the painter sometimes treats it as a stylized object. When an icon has only one tree, it might have a specific meaning in the story. The single tree in Rublev's icon *The Trinity* is the oak of Mamre under which Abraham entertains his three mysterious visitors. The word "tree" and the picture brings other thoughts to the surface: the tree of the knowledge of good and evil in the Garden of Eden, the tree of Jesse (Christ's ancestry), and the tree of the Cross. (Be careful: Not every tree in an icon means something. It is easy to become too clever for the picture and risk missing the simple thing that it is saying.)

An icon of *St. John the Baptist* might have a tree near him with an ax laid across it. It is not a narrative detail: He is not cutting wood to warm himself on a cold night in the desert. The ax is a reference to his words of judgment, "The ax is already at the root of the trees. . . ." (Matt. 3:10).

A carving on an ivory casket, dated about 420, shows Judas hanging and Christ crucified. The juxtaposition invites us to consider the contrast: a traitor who took his life on a tree, and the Redeemer who gave his life on the Cross.

At first sight an icon landscape looks like the branch-in-a-bucket technique of a Shakespearean stage set, then we realize there is more to it than that. Rocks piled in intense angularity point to the intensity of the story, and a barren desert can show the austerity of the hermits who lived there. The landscape of a *Nativity* icon includes the dark cave behind the manger, symbolizing the darkness of the world that he came to save.

An icon landscape is more than a blank setting in which the figure stands about. It can complement the figural composition, reflecting the posture of protagonists and even intensify the mood of the scene. It must also be said that after about 1300, Byzantine landscape backgrounds became much fuller and more naturalistic.

See also *Craggy Rocks*.

MANDORLA

It is not a *mandala*, which is a visual pattern for Buddhist meditation. A *mandorla* (*man*-dor-luh) is an elliptical shape behind the full-length figure of Christ. Think of it as a full-length halo. The word "mandorla" is Italian and means "almond"; Greek craftsmen called it *doxa,* meaning "glory." Circular "glories" or circles slightly pointed at the top and bottom are properly called *aureoles*, and these may be combined with a lozenge- or diamond-shaped "glory," the round glory representing the heavenly sphere, while a square or diamond one represents the created world. The intersection of the two figures in icons of Christ suggest the mystery of the Incarnation as an interface of time and eternity. Like the halo, the mandorla should be read as an enclosing area of light rather than just flat rays. Especially in *Transfiguration* icons, these rays of glory may emanate from the figure of Christ beyond the edge of the mandorla to other protagonists. This emphasizes that the uncreated divine energies that transfigure and deify Christ's human nature can also transform the disciples, including ourselves.

In Early Byzantine pictures, Christ comes in glory in a skyful of clouds that are bright pink and thunder blue like the dawn clouds of a bright summer day. Later, the mandorla indicates the divine majesty and risen splendor of Christ in, for example, the *Dormition*, the *Anastasis*, and *Christ Pantocrator Enthroned*. Only the top three-quarters of a mandorla are in the fourteenth-century *Anastasis* icon in St. Saviour in Chora, Constantinople; it looks as though the glory of God has plunged deep into the darkness. Sometimes the *Virgin Platytera* is in a mandorla; as the Incarnate is safely contained in her womb, she is safely contained in a womb-shaped radiance, an image found also in Western art.

An Anglo-Saxon picture of the *Fall of Satan* has a mandorla around the prince of darkness, the painter having misunderstood the visual language of Byzantine art. Angels and archangels are not shown with mandorlas—and anyway, Satan lost the angelic radiance he had when he rebelled against God. The iconography is not a mere decoration but a carefully thought-out, theologically precise visual language, refined over centuries.

NAILS IN THE CROSS

The first pictures of Christ on the Cross showed him standing against a cross with his feet on the ground. From about the ninth century, he was shown lifted from the ground with his feet side by side on a little shelf or footrest, a *suppedaneum* (soop-eh-*dane*-ium). There was one nail through each standing foot, and the nails were not always a feature of the picture.

Later, to emphasize his physical suffering, he was drawn as though with his whole weight hanging, dead and passive, from nailed hands. The arrangement of straight legs and feet side-by-side looked awkward beneath a slumped body: Should the knees be bent and if so in which direction? If the knees are bent, the feet looked awkward nailed flat and side-by-side, so craftsmen painted the feet crossed one over the other with one nail through both. The new type of *Crucifixion* spread from Northern Europe in the twelfth century to Italy but had already appeared independently in Byzantium by the mid-twelfth century (e.g., Nerezi in Macedonia, 1164, emphasized the physical suffering of the Passion).

Sometimes changes in art reflect new concepts in spirituality and religious sensibility. The new stress on Christ's suffering humanity, both in East and West, is a case in point.

NARRATIVE DETAILS

About the fourteenth century, narrative details threatened to take over the composition of the icon. The old device of simultaneous narration developed beyond good design, and little subplots were played out all over the picture surface.

In an icon of *The Hospitality of Abraham,* while Abraham offers food to the angelic visitors, a servant cuts the throat of an ox, and Sarah kneads dough. Though the extra figures have charm, they draw the eye and the devotional focus from the main reason for the icon. In a *Crucifixion* icon, people look up at the repentant thief; three soldiers hunker down over their dice; the good centurion is on his horse; St. Mary kneels with her pot of ointment and flowing hair; the Virgin faints in the arms of attendant ladies; Joseph of Arimathea waits to take the dead body of Christ to his own tomb; a donor kneels in a corner. There is too much to look at. Somewhere in the middle of it Christ is crucified, but our eyes are pulled all over the place and the icon lacks focus and stillness. The great moment of salvation is reduced to a series of vignettes to be read one by one, each competing for attention and each—including the crucified figure—seeming of equal importance. Later icons of the *Nativity* tend to be anecdotal, with Magi, midwives, angels, and shepherds; but if there is enough space and different scale is used for the figures of differing importance, the composition may work without looking restless. What makes the late-Byzantine narrative style unsuccessful is that all the figures are of equal size, but too many incidents and too many protagonists are also a problem. It is difficult to know where our focus is supposed to be.

With Western influence bringing an increased interest in three-dimensional picture space, an icon was painted to look like a window into the real world with crowds jostling and a lot of different things happening. The unintended consequence of such a picture is that we don't know where to fix our attention.

The elaboration of pictures with extra details developed in mosaics and wall paintings because there were large areas of space to decorate. The walls did not look crowded by the extras. The worshiper's eyes scanned across the area, taking in each part of the scene and relating it to the whole. Later, some of the details were transferred to panel icons. The worshiper now stood about an arm's-length away from the picture, distracted by too many details in one small area.

NUMBERS

Medievals read in the Old Testament: "God has arranged all things by measure, number, and weight" (Wisdom 11:20). That verse justified the idea that numbers are filled with spiritual significance, an ancient belief explored by Plato, Augustine and others.

To us, a number is only a cold measurement; to medievals, it had a moral and theological dimension. Eight was an ideal number that stood for resurrection or rebirth and for the Age to Come; that is why so many Gothic fonts are octagonal. When people described a building as having so-many pillars or so-many windows, it was more than just a description: The number was filled with a significance greater than simply reminding the viewer of what it symbolized. The symbol connected the viewer to the thing or concept itself. Medieval people lived in a more complex and interconnected world than ours; for them harmonic proportions and perfect number-ratios reflected a divine, cosmic order.

OPTICAL CORRECTION

Mosaicists used optical illusion with color. They knew their work was going to be seen from a distance, sometimes as high as the vault of a church. To make an area look green, they juxtaposed cubes of blue and yellow so the area would look green to the person standing on the ground.

Half-tones and shadows were created by juxtaposing different-colored tesserae as skillfully as a painter mixing tempera. By juxtaposing cubes of different colors, the mosaic shimmered more than tesserae of a single color would have done. In the late nineteenth century, the Pointillists did the same trick with tiny dots of paint of contrasted hue that resolved themselves at a distance to a color that vibrated. The fourteenth-century mosaic of the *Virgin and Child* on the narthex wall of St. Saviour of Chora, Istanbul, is surrounded by rows of colored diamond shapes of red, green, cream and grey. They quiver like a serendipitous color combination in a patchwork quilt. The figure of *Christ Pantocrator* in the dome at Daphni has a similar circle in diamonds of green, gold, buff, and deep red.

Making pictures for a vault or for high on walls called for special knowledge of perspective. The craftsman sometimes elongated the figures so they would have normal proportions when they were seen from the ground. Designing for a vault needed even greater skill. When we look up at a vault, we look directly at the middle of the picture as at a panel painting, and we see the edges of the picture foreshortened as though we were looking up into an open umbrella. A skilled craftsman knew how to adjust his design to allow for that foreshortening without the picture looking distorted.

That technique of optical illusion is called *anamorphosis* (ann-nah-*mor*-foh-sis), meaning "forming anew." In computer graphics, when one picture reshapes itself into another, the process is described as *morphing*. An *anamorphic* (ann-nah-*mor*-fic) picture is distorted in itself, but when seen from the proper angle it resolves into the right proportions. An everyday example is the stencil of a bicycle on the bicycle lane of a city street. When we stand above it looking down, it is tall and thin with oval wheels: when seen from the angle of an approaching cyclist, it looks "right."

Craftsmen used the technique of anamorphosis or optical correction when they were decorating the curved apse of a church with a painting or mosaic. The worshiper would not be able to stand in the middle of the curve and turn from side to side to look at the picture because the altar was there. He would see the center of the curved wall straight-on, and the two ends of the curve edge-on, along the wall. A skilled craftsman made the figures on the two ends wider than the center ones and with sideways gestures to compensate for the angle at which they would be seen. Looked at from the normal viewing point, they float forward off the wall to inhabit the viewer's space. Wide-angled photographs of such anamorphic pictures redistort the carefully planned distortion and alter the medieval craftsman's design.

In the fourteenth-century mosaic of the *Miracle of Cana* in the Chora Church, the waterpots are placed on a concave section of wall. If you see them "in person," they look the right shape, but in a guidebook photograph, they look distorted. The mosaicist who made that picture used optical illusion in the placing of highlights, making use of the natural light coming from the main door of the church to make us see pots on a concave surface as though they are rounded shapes projecting from the wall.

The Kremlin Museum in Moscow has fifteenth-century portrait palls, made to be spread over the tombs of prelates on their saints' days. Seen faced directly, the saintly churchmen have unusually broad shoulders and heads, each face seeming to have been stretched sideways, toward an oval, which gives them an Oriental look. It is the oval haloes that give the game away: These portraits were designed to be seen from the side.

OUTER DARKNESS

Frescoes of hell show skulls floating against blackness with worms wriggling in and out of the eye sockets, and other torments of the damned.

The most successful iconography of outer darkness is so simple that at first we may be tempted to laugh at it: It is a black square lurking like a black hole. We should not assume that craftsmen of earlier ages were simpletons because they painted such images of hell; if we do, we cut ourselves off from them and we don't learn any more. The process of the Last Judgment, the weighing and the separating, can be shown in a picture, but if the result for the unsaved is, in Jesus' words "outer darkness," what else can you paint except darkness? Hell is painted as a black hole without form and void; its basic simplicity bores into the mind.

PARTICULARITY

Icons made according to the iconography of the Orthodox Church are intended to communicate an aspect of Christian truth and to make present the person or event shown in the picture. They therefore are painted in a way that is designed to be timeless. Changing details of style or influences from other countries are contained within the iconography. Craftsmen had no more right to change the language of iconography than a group of Christians had of voting to change doctrine or Church practice after two thousand years. A craftsman was the servant of iconography and made icons within the specified guidelines.

A full-length icon of St. George shows him wearing armor, with a spear or lance aimed at a dying dragon. St. George has continued frequently to wear armor in icons when soldiers were going to war first in half-armor over buff jerkins, then in braided red coats, then khaki and camouflage, and now in antinerve gas suits. In icons, St. George still wears medieval war gear, pig-sticking the dragon with a lance. Because icons show eternal truth they are not tied to a particular generation.

In Renaissance painting, landscapes and buildings became identifiable, and biblical characters wore contemporary clothes. *The Miraculous Draught of Fishes* by Conrad Witz, 1444, shows the landscape of Lac Leman in Switzerland; *The Descent from the Cross* by Roger van der Weyden, 1435, has women wearing fifteenth-century gowns and wimples.

Particularity is the opposite of the timeless quality in an icon. Particularity can have a positive effect on the viewer: It shows Christian truth to be true for his own generation, rather than only for biblical or medieval people. In G.K. Chesterton's words, "To see Christ walking on the water, not of Gennesaret but Thames." A modern church banner might show Christ wearing blue jeans. In icons, donors wear contemporary costume, but Christ and the saints do not: Holy persons exist in heaven, in a different mode of reality from this world.

In the wrong setting, particularity can have a negative effect. By being tied to a historical moment, it soon fades from being a statement of eternal truth into being out-of-date. More ephemeral religious pictures, such as Sunday school leaflets, can bear particularity, whereas ones that are made to last work best when they are designed in a relatively timeless style. Icons are made to last.

PERSONIFICATION

"Personification" means that something abstract—a concept, characteristic, or virtue—is presented in the form of a person. Artists use personification to show something that is too complex or too abstract to show directly: for example, the Statue of Liberty at the entrance of New York Harbor or the figure of Britannia on British bank notes.

As Christian art developed its own language, craftsmen used figures that were familiar to them and their patrons. Some icons of the *Baptism of Christ* have a man at the bottom of the picture pouring water from a jug; he is the personification of the River Jordan. A robed, kingly figure in icons of *Pentecost* represents Cosmos, all mankind as the crowned image of God. In some manuscript illuminations, a a dark-robed woman with a veil swirling over her head is Night. A twelfth-century fresco of *Christ by the Sea of Galilee,* in Pskov, shows an old man deep in the water; he is the personification of the lake. He kneels with his hands raised in reverence, in contrast to the disciples standing in the boat; they are debating whether or not the figure on the shore is really the risen Christ, while Lake-Man recognizes his Creator.

A dark figure bound beneath Christ's feet in an *Anastasis* icon is not Satan but Death. Western art uses similar pictorial language. In a fifteenth-century carving of the *Descent into Hades* from the South Netherlands, Christ has his feet on the broken door of hell; beneath the door is Death shown as a large, black, squashed toad. There is no romanticism about death being a friend. Death is a defeated enemy.

A Russian fourteenth-century fresco shows angels labeled as virtues disposing of demons which are their opposite vices. Chastity spears Defilement, Understanding spears Unreason, Hope spears Despair, and Poverty (poverty of spirit) spears Bitterness.

Today, symbolic figures from classical art are no longer so familiar to us, so we need explanations that the dark-robed lady with the veil swirling around her head represents Night, or that the man in chains represents Death. The language of pictorial art is like written or spoken language: it can communicate only if it is understood.

See also *Classical Details*.

PERSPECTIVE

When we look at a straight road the lines on either side seem to get nearer till they join on the horizon and when someone walks away along the road he seems to be shrinking. That is one reason that very small children become agitated when they watch a parent walk away: They have not yet learned to read perspective. Perspective developed by painters during the Renaissance puts the figures inside the frame and pulls us into the frame to join them. Unless we have recently been looking at a lot of icons or examples of Cubism, our mind will be filled with pictures that have Renaissance or early modern perspective.

The treatment of space in icons is different because icons are different from other pictures. The Virgin Mary's footstool sometimes has lines that splay out from each other as they go back into the picture, the opposite of what we are used to and the opposite of what we see in a road. This is so-called "inverted perspective," though it isn't used consistently. An icon's viewpoint is different from what we see with a camera. The footstool in the icon is like a chute sliding the figure toward us.

Icons don't have perspective comparable to Renaissance one-point perspective, which constructs a spatially logical "picture box." Rather than saying the spatial composition of an icon is "wrong," try to recognize it as being merely unfamiliar. It does not show that medieval craftsmen were ignorant or could not draw. The Byzantines probably knew more about optics than their Western medieval contemporaries. Their "perspective" is designed to throw the figures forward into our world. As a rough guide, measure with your eyes the diagonal of a panel icon (corner to corner), mentally double the length and stand at that point. The icon invades our space with the lines converging at the point where we are standing. Space in the icon is the reverse of Western perspective: it includes us in the picture space by moving the figures out to meet us. As for the space in the icon itself, the further we go into it, the bigger it gets.

Byzantine artists chose deliberately to subvert spatial laws for theological reasons: Though a scene really happened, it has a more-than-historical significance. Similarly, the saints once lived in a time and space-bound world, creatures of flesh and blood just like us. But now they live in a different dimension, with body and soul transfigured by the deifying light of God. Somehow sacred art conveys this transformation—mere realism is not enough.

Picture Space

Picture space is the amount of space that there appears to be around and behind the figures in a painted or incised image. The page of this book has two dimensions: up-and-down, and side-to-side. A box has three: up-and-down, side-to-side, and depth. Painted icons have two dimensions but are sometimes painted at least in part in such a way as to seem to have three. Though the figures move forward to our space, they look as though they have space and air behind them.

Modern church furnishing provides a similar example. When an altar is placed in the middle of a late-twentieth-century church, the eye is encouraged to roam through the space that lies over and around and behind it. By contrast, an altar placed against the east wall channels and focuses the attention as the roaming of the eye is blocked by the solid wall immediately behind it.

The picture space of many icons is like an altar placed against the east wall. The figure painted on the panel confronts you from a shallow stage, often with a solid background of gold directly behind his shoulders. He relates to you and you to him; there is no escape. Even if the icon shows a landscape, it often looks as though it is a painted backdrop rather than a three-dimensional receding space.

When we watch a television drama, we are invited to step into the picture. When we watch the television news, we must relate to the newsreader who sits at a desk apparently just behind the screen. The newscaster speaks directly to us. That is how it feels when we spend time with icons. They have a sense of personal presence so powerful that we note with relief that the faces are very solemn and still. Emotions too large and raw on that shallow stage would be so strong that the audience would switch off emotionally. The shallow, forward-thrusting picture space forces us to relate to icon subjects person-to-person, while the solemnity of the faces is for our protection.

You would think that the more realistic figures would engage us on a more personal level than stylized ones.

The opposite is true because of the picture space. It is the other-worldly figures, standing in front of a gold ground, that come forcefully forward to meet us while the "more real-looking" figures that exist in more credible picture space, remain there.

PRAYING FIGURES

The word *Deisis* (*day*-ess-iss) means supplication. In its basic form, a *Deisis* icon shows the Virgin and St. John the Baptist standing in supplication on either side of Christ Enthroned. When we see an icon of a single figure turned at three-quarters to the picture-plane with hands held up in prayer, it may be the remaining leaf of a folding icon. It may be a panel of the *Deisis* tier of an icon screen in which pairs of saints (archangels, apostles, bishops, etc.) flank the Virgin and the Baptist. There is—potentially—a fourth person in a *Deisis:* When you look at the icon prayerfully, the fourth person is you.

PROFILE

A profile is a face painted as seen from the side so we can see only one eye. The Orthodox Church teaches that an icon is a privileged point of contact with the subject. Therefore, an icon of Christ, the Virgin Mary, the apostles, the saints, and angels are shown full face or three-quarter face. They either look directly at us, or they turn their faces toward us. Evil or unrighteous people like Judas, Christ's tormentors, or the Bad Thief are shown in profile, as are also Satan and his angels. The craftsman knew that we would not want to look them in the eye and would not want them to look directly at us. In the mosaic of the *Last Supper* in St. Apollinare, Ravenna, Judas's face is the only one in profile. (The tradition of bad or threatening people shown in profile can also be seen in Western medieval pictures, for example, the giants of Genesis 6:4 in the eleventh-century Anglo-

Saxon *Hexateuch*.) There are exceptions, of course; one example is a twelfth-century *Raising of Lazarus* icon in which his sisters Martha and Mary are shown in profile, but profiles-for-bad-people is the general rule.

In the West, with the development of the third dimension in picture space and with more naturalistic ways of grouping figures in a crowd, the tradition of showing bad people in profile fell out of use. With the Renaissance interest in classical art and Roman models, it became fashionable to paint profile portraits.

PROPORTIONS

Some figures in icons look "normal," that is to say, having average proportions, while others look elongated: tall and thin.

Early Byzantine figures were often proportioned just over one-in-five (1 to 5). Taking a measure from the top of the head to the chin as one unit, the whole figure was five of these units. The units were: head to chin, chin to chest, chest to crotch, crotch to knee, knee to heel. The effect was solid and confident, but the figures can look stumpy with large heads.

From time to time in Byzantine art, figures were drawn 1 to 7 or even 1 to 9. It would be like someone of 5'6" (1.68 m) growing over 10 inches (25.5 cm) taller and no wider. The figures are imposing and supernatural, towering over us. Often their feet are on tiptoe as though their contact with this world is slight and they are straining up to heaven. By being so tall, they draw our eyes and minds upward when we look at them. Whenever Byzantine art returns to classical style, feet stand flat and proportions settle down to about 1 to 5.

Cennini, a Florentine craftsman writing in the fifteenth century, recommended trying again and again till the drawing "agreed in proportions with the model." His "model," however, would have been the copy of a finished image or a picture in his pattern book, rather than a professional sitter in the studio or workshop. The image would have to be enlarged for a wall painting or reduced for a small panel painting.

An apprentice in an icon craftsman's workshop would have learned to draw from just such a proportional system. Faces and figures, drawn in the accepted proportions, would be copied from patternbooks, over and over again, as children used to be taught to copy letters in an exercise book.

The *Pantocrator* over the entrance door of the Chora Church in Constantinople has a halo 5½ times the length of the nose. (Icon faces sometimes have a distinct shadow across the bridge of the nose.) The height of the head is 1½ times the halo's diameter and its breadth is one third. The depth of the semicircular mosaic is twice the diameter of the halo. The *Virgin and Child* in a central roundel in the dome of the same Church has the diameter of the Virgin's halo 6½ times her nose length. Christ's halo is half the size of hers. Her halo fits twice into the diameter of the icon circle. When a wall was marked in preparation for painting, sometimes only the halo was marked with a groove on the plaster—so the exact size could be used as a measuring unit for the rest of the picture. (However, the whole composition would already have been worked out in reduced scale as a blueprint on parchment.)

The fact that such a proportional system existed shows the medieval craftsman's attitude to his work: He did not seize a paint brush and draw an icon as the mood took him but set out his figures in whatever proportions were perceived at the time as being the right ones.

Through the millenium of Byzantine art, from about 330 to 1453, the pendulum has swung several times between classical and "transcendental" proportions, between 1 to 5 and 1 to 8. There have been periods when secular pictures had short figures while religious pictures, made at the same time, had tall ones.

"Provincial" Style

Icons painted in a provincial style were painted some distance from major artistic and cultural centers. If a gallery catalogue describes an icon as "provincial," with the implication of "merely provincial," spend more time with that icon, rather than walking past it. Notice two things about it: It has the direct, childlike quality of other "primitive" pictures, the painter going straight to the heart of the subject, and it follows the iconography of Byzantine art, even though it does so in a simple way. Provincial-style icons have the charm of Early American "naïve" portraits.

The work of a provincial icon painter may be his best work; he painted icons because he and his patron believed they were important. That provincial icon, now in an art gallery, may have been the focus of sincere love and devotion for a family in some Eastern European village. They brought their prayers to it and looked at it long and lovingly; it gave them strength to continue in what may have been a difficult life.

When you see an icon in provincial style, stay with it until you can see its sincerity and charm. Not every icon painter was a Rublev, and not every icon painter *should* be a Rublev; a variety of styles will reach out to a variety of people.

Regional Schools

As explained in chapter two, Constantinople set the standards and style emulated by the whole Orthodox art world: Byantine art was a centralized international phenomenon. Even in outlying provinces, artists tried to do work of metropolitan character and quality; what one may be tempted to label "provincial" may just be poor quality workmanship (perhaps done for less discriminating or poorer clients). The only real Byzantine exception to the above might be the monastic murals of the rock-cut churches of Cappadocia, accomplished in the ninth to the eleventh centuries.

In the Middle Ages, regional schools evolved in the South Slav world, but it is often hard to distinguish between, for example, Serbian painting and Byzantine. Inscriptions are no help, for Greek was still the language of culture, and some artists working in Serbia were certainly Greeks. But as icons passed freely along diplomatic and trade channels, the homogenization of style increased.

In Russia, in the eleventh and twelfth centuries, work in the international Comnene style also begins to appear in Novgorod and Pskov. But in the later Middle Ages (and especially after 1453), regional schools develop in Russia, most importantly, the schools of Novgorod and Moscow. Only in the late sixteenth and seventeenth centuries can we use the word "provincial," notably regarding the so-called "Northern School" icons, which are inferior emulations of the former Novgorodian style in northern areas of Russia. In any case, by that time, regional styles had been largely absorbed into a single basic Moscow manner.

SCALE, HIERARCHY OF

Scale is the relative size of figures in a picture. An icon shows spiritual reality rather than material reality, so the relative size of the figures is not the same as it would be to someone looking at the scene through a camera. Saints and angels tower over us, while minor figures are half-size or smaller. Figures appear in doorways that reach as high as the roof, or buildings are half-size to the people standing just outside them. Looking at such an icon with eyes trained in Western perspective, the relative size of people and buildings can be confusing. In Renaissance pictures something small means something in the distance; it is part of the language of Western art that we are used to and that children have to learn.

Scale in icons has to do with spiritual hierarchy. When small figures in an icon stand directly beside large ones the difference is spiritual status rather than distance. This is what we call "hierarchy of scale."

The difference of scale appeared long before Byzantium, in Egyptian art and in Late Antique Roman sculptural reliefs. This way of showing rank or spiritual status was used by icon makers and continued in Western medieval art, with figures of donors shown half-size or quarter-size to the main figures. When a third dimension was added to icons, donors became full-size; with a more believable picture space a difference of scale works only if it shows distance.

Without having been taught anything about scale or medieval painting, young children draw people in the size that shows the child's perception of the person's importance. Like icons, children's pictures show spiritual and psychological reality instead of only the material appearance. The relationship of status to size is a perception that stays with us into adult life: If we see the Queen in real life rather than on television, we feel a moment of deep surprise and say, "She seems so small." We expected her to be larger than life-size and in our memories of the event she *will* be larger because in memory our perception will have taken over from camera sight.

SIDE OF BLESSING / SIDE OF JUDGMENT

In Matt. 25:31–46, Christ describes how the Son of Man will judge the nations of the world, separating them as a shepherd separates the sheep from the goats. Before the selective breeding of wool-bearing sheep, they and their goat cousins could look similar at a distance; in the push and jostle of a mixed flock only a shepherd could tell the difference, as Christ's listeners knew well. "He will put the sheep on his right and the goats on his left. Then the King will say to those on his right, 'Come, you who are blessed by my Father. . .'" (vv. 33–44). They had fed the hungry, welcomed the stranger, clothed the naked, nursed the sick, and visited the prisoners. "I tell you the truth, whatever you did for one of the least of these brothers of mine, you did for me." Then he will say to those on his left, 'Depart from me, you who are cursed, into the eternal fire prepared for the devil and his angels'" (vv. 40-41).

In icons of the *Last Judgment* the right-hand side of Christ (on our left when we look at the picture) is the side of blessing, and his left-hand side is where the devil and his angels live. There are *Last Judgment* icons in which Christ's right hand is extended in blessing while his left is turned palm downwards. Examples are in St. Saviour in Chora, Constantinople, and the Cathedral of the Dormition in Moscow. In some icons of *Christ Pantocrator,* there is a hint of the two sides in his face. The eye and eyebrow on his left side seem severe; the right side of his face is full of love. It is especially evident in the sixth-century wax icon from St. Catherine's monastery, Sinai.

SIMULTANEOUS NARRATION

If there are two or more episodes of one story in one picture, then the icon shows simultaneous narration. An example most familiar to Westerners is a *Nativity* picture with three shepherds on one side and three Wise Men on the other, even though, in the Gospel account, the Magi arrived when Christ was an infant, and the Virgin and St. Joseph were living in a place other than a stable (Matt. 2:9). What the artist is doing is telescoping subsequent events within the written narrative into a single composite image.

An example of simultaneous narration that looks bizarre is an icon of *St. John the Baptist,* standing (with head!) with his severed head on a plate. A fifteenth-century Moscow icon of the *Transfiguration* shows Christ leading his disciples up the mountain on one side of the main picture and down it on the other side. In the top right- and left-hand corners of the picture, angels lead Moses and Elijah through space and time to the Holy Mountain. An *Annunciation* icon shows five separate moments in one picture: the Archangel hurrying in, the Virgin startled, the Archangel announcing the will of God, Mary's acceptance, and God the Holy Spirit flying from heaven to effect the conception. On a sixth-century paten with the *Communion of the Apostles,* Christ is shown twice, handing the consecrated Host to one group of apostles and the chalice to the other. With the elaboration of iconography in the Byzantine late Middle Ages, more and more scenes or protagonists are set into one picture-space. For example, an eleventh-century *Nativity* would show only the core protagonists (Mary, Joseph, the Child, probably with the animals). But by the late fourteenth century, there would be additional scenes, prior or subsequent to the birth itself, such as the annunciation to the shepherds, midwives washing the baby, and the arrival and departure of the Magi.

Simultaneous narration may, in fact, use every part of the picture space for telling the story. In iconography the story is more important than an elegant composition of figures in a landscape. Simultaneous narration allows more of the story to be told inside one picture. The episodes of the story are not always arranged neatly from left to right as in a strip cartoon; we have to know the story before we can make sense of the picture. Though the main moment of the story is likely to be in the center, with previous and subsequent events arranged around, it is not always like that; neither do the events always move from left to right.

Simultaneous narration happens inside our heads when we think about a familiar fictional story, for example

Cinderella. At the sound of her name we see her in our mind's eye: in rags sweeping the ashes, dancing at the ball, running away at midnight with her shoe left on the stairs, and finally reunited with her prince. All the episodes flash into the mind at once. Medieval craftsmen presented episodes from the Old and New Testaments and lives of the saints in the same flash-fashion.

As incidents from the Gospels become less familiar to people in the post-Christian West, an icon with simultaneous narration becomes confusing; viewers are not sure of the order of events. Medieval craftsmen, patrons, and viewers knew the story and had no problem distinguishing its separate parts.

When particularity entered icons influenced by the West, the visual technique of simultaneous narration ceased to work. A picture was less a showing-forth of the event and its significance, and became more like a snapshot of a time-bound moment.

SKULL

Christ was crucified on Golgotha, a word meaning "place of the skull" (a place of public execution outside the city walls of Jerusalem). In icons, the "hill" is shown by a hillock or small pile of rocks into which the upright of the Cross is jammed. Sometimes the craftsman shows a skull at the foot of those rocks, set in a little black area like a tiny cave.

The skull has two meanings: It identifies the event as happening at the place of the skull, and it represents the first Adam, dead in sin. St. John Chrysostom, who died early in the fifth century, first suggested that the skull was that of Adam; and after about a hundred years the idea worked its way into the iconography of the *Crucifixion*. In some icons the Blood of Christ trickles down the wood directly onto the skull, showing that by his death the

Second Adam redeems the first Adam, who represents the whole human race.

In Western pictures of the *Crucifixion*, the significance of the skull is diminished if the artist paints only scattered bones, as though of previously crucified men. In the West, often Adam's skull is clearly there at the foot of the Cross, although surrounded by bones—these too are significant, because Christ's sacrifice has a universal redemptive power.

Stars on the Virgin's Veil

Since about the eleventh century, craftsmen have painted three stars on the Virgin's veil: one on each shoulder and one above her forehead. In Byzantine iconography, the three stars are said to stand for her virginity before, during, and after the birth of Christ. Though the star on one shoulder may be obscured by the figure of the infant Christ, it is understood to be there. The stars are nearly always gold and eight pointed. They are not integrated into the folds of the fabric as though they had been woven in, but look as if they have been added to it like pinned-on filigree brooches.

The three stars traveled through Eastern Europe to Russia where they are a firmly fixed detail of iconography. No other figure in an icon is adorned with stars, although this is not surprising; the Virgin has a unique role in the history of salvation.

❖

Some people think Byzantine art is set into rigid iconography. Iconography, yes; rigid, no. The art of the icon can absorb slow and carefully considered change. Like any spoken or written language, it can take on a new word or drop one that no longer communicates. But, as seen in previous sections, the development of the iconography of the Virgin is an example of how iconography is able to adjust itself toward clearer communication.

Next time you see an icon I hope you will be able to say with joy, "*Now* I know what it means!" But there is still more (with icons there is always more). The next chapter is about how God, angels, and people are shown in Byzantine art.

EIGHT

God, Angels, and People

RUBLEV'S TRINITY ICON

The finest picture of the Holy Trinity is St. Andrei Rublev's icon of Abraham's three visitors, an event interpreted by theologians as an Old Testament prophetic adumbration of Father, Son, and Holy Spirit. In Rublev's icon the three figures are not differentiated by a cruciform halo or by different ages. (Plate 1. *The Holy Trinity*)

It is possible to read them from left to right as Father, Son, and Holy Spirit. The figure on the left wears a robe of luminous colors, seeming to have been made of light; the central figure has a tunic with a broad stripe running down it, as seen in other pictures of Christ; the figure on the right of the panel has a mantle that is green. The central figure points a hand of blessing toward the chalice on the altar-table: We could therefore see the central figure as Christ, the great High Priest. By a subtle tilting of the heads, the left and central figures relate to each other while the figure on the right looks toward the chalice.

The identification of the three figures as (left-to-right) Father, Son, and Holy Spirit is not necessarily the only possibility, for when we consider the Trinity, we contemplate *one* God in tri-*unity*. St. Gregory Nazianzen writes that the three Persons are distinguished only by *relationship* (not function, in which all three cooperate). The artist is trying to communicate the mystery of three Persons, one in essence, power, and glory. In the end, speculation on which Person is which in the icon is pointless.

It is notable that the three angels are identical in personal appearance—probably to counteract the possible misinterpretation of the icon as *tritheistic* (proposing three separate gods). However, it must be remembered that this is not a "portrait" of the ineffable Trinity, but a symbolic Old Testament "type" or prefiguration of the Christian mystery.

The landscape details are slight: A house indicates the place where Abraham and Sarah live, a tree indicates the oak of Mamre mentioned in Genesis 18. Light flows through the figures' clothes as though through shifting layers of fine silk. The three supernatural figures are represented by three angels, filled with beauty and strength and divine youth, relating to one another in an eternal song. The icon expresses both song and silence.

Of significance is the "circularity" of the composition: The three angels' forms and glances create a dynamic circle suggesting the eternal interchange of life and love within the eternal existence of the Trinity.

GOD THE FATHER

There are no icons of God the Father because of Exodus 33:20, which reads, "you cannot see my face, for no one may see me and live;" and John 1:18: "No one has ever seen God; the only Son, who is in the bosom of the Father, he has made him known" (RSV). If you want to see the face of God, look at an icon of Christ.

God the Father, according to both the Old and New Testaments, cannot be seen by human eyes. He remains transcendent and has never manifested himself visibly to human sight. Since he is invisible, he cannot be depicted in an icon. The Greek Fathers insist that all the "theophonies" (manifestations of God) in the Old Testament were disclosures of the preincarnate Christ, the Eternal Word and Wisdom of God, who is the exclusive and sole revealer of the Father. This is why in images of the Creation or of prophetic visions (Ezekiel, Daniel, etc.), it is Christ who manifests God or is shown in the act of creating. So when humans meet God, they behold the face of Jesus Christ.

The three Persons of the Trinity are not three gods. And because God is one, each Person of the Trinity manifests the other, so that an icon of Christ implies an icon of the whole Trinity.

GOD THE SON

The earliest pictures of Christ show him as youthful, elegant, and clean-shaven like the Roman gods Apollo or Mithras. In the Middle Ages, icons still sometimes show him as the youthful *Christ Emmanuel* (the name means "God with us"), especially when the accent is on his preexistence as eternal Son. In the fifth century the bearded face became standard and has continued to be the principal way he is shown. There is a cross in his halo so you can immediately distinguish Christ from the apostles. His hand is in a position of blessing, commanding, or teaching. In some icons of the *Virgin and Child,* he is a miniature adult (though beardless) to show he had a knowledge and an identity beyond that of an ordinary purely human baby. This is precisely because he is the Incarnate Word and Wisdom of God. The Christ Child in icons usually holds a scroll to show he is God's Wisdom.

Icon craftsmen were not concerned with making a pretty picture of any mother and baby and then merely adding haloes. To paint him as an ordinary baby would be to say, visually, that he *was* an ordinary baby. Instead, the Byzantine craftsman was making a picture of the Incarnation.

GOD THE HOLY SPIRIT

In icons of the *Baptism of Christ,* the Holy Spirit is shown as a dove coming down on Christ's head, a reference to Matt. 3:16-17. In Orthodox tradition, the Baptism is given much more weight than in the West, because it is seen as the first simultaneous disclosure in time of all three Persons of the Trinity: The Father's voice is heard (as later at the Transfiguration), the Spirit visibly descends in the form of a dove, and Christ is designated as Divine Son. This is why the Greek Fathers often call the Feast of the Baptism of Jesus Christ "the Theophany"—in other words, the Manifestation of the Triune God.

In icons of *Pentecost,* the Holy Spirit is shown as twelve rays of power or tongues of flame, one on the head of each apostle. In icons of the *Annunciation* he (not "it") is coming down to the Virgin Mary as a tiny dove. She asked the archangel about the conception of the Messiah

(Luke 1:34-35): "How will this be . . . since I am a virgin?' The angel answered, 'The Holy Spirit will come upon you, and the power of the Most High will overshadow you.'" In the icon, we see it happening.

The shaft of power is sometimes divided into three points to show that the whole Trinity is at work. Where the points join there is a circle, which may have a small white dove inside if the picture is big enough.

CHRIST PANTOCRATOR

Christ Pantocrator (pan-to-*crah*-tor) means Christ, the ruler of all. (Plate 2. *Christ Pantocrator*)

The domed roof of a Byzantine church represents the vault of heaven, and originally, mosaicists may have decorated it with the Ascension.[1] By the tenth century, the figure in church domes was half-length, and the picture for a dome had changed from narrative to confrontational. It was discovered that a half-length figure fitted more easily into a circle than one of full length, and it allowed the face to be on a larger scale. The most powerful image of *Christ Pantocrator* is at Daphni, near Athens, the mosaic made about 1100. He holds a closed book, which may be seen as the Gospels or as the Book of Judgment in Revelation 20:11, 12:

> Then I saw a great white throne and him who was seated on it. . . . Another book was opened, which is the book of life. The dead were judged according to what they had done as recorded in the books.

The fingers of his right hand are bent in the position of a priest's hand of blessing and are pointing toward himself. The index finger of his other hand points powerfully across the picture, balancing the sideways glance of his eyes to his left. When we look carefully at the face of this Pantocrator, we see a difference between one side and the other. His right side, the side of blessing, is calm; his left side, the side of judgment, is fierce with an angry eyebrow. After nearly nine hundred years this awe-inspiring image still has the power to convert. Confronted with it for the first time some people react with shock: This is not a tame Jesus. The only thing that lets us off the hook is that those eyes do not look directly at us. The image is a reminder that the Last Judgment should be feared because it will be absolutely just, albeit tempered by mercy and total understanding.

The Pantocrator is not intended to represent Christ as the Jesus of Galilee, but as the awe-inspiring God-Man, the King of the Universe and terrible Judge at the end of time. By the fourteenth century, the severity of the Judge is tempered, and in icons a merciful Redeemer holds out his book with the text, "I am the light of the world" (John 8:12), or "Come to me, all you who are weary and burdened . . . " (Matt. 11:28).

THE HOLY FACE

The *Mandylion* (man-*dee*-lee-on), literally a napkin or handkerchief, is an icon of the face of Christ. (Plate 3. *The Holy Face*) According to the tradition of the Western Church, Veronica, a member of the crowd following Christ when he carried the Cross, pressed her veil to his perspiring face; the cloth held the image, the details, of Christ's face on it.

In the Orthodox tradition, there is a different version of the story. King Abgar of Edessa sent a message to Christ to come and heal him, but Christ could not come. Instead he pressed a cloth to his face, thus miraculously imprinting his image on it, and sent it to the King, who was healed by the sight of his face. The outlines of the face remained on the cloth as the "image not made with hands," and all the other icons of the *Holy Face* are claimed to have been copied from that prototype.

In 525 some workmen repairing the city wall of Edessa found a container with a cloth that had a face painted on it. It was called the image not made with hands, and was said to have been hidden in the wall by Christians when they had been persecuted. In the dry climate of Turkey a piece of linen could have been preserved for five hundred years. The cloth was taken to Constantinople in 944 and seems to have disappeared during the fourth Crusade, when the Latins sacked the city in 1204.

Why, in iconography, paint Christ's portrait as though on a cloth? Because tradition has it that the original cloth had been in contact with the holy face. No other icon portrait is painted as though it is on a cloth. For Orthodox, the special significance of this icon lies in its miraculous production by Christ himself, thereby validating the practice of making icons.

The figure of the *Holy Face* is a man of about thirty, who looks straight at us with a calm expression. He has a cruciform halo with its identifying inscription. The face floats on a piece of white fabric like linen, painted either as though lying on the panel or hung by the top corners; sometimes it has a fringe across the lower edge. A difference between this portrait and other portraits is that this image has no neck (as though it is, indeed, an image taken from a cloth pressed to a person's face which maintains the image of the face, unlike a portrait which contains a face, neck, and shoulders). The face we see is masculine and gentle. His dark brown hair is smooth on either side of his brow, and his short beard is pointed or forked. His hair descends in two locks. Orthodox tradition maintains that, here, one can see an authentic portrait of Jesus Christ.

ORDERS OF ANGELS

Archangels

The archangels most often seen in icons are Michael and Gabriel. (Plate 7. *The Archangel Michael*) Two others not often seen are Raphael and Uriel (mentioned in the book of Tobit and in the Jewish apocryphal Book of Enoch). They are shown in formal robes, in imperial dress, as God's *Vicegerents* (appointed deputies). They have wings and classical heads. Gabriel, the messenger of the *Annunciation*, carries a staff. Michael, protector of God's people, is often shown standing above a dragon, piercing him with his sword, a reference to Satan in Revelation 20:1–2.

> I saw an angel come down out of heaven, having the key to the Abyss and holding in his hand a great chain. He seized the dragon, that ancient serpent, who is the devil, or Satan, and bound him for a thousand years.

Many believe that at Armageddon, the final battle of good and evil, Michael will finally defeat and slay the dragon.

Icons of the Archangel Michael (and of the assembly of the archangels) show him carrying a circular picture of Christ, an icon in an icon. In other icons he has an inscribed orb. (The inscription reads, "Jesus Christ, the just judge": overtones of Michael's role as weigher of souls at the Last Judgment.) Gabriel, too, can be depicted outside of narrative contexts, sometimes alone, more often paired with Michael in the *Deisis*.

Although St. Dionysius the Areopagite hierarchically distinguished nine orders of angels (the purely contemplative seraphim and cherubim coming first, or highest, and the ministering, active archangels and angels last), in practice the archangels are given preeminence, as God's viceroys here below, and as "taxiarchs" (commanders of the heavenly ranks of angels). Other categories of angels (some mentioned by St. Paul, for example, principalities and powers) are basically ignored by the Eastern iconographic tradition (though they are common in Western late medieval art).

Cherubim and Seraphim

These two orders of angels are described in the Old Testament:

> The sound of the wings of the cherubim could be heard as far away as the outer court, like the voice of God Almighty when he speaks. (Ezekiel 10:5)

> I saw the LORD seated on a throne, high and exalted, and the train of his robe filled the temple. Above him were seraphs, each with six wings: With two wings they covered their faces, with two they covered their feet, and with two they were flying. (Isaiah 6:1–2)

Seraphim in icons are often painted red as in the fiery wheels-within-wheels in Ezekiel's vision. They have shadowy or fiery faces half visible through the feathers. They appear in icons of *Christ Pantocrator* and the *Death of the Virgin* and elsewhere. In some icons a single angelic figure painted red like fire represents Christ, the Wisdom of God, *Sophia*.

With the Italian Renaissance fascination with classical art, naked winged infants appear in the Christian art of the West. They are *putti*, the small genii of pagan Rome, and have been called *cherubs* since the Renaissance. They have nothing to do with the cherubim seen by Ezekiel, and indeed cherubim have tended to become supplanted by seraphim in Byzantine art.

Assembly of Archangels

How many archangels make an assembly? In icons it can take only two. An *Assembly of Archangels* icon shows two stately winged figures standing side by side, looking at us. Between them they hold either a transparent sphere with an inscription or a roundel with the head and shoulders of the Holy Child, an icon in an icon. However, other angels may be present in this scene (a beautiful fourteenth-century Byzantine example is in the Pushkin Museum, Moscow).

Angels

Angel means messenger. Angels are messengers of God and guardians of the faithful. When angels appear in the Old or New Testament, they are described as young men in white robes; therefore, following Biblical precedent it is proper to refer to an angel as "he." In icons they are young, male, beardless, and they often wear the white robes still seen in Christmas cards and church windows. They are eternal youths, ageless but also sexless, like the eunuch-chamberlains of the Byzantine court. In an icon the robes appear in whatever color balances the other colors of the picture. Angels in icons also wear court dress or military costume, for angel courtiers are part of the early practice of using the splendors of the imperial court as an adumbration of the court of heaven. Military angels are the embattled guardians of the Christian people, actively engaged against Satan's cohorts. (Plate 11. *The Angel of the Resurrection*)

Though angels in the Bible are not described as having wings, those in icons derive from the Winged Victories or *genii* of Roman art. They look like Winged Victories because such figures were part of the classical visual language known to the craftsmen and their patrons in the early centuries of the Church. Thus the visual formula of angels-with-wings-and-haloes is still understood today.

Ask any child in Sunday school (or out of it) to draw an angel, and you can be sure the figure will have wings and probably a halo.

The iconography is simple and the iconography still works. The wings make the figures immediately identifiable and since an icon is art for communication, it is important to know at whom you are looking. In an age when the fastest way for a person to travel was on a horse, people observed that creatures with wings, such as a hungry falcon or an eagle in a power dive, could travel even faster. As God's messengers, angels had wings to show them to be swift and airy travelers between heaven and earth. Angels have haloes because they are holy creatures carrying divine authority.

Because of their origins in pre-Christian Roman art, angels remain the most persistently classical figures in Byzantine art: They retain classical robes and coiffeurs, bound with a fillet, and often are shown fully modeled, even in periods of more abstract style. They can even appear quite "beefy" and masculine (especially in works of the so-called fourteenth-century Macedonian School)—strange, one might think, when Tradition insists that their forms are entirely ethereal (like fire), and the Byzantine Liturgy calls them "holy bodiless powers of heaven"!

VIRGIN MARY

In the art of the Orthodox Church the Virgin Mary is usually shown with Christ because her status and importance are derived from him.

Icons of the Virgin Mary are in several iconographic types that are known by name. The differences between them are specific and of more significance than between Western Madonnas, which may differ only in styles of dress. In Orthodox Christian art, an icon of the Virgin presents to us a particular aspect of her life and significance.

An icon type of the Virgin Mary may be referred to by the name of a town, as in the Western Church we speak of Our Lady of Lourdes or of Walsingham. For example, the *Virgin Pelagonitissa* is an icon from Pelagonia, and the *Virgin of Vladimir* (Plate 6. *Virgin of Vladimir*) is so named because the icon was in that town for over two hundred years. Virgin icons with the reputation of being wonderworking are also often named after their towns of origin or residence, (e.g., the *Virgin of Smolensk*, of Tikhvin). (Plate 6.*The Virgin of Vladimir*) Madonnas painted and sculpted in the West are sometimes crowned; Byzantine Virgins are crowned only in instances of Western influence.

Ways of depicting the Virgin Mary have developed over the centuries, from a stately Roman matron, to an equally stately Byzantine princess, or a richly dressed aristocratic lady, to a grieving and compassionate mother. In general, before the Age of Iconoclasm she was a theological figure, a visual presentation of the doctrine of the Incarnation. During those early centuries, the Church defined the doctrine of the Incarnation against heretical points of view: that Jesus Christ was not a God who only appeared to be human; that he was not a mere man who later became God; that he was not just a good man who said wise things and whose followers exaggerated and fantasized. Rather, he was a single person in two natures, wholly God and wholly man, the Incarnate Second Person of the Trinity.

In the fifth century, Cyril of Alexandria wrote to Nestorius, Patriarch of Constantinople to correct him on the completeness of incarnation:

> We do not say that first an ordinary man was born of the Holy Virgin and then the Word descended upon him, but we say that having the flesh, he accepted a carnal birth, because he claims this carnal birth as his own . . . so the Holy Fathers did not hesitate to call the Holy Virgin "Mother of God."

Whatever the type of icon, she always has the abbreviated inscription in Greek or Cyrillic letters to identify her as the Mother (or, the Bearer) of God. Iconography of the Virgin developed over generations as the Church grew in understanding of her.

Here are nine types of Virgin, and Virgin and Child icons, in roughly historical order.

Virgin Orans

The *Virgin Orans (oar-*anz), the *Virgin Praying,* is the earliest type. Unlike most Eastern Christian pictures of the Virgin, she is shown on her own, though an *Orans* icon may be only part of a group of praying figures. Even if Christ appears absent, he is present by implication as the One to whom the Virgin prays. In this type of icon we see the Virgin as intercessor and *the* type of the Church at prayer. She stands facing us with both hands raised level with her shoulders. Sometimes, for compositional reasons or lack of space, her hands are held up in front of her so her figure is a simple pillar and her hands are clearly visible against her dark clothes. Early Christian and pre-Christian pictures in the ancient Greco-Roman world show standing figures with their hands raised in prayer (the gesture is also used in the Jewish and Muslim traditions). Early Christian wall paintings of a woman holding up her hands in prayer may represent the Virgin, or the praying Church, or an individual soul. (There is deliberate ambiguity about this in the frescoes of the Roman catacombs, from the third to the fifth centuries.)

Virgin Platytera

The *Virgin Platytera* (plat-tee-*tare*-ah) is also called the *Virgin of the Sign.* This type has been made since the Early Byzantine period. (Plate 4. *The Great Panagia, called the Orant of Yaroslavl.*)

Plate 1. The Holy Trinity
Andrei Rublev (c. 1370–1430)
Credit: Scala/Art Resource, NY

Plate 2. Christ Pantocrator
Bishop Jovan, 1393
Credit: Giraudon/Art Resource, NY

Plate 3. The Holy Face
16th or 17th century
Credit: Beniaminson/Art Resource, NY

Plate 4. The Great Panagia
(Virgin of the Sign) 12th century
Credit: Scala/Art Resource, NY

Plate 5. Virgin and Child
Dronisii, 1502-3
Credit: Scala/Art Resource, NY

Plate 6. Virgin of Vladimir
Byzantine, 12th century
Credit: Scala/Art Resource, NY

Plate 7. The Archangel Michael
Byzantine, 14th century
Credit: Scala/Art Resource, NY

Plate 9. St. George and the Dragon
Russian, circa 15th century
Credit: Scala/Art Resource, NY

Plate 8. St. John the Baptist
Andrei Rublev, 1408
Credit: Scala/Art Resource, NY

Plate 10. St. Nicholas
Russian, late 15th or early 16th century
Credit: Beniaminson/Art Resource, NY

Plate 12. Baptism of Christ
14th century
Credit: Giraudon/Art Resource, NY

Plate 11. The Angel of the Resurrection
(fresco) circa 1234
Credit: Scala/Art Resource, NY

Plate 14. Christ's Entry into
Jerusalem
Credit: Scala/Art Resource, NY

Plate 13. Transfiguration from Pereslav
Russian, circa 1403
Credit: Scala/Art Resource, NY

Plate 15. Crucifixion
Dionisii, circa 1500
Credit: Giraudon/Art Resource, NY

Plate 16. Anastasis
Workshop of Dionisii, 1502–3
Credit: Scala/Art Resource, NY

The unborn Christ is in a roundel against the Virgin's breast, as an icon in an icon. Medievals did not believe that when a fetus was formed it was in the chest cavity. But a *Virgin of the Sign* icon is not an anatomically incorrect description of pregnancy; it shows that the Virgin Mary is the vehicle of the Incarnation. King Solomon prayed at the dedication of the Temple: ". . . will God dwell indeed with man on the earth? Behold, heaven and the highest heaven cannot contain thee; how much less this house which I have built!" (2 Chron. 6:18 RSV). Mary is the living house of God that by grace can contain the uncontainable Divinity; poetically, therefore, her womb is said to have become "wider (*playtera*) than the heavens." It is a way of showing the miracle of the Incarnation (cf., John Donne: "Immensity encloister'd in thy dear womb"). In the *Theotokos*' pregnancy (*Theotokos* means "God-bearer") she became the Ark of the Covenant because God dwelt in her just as he was present in the Old Testament Holy of Holies. Since the human fetus that she carried was the Creator of all things, the womb that held him was "wider than the heavens."

A *Platytera* icon shows the significance of the event as well as the simple fact of pregnancy (in icons, she is *never* shown with swollen belly).

The seventh-century Byzantine Akathist hymn referred to the mysterious fact:

> Hail, pure Mother of God, the Holy One of Israel.
> Hail, Thou whose womb is broader than the heavens.
> Hail, O sanctified one, O Throne of the heavens,
> Which the Children praised, saying:
> Bless ye the works of the Lord.

In a *Platytera* icon the Virgin may be full length (especially in church apses) or half-length (in many icons, ivories, and carved gems). She faces us directly with her hands raised in prayer. Christ has the face of a small adult and has his hand raised in blessing.

The *Platytera* type is sometimes called the *Virgin of the Sign,* in reference to the prophecies of Isaiah 7:14: "The Lord himself will give you a sign: The virgin will be with child and will give birth to a son, and will call him Immanuel."

Like the *Virgin Enthroned*, a *Platytera* is a strong dogmatic, objective statement of the Incarnation, rather than emphasizing the intimate loving relationship of Mother and Child (*see Virgin Eleousa*).

Virgin Paraclesis

Paraclesis (par-*ra*-clee-sis) means intercession. Here, the Virgin is standing at three-quarters to the picture plane and turning toward Christ, who appears in a quadrant representing part of the arc of heaven at the top of the picture. Her elbows are close to her body and her hands spread toward him with the palms up in a gesture of prayer. In one hand she may hold an unfurled scroll with a list of prayer requests. A good example is the votive mosaic in the Martorana, Palermo, twelfth century, where the Virgin intercedes on behalf of the donor, George of Antioch, who appears as a tiny supplicant at her feet.

Virgin Enthroned

Mother and Child face directly toward us, as strong as a statue. As she is enthroned on the piece of furniture, so the Child is enthroned on her lap. She presents the Child as directly as the Church presents him to us, and we should allow ourselves to read the figure as representing the Queen of Heaven as well as the historical Mary of Galilee (not one or the other, but both/and). The frontality and direct gaze is similar to the *Orans* standing figure. The *Virgin Enthroned* is an iconic type that dates from the

Early Byzantine period when the Virgin Mary was shown as a powerful Roman empress.

The enthroned Virgin and Child is a common apse subject in medieval Cypriot churches, so it is also sometimes called *Kypriotissa* (of Cyprus).

Virgin Hodegitria

The *Virgin Hodegitria* (ho-dee-*gee*-tree-ah) is a type that has been painted since the fifth century and was given its iconographic name by the ninth century. The figures are usually half-length, and Mary has Jesus in the crook of her left arm. He is shown as a small adult rather than as a child; he holds a scroll and extends his hand in blessing. She looks directly at us, extending the fingers of her right hand toward him. To understand icons, look first at the faces and the hands. It is the face and the hand that makes a Virgin icon a *Hodegitria* type: She looks at us and points our attention to him, and he, too, looks at us, so that we can meet him face-to-face. (Plate 5. *Virgin and Child*)

Hodegitria means "the one who shows the way." (The *hodegoi* were guides who led blind pilgrims to a miraculous spring near Constantinople.) In a *Hodegitria* icon, the Virgin is a guide who directs our attention away from herself; it is the iconic representation of her words at the wedding in Cana, "Do whatever he tells you" (John 2:5). A *Hodegitria* icon teaches the Incarnation, pointing emphatically to the authority of Christ, not of Mary.

There is a tradition that the original *Hodegitria* icon was painted by St. Luke, who sent it to Theophilus with his Gospel. St. Luke did paint her portrait: He painted it in words. When we see the Virgin Mary at the *Annunciation,* the *Visit to St. Elizabeth,* the *Nativity,* the *Presentation in the Temple,* or the *Finding in the Temple,* we see her as pictured in the Gospel of Luke, although it is in the Gospel of John that we hear her words at the wedding in Cana.

Virgin Eleousa

The *Virgin Eleousa* (ell-e-oo-sa) is the Virgin of Tenderness or compassion or loving-kindness. The most famous *Virgin Eleousa* icon is the twelfth-century *Virgin of Vladimir*, though the type was known before that date. It is a half-length icon with the Virgin and Christ cheek to cheek, his hand curling around her neck. Her head is turned so she looks at us with sorrow and compassion. Other Tenderness icons show him reaching up to her face or caressing her chin.

The softer, embracing Mother was especially popular as a domestic icon, in contrast to the strong doctrinal images of the *Theotokos* made for the apse of a Church. The gentler image humanized Christ and the *Theotokos* as loving Mother and Son, while still asserting the doctrine of the Incarnation in visual form. In retrospect, we can see it was a large step toward painting Mary and Jesus as an ordinary mother and baby, in terms of universal human experience and feeling. It is of a piece with a shift in the late twelfth century in the way people were shown in Eastern Christian art: Emotions were expressed outwardly, gestures were more dramatic. Even the clothes express emotion, fluttering with intensity as though the wearer's feelings have extended to the fabric.

The equivalent of the *Virgin of Tenderness* became the most popular type in later medieval Western art, where by the late sixteenth century it gave rise to a spate of weeping Madonnas, faces contorted with grief and tears dripping. To look at one of those pictures for a time is to have the emotions churned; to look at a Byzantine Virgin is to have the emotions deepened.

Virgin of the Burning Bush

The burning bush that Moses saw, burning but not consumed, was later interpreted as a symbol of the Virgin Mary because she held the Light of the world, the fire of divinity, in her womb but was not consumed by his glory. In a *Burning Bush* icon, the Virgin and Child appear in a fiery bush; we are confronted by a frontal, full-length figure often accompanied by Moses, the recipient of the vision, and by other Old Testament prophets (see remarks above, on Christ as the subject of prophetic visions).

She holds Christ in front of her, his face directly below hers. He holds a scroll and his right hand is raised in blessing. His knees are drawn up so it looks as though he is sitting on her forearm. In a *Burning Bush* icon, she presents him confidently to us.

Virgin of the Passion

In ordinary speech today, the word "passion" refers to intense feelings of rage, enthusiasm, or sexual desire. In the context of religious art, the word means strong feelings that are deliberately endured. It is an active receiving of pain rather than a passive endurance of it. The passion of Jesus Christ is the pain of betrayal and crucifixion that he chose to go through even though, as he said, he could have called upon more than twelve legions of angels to rescue him (Matt. 26:53).

The *Virgin of the Passion* was a type that developed naturally from the *Virgin of Tenderness* in the late Middle Ages. The origin may have been Serbia in the fourteenth century, unless the tenth-century *Virgin and Child* in Tokali Kilise, Cappadocia, is an example. Because of the position of the child's limbs, icons of this type are sometimes wrongly called "Virgin with the Playing Child," but the Child is not playing. In the upper corners or sometimes on adjoining icons that have been lost, angels hold the instruments of the Passion. Mary can see the whip, nails, and cross; her brow creases in distress and her eyes shift sideways as she leans her head on the Child to protect him. The Child can see them, too; one of his little feet is turned up in tension as he writhes in his mother's arms. The icon invites consideration of Simeon's words to her: "a sword will pierce your own soul too" (Luke 2:35). It questions how much the man who was God knew when he was a child. It points up the tragic inevitability of his salvific sufferings as an implication of the Incarnation.

Protecting Veil of the Mother of God (Pokrov)

The *Virgin of the Veil* is a type that has been painted since the tenth century. She stands with her hands in prayer as angels fly above her holding a veil. In the fourth century St. Andrew the Holy Fool had a vision of the Virgin in the church at Vlachernae, Constantinople. She was standing above them, praying and holding out her veil to protect Christians against invading Saracens. Also present are the imperial couple and St. Romanos the Melodist who wrote hymns in honor of the Virgin in the seventh century. This is originally, therefore, a record of a visionary experience, with profound religious and political implications—not a discrete icon of the Virgin.

It became especially popular in Russia (*"pokrov"* literally means "tent" or "shelter" in Slavonic) when in the twelfth century, Prince Andrei Bogoliubski was the recipient of an almost identical vision: a holy fool saw the Virgin, attended by angels and apostles, in her cathedral at Vladimir, stretching out her veil to protect the Orthodox ruler and people from danger. It became *the* icon of the Virgin as national defender and intercessor for Holy Russia.

How to Recognize Saints

In the Eastern Orthodox Church a saint is identified as such more by physical characteristics than by what he is carrying. (I have listed some examples in chapter seven in the section *Handheld Objects.*) It is possible to have only a head of a saint in an icon and be able to recognize him. Here are some of the ones most often seen.

St. John the Baptist

St. John the Baptist has unkempt brown hair and beard and an intense expression in his eyes, appropriate for a desert saint preaching, "Repent, for the kingdom of heaven is near." He is barefoot and is wearing a tunic made of camel skin or hair, as described in Matt. 3:2. In some icons you can see the camel's head and legs still attached to the skin. His limbs are unnaturally thin. If not in a *Baptism of Christ* icon, he carries an unfurled scroll with the text quoted above. (Plate 8. *St. John the Baptist*) The prophet Elijah looks like the Baptist but much older, with the same intense expression. They seem to have been similar in personality, and the Baptist was called the second Elijah (Matt. 11:14).

St. John the Baptist is sometimes shown with wings. The logic of the craftsmen went like this: Angels have wings (the Greek word *angelos* means messenger as well as angel [Mal. 3:1]), and the Baptist was the messenger of God's new covenant; therefore the Baptist may be painted with wings. The saint is also a paradigm of the ascetic life, considered an "angelic" life. A winged *St. John the Baptist* icon is a reminder that an icon maker shows spiritual realities rather than mere portraiture. John also frequently has his own severed head on a platter, a reference to his martyrdom at the hands of Herod.

The Apostles Peter and Paul

The apostle Peter wears a blue tunic with a yellow cloak. He has curly gray hair brushed forward and a short full beard, round pink cheeks, and a burly physique. He usually holds keys, a reference to Christ entrusting the keys of the kingdom to him (Matt. 16:19). (When an icon patron was from the Latin Church, he would instruct the craftsman to make St. Peter more prominent among the apostles than he might have been in Greek iconography.)

In icons, St. Paul is shown as a spare intellectual, holding a codex, more at home in a library than by the lakeside. His hair and medium-length, straggly beard are dark, and he is bald from the temples to the top of his head with tufts of hair showing further back.

The iconography of the two apostles (Peter and Paul) was established early because pilgrims to Rome wanted to take home pictures of them. A Roman medallion from the early fourth century shows what are already recognizable portraits. Here, St. Peter has a round head with curly hair and a full, curly beard. St. Paul has a high, domed forehead with receding, smooth hair and a ragged beard.

St. George

St. George is a warrior saint and the patron saint of England (though he never came to England). In Early Byzantine icons, he is in Roman armor with a sword in his hand. He is young and beardless with a headful of rounded, springy curls and a clear-eyed, determined expression. Georgian icons of the ninth century show his horse trampling on the Emperor Diocletian, like imperial figures on Roman coins trampling on shaggy-coated barbarians from Northern Europe. In later icons he is often on horseback killing a dragon with his lance, an epitome of the victory of good over evil. (Plate 9. *St. George and the Dragon*)

For seven hundred years—a considerable stretch of history—he was St. George without the dragon, a soldier saint like Theodore or Demetrius. The earliest dragon-slaying picture is in a rock church in Cappadocia, Turkey, painted in the late eleventh century.

Often, too, we see the saint rescuing a maiden from the hungry dragon, a legend told and retold since the sixth century. The story followed the mythic pattern of Perseus and Andromeda, and of all the hissing, scaly monsters of English folk tales from Helston to the Orkneys.

With St. Demetrius, St. George is the most popular of Orthodox military saints, considered a "great martyr" and protector of the faithful.

St. Nicholas of Myra

The third-century bishop Nicholas is shown in icons with beard and gray hair, receding at the temples. The line of his short beard emphasizes his hollow cheeks, and he has a wrinkled forehead that makes him look worried. His face is pear-shaped with wide high forehead and narrow jaw. He wears an *omophorion* with black crosses on it to show that he is a bishop. He carries a codex, and his hand is raised in blessing. His expression is calm and direct, benign but sometimes with a touch of severity. (Plate 10. *St. Nicholas*)

A *Life of St. Nicolas,* written in the fifth century, describes him as "meek and gentle in his disposition and humble in spirit." He is the patron saint of Russia, and also of children and students.

There are more extant icons of St. Nicholas than of any other saint except the Virgin—an indication of his huge popularity both in East and West.

Unfamiliar Saints

To see unfamiliar saints is a reminder to Western Christians that there are many more specially dedicated holy men and women in the East than the ones recognized as saints by the Western Church. For instance there is St. Paraskeva (in Russian, *St. Piatnitsa,* meaning Friday). Since Friday was market day, she became the patron of stall holders who sell groceries and wares, and of women who buy them. Among the many others are Saints Cosmas and Damian, familiar in Tuscan art as patrons of the Medici. These are doctor saints, shown in icons with spatulas and medicine boxes. And there are countless more.

Many icon saints gaze directly at us, silently willing us to be strong. The Seventh Ecumenical Council, 787, justified the use of icons in Christian devotion: "For each time that we see their representation in an image, we are made to remember the prototypes, we grow to love them more. . . ."

HERMITS, ABBOTS, MONKS, AND NUNS

Many icons celebrate those who have set themselves apart for the religious calling. Some were founders of monastic communities, some famous theologians or ascetics.

Men and women from all levels of society made a decision to step apart from the pleasures and pressures of Roman society, to live in simplicity before God. Two of the first hermits recorded were St. Paul of Thebes and St. Anthony of Egypt, third century. St. Pachomius of Tabennisi first organized a group of hermits into a common life with a daily rule of prayer and manual work, similar to the Rule of St. Benedict in the Western Church. The solitary and communal life were combined in Palestine in the Lavra, in which monks lived in separate cells and met on Saturdays and Sundays.

The landscape of Byzantium was dotted with small monastic houses and hermit caves. In Cappadocia, entire churches were carved out of solid rock, complete with pillars, domed ceilings and blind windows. Icons of hermit saints show the men who chose to live in such rocky landscapes; they were shown with emaciated arms and faces, reflecting their prolonged fasting and self-mortification.

The lives of some solitaries may seem extreme to us, but entirely reasonable to them. They survived mainly on pulses, bread, vegetables, and water. One lived in an iron cage till his feet froze to the floor. Some, called "Stylites" (e.g., St. Simeon, St. Daniel), escaped from the world vertically as well as inwardly, living on small platforms at the tops of pillars with every aspect of their lives open to the public gaze. Other hermits, called "dendrites," like David of Salonica, lived in tree houses. St. Neophytos made his home in a cave for more than fifty years. St. Mary of Egypt, a former prostitute, wandered in the desert dressed only in her hair; in icons she is as skinny as a cadaver, her hair flowing to her knees.

The hermits' steely commitment to Christ was something that has never been easy to comprehend. Icons of hermit saints are a challenge to Christians and to Western society. The figures face us calmly, some of them holding a scroll with words of exhortation or a Bible verse. They are emaciated and determined, magnificently out of step with society.

Perhaps because of their self-marginalized position, such hermits frequently exercised a prophetic witness in society, able to rebuke the powerful with impunity. People came to them to seek spiritual counsel and healing—but keep in mind that Orthodox monks are first and foremost contemplatives, not teachers or social workers.

An icon of a hermit saint invites salutary consideration of the relationship between sanity and holy folly, and of a vision of glory so vivid that it influences life in this world.

HOLY FOOLS

Holy Fools are a special category of solitaries and of ascetics, pictured in icons, especially in Russian icons. They are solitaries in the sense that they have separated themselves from ordinary society and are homeless, constantly wandering and living on alms. They lack proper clothes and invite scorn for the sake of religious calling, even feigning madness. This is perhaps the most radical form of ascetic self-stripping and radical dependence on God, going even further than the hermit in his cave, let alone the monks with their life of corporate stability and property. We recall that St. Paul was proud to call himself a "fool for Christ's sake" (1 Cor. 4:10). In recent years holy fools have received more attention as a result of the novels of Dostoyevsky (e.g., the characters of Alyosha in *The Brothers Karamasov* and Prince Mishkin in *The Idiot*).

BISHOPS

In icons of bishops, we see those saints who serve as church leaders, preside over the Divine Liturgy in the Orthodox Church, and have the special charism to expound the true faith. They are recognized through their ecclesiastical garb, their vestments. These vestments consist of an alb (tunic), long chasuble often covered in crosses, and a wide episcopal stole. In fresco programs there are more bishop-saints than any other category, and include most of the great theologians of the Church, notably the Doctors of Orthodoxy, Sts. Basil, Gregory Nazianzen, Gregory of Nyssa, Athanasius, and John Chrysostom. All these Fathers of the Church are commonly found in the lowest frescoed tier of the apse of a Byzantine or Russian church, concelebrating at the Divine Liturgy. Since they were popular name-saints for boys, we frequently find them also among family icons.

PRIESTS AND DEACONS

There are surprisingly few popular priest-saints in the Byzantine tradition, probably because the most able and saintly usually became bishops. The abbot St. Theodore the Studite, a great eighth-century monastic organizer and champion of Orthodoxy against the iconoclasts, is a notable exception. A lot of monastic saints (portrayed in their habits, not in eucharistic vestments) were also abbots or priest-monks, like the distinguished hymnodist and theologian St. John of Damascus (also an antagonist of iconoclasm).

The deacon-saints common in art are mostly early martyrs (e.g., St. Stephen the Protomartyr, St. Lawrence); they wear albs with a long, thin stole over the right shoulder and frequently are assisting bishop-saints at the altar in images of them in the fresco-decoration of the sanctuary.

CHILDREN

Medieval children were thought of as miniature adults to be formed into adulthood quickly. Though children were loved, and—when they died young—grieved for, they were treated and dressed as protoadults.

Children appear in icons and frescoes, with their parents, as donors. The family is usually being presented to Christ by their patron saint.

In some icons of the *Baptism of Christ,* small figures swim around Christ's feet; they are newly baptized Jewish Christians (of any age) rejoicing in their renewed life. In icons of the *Day of Judgment,* small, white-robed figures are saved souls (they appear as children in Abraham's bosom); in icons of the *Death of the Virgin,* Christ holds a small white-robed or swaddled infant who is the Virgin's soul.

In a scene where a tall figure is accompanied by smaller ones, the smaller may not be children at all, but represent adults drawn to a different scale to show lesser rank than the main figure. Since adults and children were dressed the same, it is not always obvious which are which, and it is safer to assume they are lesser-rank adults rather than children (medieval people did not see much difference between those two categories). There are also a few child-martyrs, such as St. Kyriakos (usually shown with his mother St. Julitta), victims of the third-century persecution of Christians under Diocletian.

SATAN AND HIS ANGELS

In icons the figures of Satan and his demons (demons are the angels who rebelled against God before the creation of Adam and Eve) are skinny and jet black with horns, leathery wings, straight upstanding hair, and short, upturned tails like goats. They have goatish tassels of hair on chins, elbows, and knees. Sometimes they have hooves, sometimes monkeylike paws. Satan is distinguished from his followers by wearing a short, black robe and by his larger scale. He and his followers are about half-size to the human figures in the picture.

Because of the Orthodox belief that an icon is a privileged point of contact with the heavenly world, Satan and his angels are seldom shown. If they are, they appear in profile and in pictures of the *Last Judgment*. They also appear in the *Temptation of Christ* and other narrative New Testament subjects in manuscripts, frescoes, and (rarely) icons.

In an eleventh-century icon of the *Ladder of Perfection* at Sinai, devils are trying to prevent monks from ascending the ladder to heaven; their demonic armaments include hooks, and bows and arrows. In the Latin Church and sometimes in the Christian East, hell is shown as an enormous, lipped mouth like the mouth of a fish, opened wide to receive the damned. Satan's angels, in and around that mouth, are in violent, disorganized movement, as though held forever in clanking, chaotic noise. By contrast, God's angels and saints are in control and usually calm.

In an eleventh-century icon of the *Last Judgment,* Satan is sitting on a throne made of a seven-headed serpent, like the seven-headed beast in the Book of Revelation. Behind him is a wall of flames. He looks like an infernal version of Abraham, who sits on the opposite side of the picture, cradling the saved on his lap. The devil has a lost soul (probably Dives, the rich man in Luke 16:19-31) on his knee and is welcoming other souls to that ultimate horror, a party to which no one wanted to go and that will never end.

Some icons are statements of heavenly realities, such as *Christ Pantocrator,* or praying saints. Other icons are about historical events, especially key moments in the life of Christ that Christians believe are of permanent saving value to humanity. You may or may not have read the New Testament with the aid of icons. The following chapter is about icons that show scenes from the Gospels and from Church tradition, notably those events celebrated liturgically as the red-letter feast days in the Church's calendar.

NINE

New Testament Scenes in Icons: The Festal Cycle

INTRODUCTION: TWELVE FEASTS

The twelve feasts often shown in icons are the *Annunciation, Nativity, Presentation in the Temple, Baptism of Christ, Raising of Lazarus, Transfiguration, Entry into Jerusalem, Crucifixion, Anastasis, Ascension, Pentecost,* and the *Dormition.* But twelve does not always mean twelve. Feast icons may also include the *Virgin Mary*

Entering the Temple when she was a child and other Marian scenes; the *Adoration of the Magi, Washing of the Feet, Last Supper,* or *Doubting Thomas.* However, these ancillary scenes should be read as supplementary to major feast-scenes—for example, the *Magi* as pendant to the *Nativity, Doubting Thomas* to the *Anastasis* (Resurrection). Only in polyptych icons are all twelve feasts presented; in fresco cycles, a selection is made to fit the architecture of the church.

The festal cycle is liturgical rather than biographical: It celebrates those key events in the life, death, and exaltation of Christ and his Mother, which by the sixth century were identified as worthy of commemoration because of their doctrinal importance as major feasts ("red letter days") in the Church's calendar.

The basic twelve feasts took many generations to be established because iconography is not fixed like cement, but grows like a tree. You may see one festal icon and identify all the parts of it, then see another and notice that one or two of the feasts are different. Flexibility was permitted. Iconography allows variations on its themes. Icons of the twelve feasts (or fourteen or sixteen) were sometimes made into folding icons called polyptychs or (more rarely) were set as a frame of pictures around a central figure of Christ. A full iconostasis has them in a horizontal row along the first tier above the pillars on the upper walls of the Church.

New Testament scenes are frequently addressed in icons. The following listing includes the twelve feasts, as well as other common themes, here given in chronological order.

ANNUNCIATION

The *Annunciation* was the announcement by the angel Gabriel to the Virgin Mary that she was to be the mother of Christ (Luke 1:26-38).

The simplest and earliest *Annunciation* picture is from the third century in the catacombs in Rome. Like the other twelve feasts of the Orthodox Church, *Annunciation* icons show a decisive moment in history. There is a background of buildings, and the scene is identified as happening inside (indicated by a red drapery looped over part of the architecture).

From the sixth century, the iconography was fixed, with the archangel Gabriel entering usually from stage right. His knee is bent in the action of running or landing, and in many *Annunciation* icons his feet do not touch the ground. It gives him an air of urgency and of coming from another part of reality instead of walking across the floor.

In later *Annunciation* icons, his knee may be bent more and he sometimes kneels before the Virgin. He may wear a deacon's dalmatic, or be dressed as a member of the imperial court in rich cloak and tunic. He carries a staff to show his authority and his hand is stretched out in greeting. He comes as an Ambassador Extraordinary, a representative of another country who is sent on a special diplomatic mission.

The Virgin Mary is usually standing on the right of the picture. Her veil (*maphorion*) covering her head and upper torso is Byzantine purple, her tunic may be blue, and she wears the red slippers associated with Byzantine royalty. She stands on a footstool drawn with a perspective that looks strange if you are used to Western, post-Renaissance art, though not strange if you are used to Cubism. She may look surprised or very composed and may have a hand raised in greeting, or both hands folded in acceptance of God's offer.

God the Holy Spirit comes from the top of the picture, either in the form of a dove or as a shaft of divine power coming down onto the head of the Virgin. Sometimes the shaft of power ends in three rays of light to show that the whole Trinity is at work. It shows that the power of conception was from God and that the archangel was only a messenger. As soon as Mary had said, "May it be to me as you have said" (Luke 1:38), the angel departed from her and the Child took root in her womb. *Annunciation* icons show the three parts of the event: the announcement, the acceptance, and the conception, which occurs at the moment of her assent, through the action of the Holy Spirit (this is the miracle of the Virgin Birth).

NATIVITY

The Nativity is the day of Jesus Christ's birth. In a *Nativity* icon, the Virgin Mary reclines on a kidney-shaped mattress. (An icon of the *Birth of the Virgin* also has a reclining female figure, but she is St. Anna, and is inside a house and in bed.) In a *Nativity* icon, the reclining figure is in a landscape.

There is a cave behind the Virgin represented by a black shape; in Orthodox art, Christ is born in a cave rather than a wooden stable, because he is light born into darkness. The heads of an ox and ass peer over the manger, showing that this cave is where domestic animals live (this detail, which we take for granted, is not in fact mentioned in the Gospels, but comes from a verse in Isaiah [1:3]: "The ox knows his master, and the donkey his owner's manger"). A shaft of light from a segment of circle, the arc of heaven, comes down to the Child in the manger. The Virgin is the largest figure, the still center of the icon. If she is shown sitting rather than reclining, it is to teach that the Virgin bore Christ without pain. There were times when it was important for the Church to emphasize the difference of her motherhood from other mothers, and times when it had to emphasize the ordinariness of Jesus' birth.

A *Nativity* icon in its fully developed and late medieval form shows several events in simultaneous narration. Near the top of the picture, angels appear to the shepherds, who hear and hasten to attend. The shepherds are identified by their woolly cloaks and shepherd's crooks. In some icons the sheep or a shepherd's dog looks up at the angels, reminding us that the host of heaven actually was visible and was not just a religious idea in the minds of the simple faithful.

In the bottom corner, St. Joseph sits by himself, his hand held to his face in distress and confusion about the virgin birth. In some icons a man is speaking to him; the man is sometimes interpreted as being one of the shepherds, or as Satan in disguise coming to increase his doubt about the miracle.

Also near the bottom of the picture, two women prepare the Child's first bath, one testing the temperature with her hand in a gesture familiar to all mothers. The Child is in the manger in the center of the picture and in the midwife's arm at the bottom of the picture, an example of simultaneous narration. The midwives first appear in icons in the seventh century; they are from a story in the second-century apocryphal Gospel of James in which St. Joseph goes to find a Hebrew midwife. She realizes that the young mother in labor is a virgin and says, "My soul is magnified this day, because mine eyes have seen marvelous things: for salvation is born unto Israel." A second midwife doubts her till she has examined Mary for herself. Procuring a Hebrew midwife to assist and say the proper prayers during the birth is what any good Jew would do; a midwife's services were so highly valued that the Talmud allowed her to travel even on the Sabbath to attend a birth.

In some *Nativity* icons the Magi arrive, identified by Persian trousers and cap. They were not kings in Eastern tradition but wise men (astrologers). Byzantine icons did not put them in as prominent a position as pictures in the West. Till at least the twelfth century, they were shown riding horses rather than camels. The more exotic animals are so associated with them that it is difficult for us, in the West, to imagine them riding anything else. The number of Magi is not specified in the Gospel; painters assumed there were three because there were three gifts: gold, frankincense, and myrrh (Matt. 2:1–12).

PRESENTATION IN THE TEMPLE

Icons of the *Presentation in the Temple* commemorate the day Christ was taken to the Temple in Jerusalem to be presented to God as the first-born son (Luke 2:21–39, Exodus 13:2, 12).

Icons of the *Presentation* have been made since the fifth century and fixed in iconography from the ninth century. The composition closely follows the Lucan account. There are buildings and drapery indicating an inside scene. The Virgin Mary hands the Child to an elderly man whose hands are veiled in respect. He is Simeon, who recognized the Messiah in the tiny child and said, "Lord, now lettest thou thy servant depart in peace . . . for mine eyes have seen thy salvation" (Luke 2: 29, 30 KJV). Christ is no longer shown as a swaddled newborn but as a small child, though actually only forty days old. He is sometimes drawn as a tiny adult to show he is the Word and Wisdom of God Incarnate, as well as an ordinary, fully human baby. There is an altar in the middle of the picture to turn our minds to thoughts of sacrifice (offering and dedication, even to death).

In the background is the aged prophetess Anna, stooping and with lined face, holding out her hands to the Child. St. Joseph, standing on one side, holds a basket containing two white doves, the Temple sacrifice of a poor man (Lev. 12:6-8, Luke 2:24). The Presentation in the Temple was when Christ was brought to the Temple in thanksgiving at forty days old, was dedicated to the service of God, and was recognized as the Messiah by Simeon and Anna. The incident should not be confused with the Finding in the Temple, when he was twelve.

BAPTISM OF CHRIST

The Baptism of Christ marked the beginning of Christ's teaching ministry when he was baptized in the River Jordan by St. John the Baptist. Christ stands in the middle of the picture in what looks like a mound of water in the midst of a wide, deep chasm which is the dark world. Christ's right hand is held downward in blessing like a priest who invokes God's blessing on the water in a baptismal font. Above him God the Holy Spirit comes down as the Baptist reported, "I saw the Spirit come down from heaven as a dove and remain on him" (John 1:32). At the top of the picture is a segment of a circle, which represents the arc of heaven, from which appears the hand of God the Father or a descending ray of light and grace from him, containing the Holy Dove in a roundel. (Plate 12. *Baptism of Christ*)

Baptism icons reveal or at least suggest the Trinity, with Christ Incarnate standing in our world and the Father sending down the Spirit. The Trinity appears in icons either as Abraham's three angelic visitors (which emphasizes the three Persons' eternal relationships to one another), or in the Baptism of Christ where we see the three Persons as they relate to our world, revealed in the scriptural account.

In some icons of the *Baptism* there is a gray-haired man, with or without a fishtail, in the water by Christ's foot, a remnant of the personifications of classical art. He is the Jordan. Sometimes there is a female turning and swimming away: she personifies the Sea (Ps. 114:3–4, 7–8):

The sea looked and fled, the Jordan turned back; the mountains skipped like rams, the hills like lambs. . . .

Tremble, O earth, at the presence of the Lord, at the
presence of the God of Jacob, who turned the rock into
a pool, the hard rock into springs of water.

On both banks of the Jordan, angels with classical heads
and robes stand with hands veiled, facing the center of the
picture and holding Christ's garments. St. John the Baptist
stands on the bank with one hand raised in the act of pouring water on Christ's head. He is thin with tousled hair and
beard, and he wears a hairy tunic. There is a sketchy landscape with small bushes and craggy rocks. There may be a
felled tree near the Baptist's feet with an ax lying on it.

TRANSFIGURATION
The Transfiguration is a scene in the New Testament when
Christ led three of the disciples up a mountain and these
disciples saw the glory of God shining from him (Matt.
17:1–8).

The change was not in Christ (because he was always
filled with glory), but in the disciples' eyes, enabling them
to see reality. In a similar way the servant of Elijah saw the
armies of God in response to the prophet's prayer, "O
LORD open his eyes so that he may see" (2 Kings 6:17).
God's protecting armies did not spring into existence at
that moment: The only change was in the servant's eyes.

Because of the Orthodox belief that God's power can
be expressed sacramentally in and through the material
creation, there are more pictures of the Transfiguration
in Byzantine than in Western art. A *Transfiguration* icon
shows Christ in the upper part of the picture, backed by
a mandorla and with rays of light flaring out in six directions as from a star. His hands are raised in blessing. In
some icons there are clouds and cherubim. The landscape
has a few scrubby trees and the rocky hills leap upward.
(Plate 13. *Transfiguration from Pereslav*)

In some *Transfiguration* icons Christ is standing firmly on the ground, in others he floats above the earth in a mandorla. The light that flares out from him touches trees and rocks, showing that it was not a religious idea expressed in historical terms but an event in history as objectively real as yesterday's breakfast was for us. It is that historical reality that leads us through to the spiritual reality.

The figures standing on either side of Christ are identified by faces and inscriptions as Moses and Elijah. Their hands are held toward him in prayer, the group of three praying figures resembling a *Deisis*. Moses is present because he gave God's people the Law; Elijah is present because he represents the prophets. The three figures together show us God's plan in history: the Law, the Prophets, and the Incarnation. In the lower part of the picture the three disciples cower to the ground as though flattened by the weight of glory. They represent the New Testament Church of which all Christians are a part.

If there is one icon that sums up the whole theology of icons it is the *Transfiguration*. It shows that matter can be transformed by the power of God and can mediate God to us. The icon painter takes the most mundane materials— wood, minerals, lime, oil—and by his God-given creative imagination transforms them into a luminous image in God's praise, through which we can glimpse living glory and meaning. For Orthodox, the Transfiguration is also the visible model of human sanctification (they would say, "deification": being made participators of the divine nature, body as well as soul, a process which in the saints begins even in this life). The shining body of Christ, refulgent with uncreated light, is a living icon of the Christian hope of glory, in which the whole world shares.

RAISING OF LAZARUS

The Raising of Lazarus is the miracle Jesus performed of bringing Lazarus back from the dead. Lazarus comes out of the tomb, alive after being dead for three days (John 11:1-44).

The earliest picture of the Lazarus miracle is from the third century in the catacombs in Rome. In Early Byzantine images, Christ points to the dead man with a staff, a reminder of how Moses struck the rock with his staff and water came out. Jesus strikes the door of the tomb and the dead man walks out.

The icon shows several incidents as though happening simultaneously, and Jesus makes a gesture of authority toward the dead man, who stands wrapped in grave clothes. His commanding hand is the gesture of power: "Lazarus, come forth!" Several disciples stand behind Jesus, the number depending on the space available in the picture. At least one attendant holds his sleeve to his face, indicating disgust at the stench of a body that has been dead for three days in a hot climate. Lazarus' death was a real death that Christ reversed by his commanding word.

One or two attendants drag the lid of the coffin to one side. There is some indication of landscape to show that the event is taking place out of doors. St. Thomas is present because, at the news of Lazarus' death, he had said, "Let us also go, that we may die with him" (John 11:16), fearing that the Jewish leaders would try again to kill Jesus if he went back to Judea.

At Jesus' feet are two women, Martha and Mary, sisters of the dead man. One may be crouching or kneeling. The other may kneel with her body flat on the ground and her hands stretched out in front, the *proskynesis* (pross-*ken*-nee-sis), a prostration of deepest reverence. One of the women is talking to him, a hand raised to emphasize her words,

"Lord, if you had been here, my brother would not have died" (John 11:21).

Lazarus' face is visible framed by the head-cloth or bandages, his body covered with criss-crossed wrappings similar to an Egyptian mummy. He stands outlined against an upright black tomb with a gabled roof. It looks like a sentry box and focuses the eye on the drama of the moment: a man in a shroud standing against blackness. It is not a photographic description of the scene—Lazarus was buried in a rock-cut tomb, not in an upright box—but is a visual description of the event: Lazarus walked out of his tomb. In some icons, one of the attendants is holding one end of Lazarus' grave clothes, as in Jesus' words, "Take off the grave clothes and let him go" (John 11:44). Some icons show the resuscitated man in grave clothes bowing to Jesus, thanking him for the gift of life.

ENTRY INTO JERUSALEM

The *Entry of Jerusalem* refers to the day Jesus rode on a donkey into the holy city and was greeted by crowds waving palm branches (John 12:12–15).

A fourth-century sarcophagus has a picture of the *Entry into Jerusalem,* and icons of the event are the same for hundreds of years. Christ is on a donkey as recorded in the Gospels, though in some icons it looks like a mule or a horse. He usually crosses the picture from left to right with crowds close on all sides. His hand is raised in blessing.

In icons the figure leading the donkey is just a human being, a member of the crowd. People wave palm branches that look like enormous feathers, and clothes are spread under the donkey's feet. Little boys climb palm trees to break off branches. Jerusalem is represented by a group of buildings with a doorway and people coming out of it. (Plate 14. *Christ's Entry into Jerusalem*)

Communion of the Apostles

This subject is not one of the twelve feasts, but largely takes the place of the image of the Last Supper common in Western tradition. It shows Christ as institutor/minister/victim of the Eucharist in terms of Byzantine liturgical practice. Its primary place is in the frescoes or mosaics of the apse (sanctuary), below the Mother of God and above the concelebrating bishop-saints. The whole iconography of the apse conveys the doctrine of the Eucharist (a sacrament instituted by Christ and continually celebrated in the Church until the end of time) as an extension of the Incarnation (shown forth by the Virgin and Child above).

The *Communion of the Apostles* usually appears in such a monumental context and is rare in portable images. In the church program, the scene of the *Last Supper* may appear as a pendant, showing the actual historic event described by the evangelists.

Icons of the *Communion of the Apostles* show the Eucharist to be a continuing event linking heaven and earth. *Communion of the Apostles* images date from the mid-Byzantine period. There is an altar in the middle of the picture with vessels on it and a canopy over it. The disciples approach from both sides in two rhythmic processions of six on either side, bowing low with hands held out to receive the sacrament. In most icons Christ is pictured twice, handing the chalice to the group on one side and the Host to the other, an example of simultaneous narration. In the continuing heaven-and-earth event of our Sunday morning, the priest is Christ, the deacons are the angels, and the disciples are us. In many images of the *Communion of the Apostles,* angels assist in the liturgy, as Orthodox deacons do in the Orthodox Liturgy, where Christ is described as "He who offers and he who is offered": the Great High Priest of the Epistle to the Hebrews, who at the altar in heaven continually offers himself to the Father.

CRUCIFIXION

The image of the Crucifixion has been a part of Christian art since at least the fifth century, when a crucified Christ was carved on an ivory box (now in the British Museum). The earliest pictures are of Christ fixed to the Cross, standing on a wooden footrest (*suppaedaneum*), his eyes open, his two feet nailed separately, and his legs straight. He presents himself to us, floating forward from the surface of the icon into our space. When he is shown upright with his eyes open, the emphasis is on his victory over death.

Slowly the iconography for painting the *Crucifixion* changed in the art of the Eastern and the Western Church. The first change is that he turns his head to the watching Virgin Mary, then his eyes are shown closed, then the weight of his body slumps from the nails. Eventually the new iconography is fixed: He is naked but for a loin cloth, and dead, with head bowed, body inert, and lines of blood running to the ground. (Plate 15. *Crucifixion*) In its most economic medieval form, the Crucified is flanked only by the mourning Virgin and St. John.

From the twelfth century, icons often also show holy women and disciples mourning the dead Christ, and Longinus the centurion witnesses to Christ as Son of God. In the fourteentth century we may also see the two thieves, crowds of Jews and Romans, and the soldiers casting lots for Christ's robe. The Western part of the Christian Church places more emphasis on his physical suffering than the Eastern. The little shelf for Christ's feet has disappeared from a Western crucifix; the feet are crossed and impaled with a single nail. Orthodox Tradition includes four elements in drawings of the Cross: The first three are the upright, the crosspiece, and the short crosspiece near the top for the superscription, the sign that Pontius Pilate had fixed with the words "Jesus of Nazareth, the King of the Jews" (John 19:19). The fourth element is a sloping line near the bottom, lower on Christ's left side, the side of judgment; it represents the shelf for his feet.

SPICE-BEARING WOMEN

The spice-bearing women are those who took embalming spices to Christ's tomb and were told by an angel that the tomb was empty.

This incident from the Gospels is not often pictured in Western art. The iconography was established in Early Byzantine art as the first Easter icon. Three women walk in, close together, at least one of them carrying a jar of ointment. The seated figure is the angel of the Resurrection, who says, "Do not be afraid, for I know that you are looking for Jesus, who was crucified. He is not here, he has risen, just as he said. Come and see the place where he lay" (Matt.28:5–6).

From the fifth century, icons may show an elaborate building with a cupola, carefully drawn brickwork, and decorated doors; we can see this is the *Anastasis*, the rotunda that the Emperor Constantine built over Christ's tomb. Two icons, dated from the early fifth and ninth centuries, have almost identical tombs and groups of walking women, the iconography having been repeated from patternbook to icon, and from icon to icon, for four hundred years. In the case of icons, the principle is: "If it works visually and theologically, don't change it." The thought is: "If a visual image continues to communicate clearly from one generation to another, repeat the image."

If the picture has enough room, there are two or more soldiers slumped in sleep near the tomb; they are the guards who were supposed to keep watch. These soldiers afterward affirmed, "His disciples came during the night and stole him away while we were asleep" (Matt. 28:13). Near the tomb, an angel sits on a pile of stones or on the one large stone that was rolled away from the door of the tomb, and inside we can see Christ's empty grave clothes.

ANASTASIS

The *Anastasis* (an-*ass*-ta-sis) is the Resurrection of Christ, shown as his descent into Hades, during the period between his burial and resurrection, where he went to preach to the souls who had died before he was crucified (1 Pet. 3:19).

The *Anastasis* is related to the phrase in the Creed: "He descended into hell." In Western medieval drama, the event is called the *Harrowing of Hell,* from an old verb meaning to plunder. Western pictures of Christ's Resurrection show him stepping out of a tomb into a garden; icons of the *Resurrection* show him raising the whole human race and triumphing over sin and death. Note that in the medieval West, the location is definitively hell, with its flames, gaping jaws, and hideous demons. These features are absent in the icon: We are looking at Hades, simply the unredeemed place of death where John the Baptist and the prophets, patriarchs, and the just of the Old Dispensation await liberation.

Christ stands in the center of the icon in a vigorous attitude; in most icons he is backed by a mandorla. Under his feet are broken doors and a medley of hinges, nails, and locks. The gates of hell shall not prevail against his Church: In the icon we see him treading them under his feet. (Plate 16. *Anastasis*)

If there is a chained figure beneath his feet, he is not the individual fallen angel who is Satan, but the personification of Death or Hades, the last enemy to be destroyed (1Cor. 15:26). Death is not merely kneeling in submission; he has been immobilized. Death's ankles are tightly bound and a rope around his neck goes down to his two wrists held behind him. Here we see Christ's victory over sin and death, celebrated by the Eastern Orthodox Christians, notably (for example) in the Easter *Troparion:* "Christ has risen from the dead, trampling down death by death, and to those in the tomb he has given life." The *Descent into Hades* icon is, indeed, *the* Orthodox Easter icon.

In the icon, Christ has seized an old man by the wrist, pulling him upward from an open coffin, while an old woman waits, her veiled hands raised in supplication. They are Adam and Eve, representing the whole human race. They are clothed, because that is how they were after the Fall; they are shown as an old man and old woman because the human race is old. In my favorite *Anastasis* image, Christ has seized Adam's wrist with one hand and Eve with the other. On either side of Adam and Eve are saints and prophets, including St. John the Baptist, the last prophet of the Old Testament era. He is pointing to Christ, as if saying, "Look, the Lamb of God, who takes away the sin of the world!" (John 1:29). Standing just behind Eve is Abel, the first just person in the world to be killed (Gen. 4:8). In addition, unidentified people appear with whom we can identify. They are the righteous from down the centuries, who were born before the coming of Christ; he is now liberating them from the realm of death.

In a sixteenth-century *Anastasis* icon from Novgorod, Death grabs Adam by the foot, trying to hold on to him, but Christ's foot is on Death's head. The image recalls the first prophecy of salvation in Genesis 3:15, that the seed of woman would crush the serpent's head. In a Russian *Anastasis* icon from the fourteenth century, Death sticks out his tongue in a final, futile gesture of rage. It is too late, his power is finished: His wrists and ankles are chained, one angel poises a spear at his head, another kneels on his back to tie a cord around his neck.

ASCENSION

All the dramatic imagery in icons of the *Ascension* is derived from Church tradition, notably the apocryphal Gospel of Nicodemus and the rich collection of liturgical texts celebrating Christ's victory. The iconography does not evolve till the ninth century.

The Ascension is the occasion when the resurrected Christ met his apostles on the Mount of Olives and then was taken from their company into heaven as they watched (Acts 1:6–12).

The earliest *Ascension* picture known to us is from the fifth century, stamped on portable metal flasks (*ampullae*) that pilgrims used to carry oil from the holy places. The outdoor setting is indicated by trees behind the group of figures. Christ is at the top of the image in a mandorla, supported and carried up by two flying angels as he blesses the apostles.

The Virgin Mary is in the center of the icon, usually looking out at us with her hands raised in prayer. She is the praying Church. Six apostles stand on either side, some with their hands to their foreheads in surprise. In fact, only eleven apostles were present at the event because Judas had hanged himself several weeks earlier, and the apostle Matthias had not yet been chosen to make up the number (Acts 1:23-26). The icon shows twelve either to authenticate the apostleship of Matthias or, if the figure is St. Paul, because he was called to be an apostle by the Risen Christ after the Ascension. To show the new apostle or St. Paul at the event is an example of how an icon can transcend historical time and place even while it shows an historical event. Likewise, the inclusion of the Mother of God, not attested in the Acts of the Apostles, indicates she is symbolically "present" as Mother and type of the whole Church.

As recorded in Acts 1:10–11, two angels were present. They stand just behind the Virgin, one on either side. They may look at the apostles, their fingers raised as though admonishing and teaching them, or they may look at us.

PENTECOST

Pentecost is the day God the Holy Spirit came upon the apostles to fill them with grace for their mission, and they were able to speak in and be understood immediately in other languages. Pentecost was a unique event, an overturning of the judgment of Babel so that the Gospel could be heard by many nations.

An icon of *Pentecost* shows the twelve apostles ranged in two half-circles, seated on benches to the right and left of the picture. Some Early Byzantine icons include Christ's prepared throne awaiting his return. There is a half-circle at the top of the picture, with the hand of God extended from the arc of heaven or with God the Holy Spirit present in the form of a dove. Rays of divine power point toward each apostle or extend from the top of the picture to touch each head. Drapery over an architectural feature shows us that the event is taking place inside a building.

Though Acts 2:2 describes the sound of a rushing mighty wind, iconographers made no attempt to show a physical wind blowing through the room. Rather than just the particularity of the historical event, the icon shows the continuing presence of the Holy Spirit with the men who were chosen to lead the Church. This icon, like others, shows the historical event and the continuation of its reality: the root and the tree.

A crowned figure in the lower center of the picture holds a cloth with twelve scrolls balanced on it. He is Cosmos, representing humanity as the image of God, awaiting restoration to full likeness and friendship with God by the gift of the Spirit. He is crowned because humanity is the crown of God's creation, made in his image (his living icon) and retaining an essential rational and moral consciousness (unlike other animals). If he is standing against a dark area, such as the entrance of a cave, it is to emphasize the darkness of the world into which the Holy Spirit has come. The Spirit is in waiting to grant humanity the power slowly to recover that likeness of God that was originally intended, and which was lost in the Fall: the capacity for unmediated, direct awareness of God, the transforming contemplative vision that is the work of the Spirit.

LIFE AND DEATH OF THE VIRGIN

A later Byzantine development from the fifth century onwards, (remember that iconography develops over generations and centuries) is a *Cycle of the Life of the Virgin*. The images (usually frescoes) show key incidents from her life, taken from the Gospels, and the Apocryphal Gospels. They include her Birth and Presentation in the Temple, the Annunciation, the Presentation of Christ, the Nativity of Christ, and the Dormition, with variations between one Virgin Cycle and another. Of these events, Annunciation, Presentation of Christ, and Nativity derive from the Gospels and will be familiar to contemporary Western Christians.

The stories of the birth and girlhood of the Virgin derive from later apocryphal writings, notably the so-called Gospel of James; these are narratives not part of canonical Scripture but important for Orthodox liturgy, hymnody, and art. Two (Birth and Presentation of the Virgin) are major Marian Feasts, as is the Dormition (death) of the Virgin, second in popular devotion only to Easter.

Here's what to look for in the icons of the Virgin Mary derived from Church traditions:

Birth of the Virgin

St. Anne lies in bed, attended by maids. In the foreground, midwives wash the newborn infant, and may sometimes fan her in the cradle (her father Joachim is sometimes present as onlooker). You can easily distinguish the birth of the Virgin in art from that of Christ, because the former takes place in a furnished bedroom, the latter in a cave.

Presentation of the Virgin in the Temple

The child Mary, attended by maids of honor and her parents in procession, approaches the Jerusalem Temple, where she is welcomed by the High Priest(s). Above, to the right, at the top of a flight of steps, the enthroned child-Virgin receives a loaf of bread from the hands of an angel.

Death of the Virgin Mary

The *Dormition* (literally "falling asleep') is not an event recorded in the New Testament, but is celebrated by the Orthodox Church as poetic truth and theological "fact." Again, the source is Church tradition and a sixth-century apocryphal writing attributed to St. Meliton. The iconographic details derive from vivid seventh-century homilies by Sts. Andrew of Crete, John of Damascus, and other Fathers.

The Virgin Mary is lying on a bed, her head and shoulders slightly raised, her eyes closed, her hands covered by her dress. The apostles are grouped behind the bed and on either side, expressing shock and grief. Though she is very still, she is the center of attention in the crowded room. In later icons of the Dormition the iconography follows an apocryphal text describing St. Peter at her head and St. John at her feet, ready to carry her body to her tomb and watch over it for three days.

A *Dormition* icon shows the moment of death. St. Peter swings a censer in reference to the liturgy of the Orthodox funeral, and also perhaps a reference to the incense-bearing angel in Revelation 8:3-4:

> He was given much incense to offer, with the prayers of all the saints. . . . The smoke of the incense, together with the prayers of the saints, went up before God from the angel's hand.

In some icons, one of the apostles (perhaps Luke) draws near to peer into the Virgin's face or leans his head on her chest. Both were actions of a medieval doctor before the invention of the stethoscope and were familiar to medieval people. In the *Dormition* mosaic in the Church of St. Saviour or Chora in Constantinople, St. Luke (?) holds the edge of the bedclothes in both hands, as if about to cover her face after death. The icon shows us the exact moment of her passing from this world to the next.

In the upper half of the picture, the Risen Christ stands behind the bed, holding up what looks like a small, swaddled child. It is the Virgin Mary's soul. He holds her as though he has just that moment picked her up; it is a reversal of the icon of the *Virgin and Child*, in which she holds him as a small boy. That gesture and the arrested movement of the swinging censer shows that death is not a process but a moment. In full-scale images, mourners may also include bishops and "daughters of Zion," and in the sky we see the open doors of heaven (e.g., the great fourteenth-century fresco-cycle at St. Clement's, Ochrid). Angels fly above, and six-winged seraphim all escort the Virgin's soul to heaven. The lower part of the picture is about sorrow, loss, and physical death. The upper half of the picture is about joy, victory, and life.

What is the theological message? That in the person of Christ's Mother has been anticipated that total glorification of body and soul that awaits all God's people in the End. With the *Dormition* the cycle of twelve feasts comes to an end.

The *Dormition* is the Orthodox equivalent to the Catholic Assumption of Our Lady: The Eastern emphasis is on the reception of her soul by Christ and the reality of her death, not on her triumphant ascent, body and soul, into heaven, borne up by angels.

LAST JUDGMENT

In Early Byzantine mosaics, Christ returns to earth on clouds of glory that are red and blue striations against a deep blue sky. In other images (mosaic and fresco), an empty throne awaits his return with its silent reminder of judgment—the second coming.

Motifs from the Book of Revelation are difficult to present in visual form because of their visionary, eschatological character. The icon maker illustrates them literally. An angel flies through the air, rolling up what looks like a wide strip of parchment in a bookbinder's workshop. It is a memorable way of making an image of Revelation 6:14: "The sky receded like a scroll, rolling up. . . ." Christ sits on a judgment throne extending his right hand in acceptance and turning his left hand downward in rejection. It is a visual image designed to warn and to disturb.

❖

By now you will have discovered that icons have special qualities not found in other religious pictures. Those qualities are what the next chapter is about.

❖ TEN
The Special Qualities of Icons

Direct Communication

Spoken words go to the mind by way of the ear, and then they go to the heart; written words go first to the mind by way of the eye, and then to the heart. Icons, music, chore-ography, and fragrances are different from words because they are means of direct communication. The art of the icon communicates the sacred tradition of the Orthodox

Church, which is why painters had to—and still have to—keep within the iconography that has developed in the Church. This iconography must sometimes be explained in words (as in this book), but once we know the essential meaning we do not need to repeat it to ourselves in front of every icon. The image is able to go directly from eye to heart.

OBSERVING FACES IN ICONS

The faces in some icons look more like those of owls than of human beings. The eyes dominate; they are almond-shaped with strong brows and deep shadows beneath the lower lid. The nose is a long, thin line, sharp as a shinbone and seemingly incapable of drawing a breath of real air. The mouth is not much wider than the tip of the narrow nose and looks as though no real sound could come from it. Faces made in this style are not meant to look like real people but are spiritual portraits. The eyes dominate because they are the windows of the soul; other features are of less importance.

Whenever the classical style is revived, faces are shown with rounded shapes, looking what we would call "more real," meaning more like people we see around us every day. They show more emotions. When figures become more stylized like figures on playing cards, they acquire a special spiritualized dignity, solemnity, and stillness.

People's perception of religious art changes from generation to generation. In the West, the more emphasis that is placed on religious pictures being beautiful in their own right, the more 'real' they are painted. Their appearance depends on the style current at the time. The more emphasis that is placed on religious images being a timeless bridge between the subject and the viewer, the more stylized the faces tend to be.

Ernst Kitzinger writes:

> when the desire to pray, the urgency to communicate
> with Christ and his saints are great enough, there is no
> need to elaborate the physical features of the holy per-
> sons. In fact, too much realism can be an impediment.

The stylized faces of icons are startling to Western people who are not used to such pictures. The faces are above any changing fashions in the perception of beauty. They make the art of icons relevant for all people at all times.

THE QUALITY OF LIGHT IN ICONS

The earliest Byzantine images were in the same style as art in pagan Rome. Figures look as though they are modeled in low relief with simple shadows as from a high, front light, while the gold background in icons represents the uncreated light of God. The figures seem to be standing on a narrow stage. Some have short shadows cast backward from their feet as though they are carved figures standing on a ledge.

In the seventh century, figures became taller and flatter; people used to Western art might say that they looked less real, that is, less like people who would be able to step out of the picture. They cast no shadows, being painted as existing in no-time. After all, a shadow is a way of meas-uring time: It moves as the sun moves.

An icon of the *Transfiguration* shows light coming from Christ to illuminate the figures of Moses and Elijah standing on either side of him. Both prophets appear as though facing toward a lamp; they have light on their faces and shadows at their backs. The light from Christ also lightens the faces and clothes of the disciples below, to show that it was not only an inner experience but real to their retinas. In later icons of the *Transfiguration,* beams of light hurl the disciples to the ground as though they had the power of a physical blow.

An icon was painted to be seen in the low light of a church, the brightness of the colors toned down by the subtle, fluid light of lamps and candles.

The gold leaf in icons was burnished with care by medieval craftsmen. They studied the chief direction of light by which the icon would be seen and rubbed the burnisher over the gold in the direction that would bring out the reflection to best advantage. Light was one of the picture's components, its inner energy. Unlike the static physical components of the icon, light was an active element; it was something that had life because all light is from God. In a Byzantine church, the light flowed down and sideways, filtering through small windows. At the same time it beamed gently upward from lamps just below the icon. Cool, gentle daylight, therefore, was met by warmer candle and lamplight. The light from lamps and candles was in constant, subtle movement from the currents of air inside the building, creating here and now a feeling of living art.

Just as there is a certain quality of light from within icons and from the exterior light that is reflected and refracted, there is also a certain quality of silence and stillness. Not only are these attended to within an icon, but we, as viewers are intended to come to an icon in silence and stillness. More discussion of this will be given in the next chapter on Icons and Prayer.

TIME AND PLACE

The art of icons communicates Christian doctrine; that is why it does not try to change from one generation to another. It expresses superiority to time by being painted according to the rules of iconography and by the use of simultaneous narration. Even when the image is of a historical event, an icon is independent of time and place.

Time

In Western Renaissance art, Jesus in his mother's arms is painted looking like a real baby, but for centuries before contact with the West, icon craftsmen showed him in his mother's arms looking like a miniature adult. They were not ignorant of what babies looked like, for there were as many babies in the Byzantine Empire as anywhere else. They were painting the doctrine of the Incarnation: How else could they show that Christ was and had always been One of the Trinity, the all-powerful and almighty God? He was not just an ordinary baby: He was God incarnate. They were painting an actual historical reality that had timeless implications.

An icon of *St. Sergius* shows the military saint on a galloping horse, his pennant flying in the wind as he rushes forward. A small, black-veiled woman who is the donor is kneeling and holding the saint's foot. No one can hold the foot of a man on a galloping horse because they would be trampled in a split second, but that fact is irrelevant to the icon. St. Sergius, his horse, and the donor have been on the panel for six hundred years without moving. The icon shows a moment of devotion that transcends time.

There are icons that show momentary, and unrepeatable, events that have significance only because they are historical: for example, the *Annunciation* or the *Nativity*. They show us the moment when something decisive *happened*, an intersection of our world and the spiritual world. There was a "before" and there is an "after," but the efficacy and significance are timeless.

Medieval perception of time was different from ours. A man may not have known his exact age because he did not need to. The mechanical measuring of small amounts of time, to minutes and seconds, has made us into impatient people, but the medieval laity did not live that way. To measure their day in minutes would have been strange to them. That meant that the artistic convention of simultaneous narration was easier for them to absorb, the timeless quality of icons was easier to understand, and eternal life was easier to contemplate. If we in the West are to draw close to an icon, we need to rediscover the medieval perception of sacred time.

Place

In the Catholic West, as in the East, the liturgy communicates the reality of sacred time as an eternal *now*: "Today Christ is born!" "Today the Savior is risen from the tomb." The celebration of the liturgy cuts across time and place, and makes what happened then (once and for all, in history) a living, present reality. Icons, as integral parts of the liturgical space, have a similar sacramental power to communicate what they depict. In and through the icon, Christ and his saints are made present to us and we to them, and we can participate in the great events in the history of salvation (the Nativity, the Resurrection).

Icons are independent of place. The landscape in which figures move is not any particular landscape; they are associated with tree-shapes and hill-shapes that means "outside," or a compacted group of buildings with a piece of drapery over a roof that means "inside." In icons of the *Flight into Egypt,* one or two date palms may suffice to identify the country as Egypt, and there may be a small picture of what were believed to be the grain silos of the patriarch Joseph (we recognize them as the Pyramids).

Many icons of saints or archangels have a plain, gold background. There may not even be a horizon line behind the legs, just a figure floating upright in a sea of gold. The saint exists in the light of God; that existence and that "place" are what matters. To paint the figures in icons as though in no-time and in no-place is not because they never existed in history, but the reverse: Like the Christian gospel, they are for all people everywhere, because they now fully exist in heaven, out of our limited time-space continium.

RESPECTING ICONS

Icons are not Western; they grew out of pre-Christian classical art and developed in Greece, Asia Minor, the Levant, Eastern Europe, and Russia. There are Christians from those countries who love icons passionately. They call them "holy icons" and shudder to think that Westerners might send reproductions of them through the mail as postcards or Christmas cards, or nail one on an office wall, or think of them as part of art history, or try to learn how to paint one.

By an act of imagination I can understand a little how they feel. For me, the line of acceptability stops short of icons reproduced as wrapping paper or jigsaws, since the purpose of wrapping paper is to be torn or crumpled and the purpose of a jigsaw is to be dismembered. I am not happy about a detail of an icon marketed as a postcard as though the part was the whole picture. An enlarged detail belongs in an art history book where the purpose of cropping the picture is more likely to be understood by the reader.

Some Orthodox believe or imply that an individual needs a certain level of spirituality or must be a member of the Eastern Orthodox Church before they can understand an icon. Some Eastern Christians, out of their great love of icons, have become protective of the use of icons, which they feel should be solely for religious purposes and not relegated to the art world. But to say that icons are not part of art history is to draw down a thick veil in front of them. A person may view an icon in a museum—it might be a famous one, such as the *Virgin of Vladimir* or

Rublev's *Trinity,* or a more simple one in provincial style— and respond at a profound level. The eye (like the ear) is linked to the mind; it reasons and sometimes rejects. But the eye is also linked to the heart, receiving light in a time- less quietness that goes deeper than the mind. So icons can act as silent revealers of Orthodox truth to the Western beholder. Already in many parts of Europe and the United States, icons are appearing in public churches (especially Catholic and Anglican) and in homes as foci of devotion and Presence. Gradually we're assimilating icons as part of the common tradition of the universal Church.

Of course, Orthodox feel that icons should be moved from museums and galleries back into churches, their true homes. It is painful when, in the West, icons are sometimes treated as simply commodities on the art market, or as art investments. Yet the high prices of the finest icons currently for sale attest to their recognized cultural value, and most will probably end up in the public sphere, in galleries. And icons in galleries enable Orthodox sacred art to speak to a new audience.

Someone might stroll past such an icon for weeks or months, accepting it almost as though it were the wallpaper. Then one day they might stop, and look and say, "*I like that*" or "*What does it mean?*" And a person's interest and devotion could begin this simply. Orthodox Christianity says an icon is a way through to the spiritual world. This is the place for the Western mind to begin to consider these doors or windows of eternity.

Because I believe questions such as "What does it mean?" should be answered, I wrote this book, hoping people in the West might (as many in the Christian East do) enrich their lives with icons, because the art is God's art and because he speaks through it to all humanity.

THE TRUE CONTEXT OF AN ICON

To the question, "Where does an icon belong?" the obvious answer is, "In a church, to be an integral part of the Divine Liturgy, or in a Christian home as a devotional focus."

The ninth-century patriarch of Constantinople, Photius, described the interior of a great church (St. Sophia Cathedral in Constantinople), glorified with mosaics, through which the senses become translucent and elevated by beauty. He writes:

> It is as if one had entered heaven itself with no one barring the way and was illuminated by the beauty in all forms shining all around like so many stars, so is one utterly amazed. Thenceforth it seems that everything is in ecstatic motion, and the Church itself is circling around. For the spectator, through his whirling about in all directions and being constantly astir, which he is forced to experience by the variegated spectacle on all sides, imagines that his personal condition is transferred to the object.

Many of us have to see icons in museums and art galleries or have first come across one in an art history book or a postcard shop. The pictures are outside their intended context, but they have a missionary role: By being accessible to non-Orthodox Westerners they may draw people to the messages icons can bring to us. Many who have learned to love them had never been inside an Orthodox Church, but through the icons are led to explore Orthodoxy and to experience the art in its liturgical context by attending Orthodox services.

If you can go to Russia or Eastern Europe, you can see icons in the buildings for which they were made, but when the buildings have become museums for tourists there is a sense in which the icons' proper context is distorted. They are still where they were made to be; they have not changed, it is the *where* that has changed around them.

Icons in a gallery are more accessible to more people than if they were still in churches in Eastern Europe, scattered here and there in tiny villages. They are also safer and better preserved, kept at a steady temperature and humidity and examined regularly to see if any further degeneration of the physical structure has taken place. However, we must always remember the gallery or museum is not their natural site, which is the Orthodox Church or home.

GETTING TO KNOW AN ICON

To understand the true context of an icon, get to know one—to begin with, just one. An illustration in an art book or even a good postcard is a simple place to start. Look at it quietly for three whole minutes (that time is longer than you realize). Let your eyes flow without hurry across the upper part of the picture from left to right, then back to the left a little lower down, then across again, then up and down. Go on moving your eyes slowly and gently back and forth over the picture, taking in as much as you can. If you prefer, just look at the whole surface intently for three minutes. Then put the icon aside and immediately describe it to someone. They should only listen without prompting you. Or write a short verbal summary of the icon's contents, or attempt a rough sketch from memory.

Take as long as you like, describing the main figure, the colors, the event, the gestures, the foreground, the background, the corners—anything and everything that you can see in your mind's eye. There are no prizes to win or lose, so there is no hurry or worry: It is a simple exercise in learning to look. You will be surprised at how much your mind has retained. Repeat that simple exercise several times a day for several days with one picture and you will fix it in your mind. It's like taking a mental photograph with a long exposure! If you ever see that icon in its reality, in a church or art gallery, there will be a strong sense of personal recognition. It will be like seeing someone in a colored photograph, then meeting them in the flesh. You will feel like crying out with joy, "I *know* you!"

To begin with, get to know just one icon and you will learn to love it. Get to know it so well that you can recreate it in most of its details any time you like on the mental slide projector that is called memory. Then it will become lovingly yours in the way it was intended to be. The true context of an icon is the heart.

In the next chapter, in keeping with this context of the heart, we will look at icons for devotion and prayer.

ELEVEN

Icons and Prayer

Icons, in the Orthodox tradition, are made by praying artists for the distinct purpose of prayer. They are considered windows to spiritual truth. No book introducing icons would be complete without mentioning how one might begin to pray with icons and appreciate them as an aid to prayer. The icon acts as a two-way channel: It communicates to the worshiper something of the presence and grace of the one depicted, and conveys to the sacred person the "prayer of the mind."

What makes it an icon is its special iconography and theological aesthetic, a way of presenting the great people and events of Christianity that is above art fashion and is therefore never going to look out of date. It is not meant to be a realistic picture like something seen through a camera lens, because it is more important than that; it shows the spiritual reality as well as the outer aspect. Some icons have several events of Old or New Testament history in one picture, because the whole event is important; some dispense with background and show a saint standing on tiptoe against a sheet of gold, because he is living in the light of God. Icons should never show God except as Incarnate Son. In prayer and stillness before icons we see this incarnational light.

LOOKING AT ICONS IN SILENCE AND STILLNESS

The first response to an icon should be silence. Later there can be time to analyze the details, admire the composition, or try to work out what pigments the craftsman used. First it is best to look in silence and let the icon say something to you. Look at the faces, then at the hands. Read the inscriptions if you can, but look longest at the faces and the hands. The first meeting with an icon is similar to a first meeting with a cat: Approach with courtesy, and let the cat open the conversation.

In their stillness icons call into question our self-important bustle, our inner lack of integration and central calm. What the American writer Tom Howard has written about structured prayers applies to the formal dignity of these images:

> One does not bustle into the Divine Presence with a frantic agenda of personal concerns. One takes one's place with the morning stars who sang together, with the archangelical host of heaven, and with all the

company of the faithful, doing the thing that Adam was placed in the garden in order to do, namely, to bless God. The sheer horizons of one's imagination are enlarged.

What I love about icons is that they do not allow us to bustle. They quieten us. They enlarge us. Even though some of the figures are painted as in movement, icons have a quality of stillness. They invite a quiet looking, and people who walk around an icon exhibition, where they can see a lot of icons close-up, feel that stillness.

The famous Novgorod icon of *St. George* shows him in the act of pig-sticking the dragon. The saint is mounted on a leaping horse, and the dragon's long tail coils in death, but in spite of the action there is a stillness. There is no third dimension in the picture space: The horse is painted without modeling; there is only a flat, horse-shaped white area silhouetted against a red sky. St. George's pencil-thin lance is unrealistically long and he is poised on the horse as though he had no weight. Both saint and horse have an expression of compassion. It is possible to look at that icon for some time without feeling restless. A distinguished Russian theologian observes:

> The saints are shown in stillness because they are becalmed in God; their eyes are open because they are keenly and prayerfully aware of our world. The less the body moves, the better do we perceive the movement of the spirit, for the corporeal world becomes its transparent shell. By expressing spiritual life with nothing but the eyes of a perfectly motionless figure, the artist symbolically conveys the immense power of the spirit over the flesh. One gets the impression that all corporeal life is stilled, waiting for the highest revelation, listening for it. (E.N. Trubetskoi)

The search for holy stillness has always existed in the Christian Church. One place for a Westerner to discover it is in icons.

WHAT IS PRAYER?

Silence is a form of prayer. But it leads naturally to other forms of prayer. Don't be overwhelmed by praying with icons. Think about simply growing toward prayer from that place of silence to a new place, as gently and naturally as the growing of a plant.

This is one place we learn to know God. We come to know God in the same ways we learn to know another human being. When you stop to think about it, how else could we know the Incarnate Christ? We look and we like what we see; we spend more time together in speech and in silence; we meet one another's friends and find interests in common. If anything has been written, we read it with attention; we share experiences, good and bad; we listen to what mutual friends say and watch how our new acquaintance speaks and acts with someone else. We grow closer to that person, unconsciously reproducing in ourselves what we see as the best in them. Slowly we become more involved in the relationship until we commit ourselves to the one we have learned to love. And it is this communion that is essential:

> The icon . . . fills a constant task, which has been that of Christian art from the beginning: to reveal the true relationships between God and man. . . . To the disoriented world the icon brings a testimony of authenticity, of the reality of another way of life. . . . The icon [can teach us] about God, man, and creation, a new attitude toward the world. (Leonid Ouspensky, *Theology of the Icon*)

THE TERRAIN OF ICONS, THE TERRAIN OF PRAYER

When we meet God through the veneration of an icon, that is, through prayer, he sees to it that we meet ourselves. For many people it is hard to know which confrontation is the more unnerving. This stillness of looking at an icon can turn into prayer, and into understanding, sometimes into confrontation.

People outside the Christian world think that prayer is an occupation suited to the old and the sick, a harmless pastime like eating baby food and being wrapped in a shawl. In fact, we see when icons confront us in our silence that there is a more bracing world out there, a great, wild, rich landscape that saints and mystics have explored. Some of them have sent messages back to base, describing the terrain, warning of dangers, and mapping some of the paths. We see those messages outlined here with icons.

> Those who pray must be deeply engaged with the spiritual realism the icon offers them; if not, they will never approach its mystery and it will for them only be a design without a soul. And for the one to whom it is given to contemplate God in the holy icon, it becomes an unerring path toward a transfiguration in Christ. (Georg Wunderle, *Um die Seele der heiligen Ikone*)

PRAYER IS NOT SAFE BECAUSE GOD IS NOT SAFE

The apostle John described what he saw in the Book of Revelation:

> . . . someone "like a son of man," dressed in a robe reaching down to his feet and with a golden sash round his chest. His head and hair were white like wool, as white as snow, and his eyes were like blazing fire. His feet were like bronze glowing in a furnace, and his voice

was like the sound of rushing waters. In his right hand he held seven stars, and out of his mouth came a sharp double-edged sword. His face was like the sun shining in all its brilliance. When I saw him, I fell at his feet as though dead. (Rev. 1:13–17)

The man who wrote those words had come face-to-face with the blinding glory of the risen and ascended Christ: He speaks of what he had seen and heard. In icons we see some of these words given an image, a physical meaning. When we come to icons in prayer, we are approaching this God and not anyone less: A sense of awe in entering his presence is an excellent beginning. "It is a dreadful thing to fall into the hands of the Living God" (Heb. 10:31). Yes, God is our loving Father, but also a God of awful majesty, before whom even the angels veil their faces. In Christ, we can approach him with confidence, but never with familiarity. "God is not a pussy-cat," Archbishop Anthony Bloom warns us.

Praying with icons opens up windows of relationship. It is a relationship so rich that we need to bring all of ourselves to it: It will involve heart and mind, eyes and ears, speech and silence and movement, our own words and the words of others; there will be exploration and evaluation, discovery, and delight.

FEARFUL LOVE

Fear and love seem like opposite ends of a line, but in prayer that line becomes a circle. Begin where you are, travel in either direction, and you will come to the other side. Fear and love, love and fear, are like the wheels whirling within wheels that Ezekiel saw (Ezek. 1:15-28). To love what is greater than ourselves should be a fearful experience if we have a proper sense of proportion. Some people have ridiculed Western medieval artists for portraying God as a bearded old man, but are we any better in imagining the Creator of the universe as a benevolent Daddy at our beck and call? The prophets and apostles and the makers of icons would weep and howl at such presumption. We may become so busy being friendly with God that we forget who he is—and that would be dangerous.

Byzantine craftsmen pictured Christ as the Ancient of Days, and depictions of the Last Judgment show him with the abode of the eternally blessed on his right hand and everlasting hell on his left. Worship was not presented as an easy activity, and there was no attempt at making it fun. One look at the *Christ Pantocrator* and you fell to the ground with *adoration,* a word that suggests fearful love. The greatest icons of Christ hold together the apparently antithetical qualities of justice and mercy. They are never harshly formidable, but neither are they ever sentimental.

LOOKING AT GOD IN ICONS

Historically and theologically, the West has erred in visualizing God as a bearded old man sitting on a cloud. Neither Jews nor Eastern Orthodox Christians tried to make a picture of God the Father himself. It was forbidden. St. John tells us that no one has seen God at any time, but he (Christ), who dwells in the bosom of the Father, has revealed him (John 1:18). If we ask an Orthodox, "What does God look like?" he shows us the icon of Christ. God Incarnate, Jesus Christ, could be pictured in divine humanity, and the Holy Spirit could be shown in symbol by a dove or by tongues of fire. The Trinity could only be depicted in symbolic prefiguration as the three angels entertained by Abraham at Mamre (Genesis 18).

But to look into icons is to find a window to God. It is to look at God, to learn of God without seeing a picture of God the Father, but observing something about the nature of God or faith or sanctity. To look at God means simply "to look": I cannot explain it any other way. Give your attention to him and let your soul smile. I know that may sound fanciful and what some people would derisively call "a bit mystical," but it is something that must be done if prayer is ever to be more than either recitation or chatter. So do not analyze what it means to look at God: Just do it. The facility has been built into you by the God who created you.

Do not think, though, that you must speak God's name in order to get his attention: He is already nearer to you than the air you are breathing. In any case, the names you address him by will vary from day to day, depending on how you are to him and on how he is to you. Often a loving look will be enough.

If these loving looks, the glancing prayers, are your only way for the next part of your pilgrimage into prayer, you will be moving forward. The pace may seem ludicrously slow compared with that of saints, but if you play the comparisons game, you will lose. You can meet God where you are now, wherever that may be, by looking. As you spend prayerful time with an icon,

> Look at and be looked at by the great God, Who in Trinity is worshiped and glorified, and Whom we declare to be now set forth as clearly before you as the chains of our flesh allow, in Jesus Christ our Lord, to Whom be glory for ever. Amen. (St. Gregory of Nazianzus, fourth century)

For Christians, for whom Christ is the living, incarnate image *par excellence* of the invisible God, surely the best and first choice of images before which to pray must be the icon of Christ, in whom "the whole fullness of God came to dwell bodily."

TIME AND PLACE

The way to begin with prayer is the way one begins to look at icons: slowly. I advise five minutes. That may feel short, but it is better to get a short time established than to begin with a longer one that you give up later.

Consider going into a church that has icons, so that the atmosphere is attentive to prayer. Some churches are open during the week, so anyone can go in to be quiet, look quietly, pray. Concentrate on developing the prayer of looking during these short times, and as the shape of your life changes, you can go on to a more sustained and focused time.

> In icons, everyone will find rest for the soul. They have a good deal to tell us westerners; and they can arouse in us a holy orientation toward the supernatural. (Review of Ouspensky and Lossky in *La penseé catholique*)

When you have set yourself a time to be still before icons and to pray, and have kept to it, you will begin to discover a sense of order. You will find that the pattern of the day has brought with it an element of expectancy.

Train yourself to stick with five minutes a day for several months, and then extend the time to only ten minutes for several more months. There is no hurry. In the Western world today, and in countries influenced by the West, we live in an atmosphere of such speed and pressure that it is always safe to tell ourselves to go more slowly than we feel we should. Extend your time to fifteen minutes or longer only when you are sure you can use the time fully.

None of your prayer should be committed to paper, because this technique is a way of praying with the living flow of your thoughts, an image of an icon. Take it slowly and you will find that a rhythm is set up. Spontaneity and repetition balance each other, while the flow of thought is like the rhythm of breathing.

We can bring the prayers of the ages to our stillness before an icon. Here is a simple prayer from a Book of Hours, one of the books of private devotions used by the aristocratic laity in the late Middle Ages. The date of this one is 1514:

God be in my heart, and in my understanding;
God be in my eyes, and in my looking;
God be in my mouth, and in my speaking;
God be in my heart, and in my thinking;
God be at my end, and at my departing.

In times of great emotion, people return to the forms of prayer that they know best. A form the Jewish Christians would have known in addition to some of the psalms was the Eighteen Benedictions. Enrich yourself with such strong phrases from that ancient prayer as, "Heal us, O Lord, and we shall be healed. . . . Save us, and we shall be saved. . . ."

Follow the pattern with your own thoughts and needs, "Encourage me, O Lord, and I shall be encouraged. . . . Humble me, and I shall be humbled. . . ." Establish a verbal pattern and let your prayers flow within it.

Here is another prayer from the Eastern Orthodox Church; it is a threefold invocation called the *Trisagion*:

Holy God,
Holy and strong,
Holy and immortal,
Have mercy upon us.

PRAYING WITHOUT WORDS

Don't be afraid of using your senses in prayer, in responding to something material.

C.S. Lewis wrote, "God likes matter, he invented it." In those six words he summed up the theology of the Creation and the Incarnation. Christianity is an incarnational religion, and icons focus on that theological center via a visual focus.

There is an inescapable physicality in Christian prayer and worship; it involves unspoken words formed in the mind by a complex process that not even neurologists claim to understand; worship involves words spoken with the tongue and the larynx; music produced by controlled breath, and instruments that make sound; limbs that walk, dance, sit, kneel, bow, prostrate, and trace the shape of the cross; taste buds that receive the dissolving texture of the Eucharist; eyes that notice the visual truth of an icon; ears that hear; noses that smell fresh flowers and (in some churches) incense and beeswax candles.

Consider that all wood and metal are special now because the Cross was made of wood and nails, that all water is special now because Christ was baptized in it, that all the ground is special now because he walked on it, and so on with every physical part of the world we live in. Rather than being evil, the material world, which includes our senses, is part of what our good God has made. Although it had been wrenched by the Fall, like a limb out of joint, the Incarnation took place in it and has changed it forever.

THE SENSE OF SIGHT

Sight has been used in godly worship from the beginning. The Old Testament is filled with pictorial object lessons: the garments of skin made by God for Adam and Eve, the lamb offered by Abel, the Temple adorned with sculpture, metalwork, spinning, dyeing, and weaving. The sense of sight has been used in Christian worship from the start, from a simple third-century picture of the Virgin and Child with a star in the Roman catacombs, to the windows of Chartres Cathedral ablaze with light, and on to some of the better examples of visual art in modern churches.

Medieval Christians valued sight as the highest of the senses because it is connected with light, and God is light; that is why they brought light into their places of worship, filtering it through glass pictures that showed his glory. Before Gothic architecture with walls of light-transmitting glass, churches had the iconostasis and frescoed walls that were bright with pictures. Worshipers saw the Old Testament prophets, guardian angels, and events from the Gospels; every time they went into their church they watched saints and sinners being divided as sheep from goats at the Last Judgment. They saw icons of Christ and his Mother and of their favorite saints. Those pictures stayed in their minds and hearts to correct, to guide, to warn, and to inspire.

Praying with Icons

Before the eighth century and from the ninth century to today, Eastern Orthodox Churches have contained special icons of the Christ, the Virgin, the saints, and scenes from the Old and New Testaments. Orthodox Christians reverence their icons as doorways to the world of the spirit, believing that honor paid to them is honor paid to their prototypes. This veneration of icons is not an idolatry, as the Russian Orthodox priest Father Arseny notes,

> Every Russian icon is inextricably connected to the soul of the Christian iconographer, of the believer who comes to the icon as a spiritual, symbolic representation of Christ, his Mother, or his Saints. The Russian people

do not approach icons as idols, but as the spiritual image of the one to whom his soul addresses itself in sorrowful or joyous prayer. (translated by Bouteneff)

The honor that Orthodox Christians pay to an icon passes through the physical medium of the picture to the heavenly reality. They look toward an icon when they pray, believing that it is a door—no more, no less. You may find that an icon helps you to pray by being a door, or simply a means of focusing your eyes and your mind.

If you come to find that it is a help, you will be joining millions of God's people who are allowing icons to help them pray.

A REFLECTION

These sorts of reflections and prayers, when standing still before an icon, go well beyond the scope of art, into the arena of the spirit.

Yet for the one using an icon as a stimulus to prayer, there is a mixture of the visual and the spiritual that lends itself to pondering and listening. Where to begin? Begin here, with Father Arseny's simple reflection on an icon. his approach is both as an art critic and as an Orthodox priest, responding here to an icon of the *Theotokos:*

When was it painted? In the beginning of the seventeenth century. Where? Who was its iconographer? God alone knows, the God who inspired the artist. The board is very old and has been painted over many times, one icon on top of the other. This last icon was restored, but a very long time ago. All this is totally unimportant, because the spirit of God lives in this icon. Look! What peace radiates from the faces of both the Mother and the Son. The icon painter was full of love and faith in Christ, so that he increased his talent by faith and love.

That is why the face of the mother is so spiritual and so real that it consoles all who are oppressed by sorrow and sadness, those who are deprived, naked, orphaned, imprisoned, those who have almost lost faith in human justice, those who are weak. It gives life to such people, it restores their hope, it reminds them that there exists another life, free from horror and fear, from blood and the evil of this world. The face of the Mother calls us and gives us the hope of salvation. (translated by Bouteneff)

Allow your eyes and the eyes of your heart to enter into the colors, pictures, images of an icon. Join in the prayer, as Father Arseny did, in a simple and deep reflection.

❖ TWELVE
Windows of Eternity:
The Theology of Icons
Dr. Nicholas Gendle

For anyone venturing for the first time into a modern Orthodox church, be it in Greece, Russia, or America, the most immediate visual impression would probably be the sight of the icons. Coming into the church by the west door from the narthex or vestibule, you are confronted with a great screen of icons stretching the width of the church in front of the altar. Even though today few churches can afford frescoes, icons presented by the faithful can be seen everywhere in the building, hanging on walls and pillars.

From its very nature, the art of the icon is a *liturgical* art: "the mystery enacted (the eucharistic liturgy) and the mystery depicted are one."[1] The central truths of faith, continually re-presented or celebrated in the liturgy, are also visually set forth in the icons: the Trinity, the Incarnation, the victorious death and Resurrection of Christ. Far from being mere ornamental extras, the icons are an essential and integral part of Orthodox Christianity, "one of the instruments of the knowledge of God, one of the means of communion with him."[2]

Icons, then, find their primary meaning in the context of worship. No Orthodox home is without icons. Again, domestic icons are not just attractive art, objects to decorate a room. Usually gathered together in a cluster on special shelves in a glass cupboard or hanging in a corner (what the Russians called the "red" or "beautiful" corner), often with a lamp burning before them, they serve as a focus for devotion, a reminder of Divine Presence, a means of sanctifying mundane reality.

Some years ago, the BBC ran a program about icons and their owners. People were asked, What difference did it make to have icons in their homes, how did they regard them? Some spoke of the artistic value of their icons, others of their ability to recall their ancestral country; finally, an old Russian prince simply replied, "I pray in front of them." Of course, some icons are great works of art: Many are rightly prized as masterpieces in state museums. But in the end, an icon divorced from the milieu of prayer and worship is no longer functioning as an icon.

When we pray before an icon, we enter into communion with the holy person(s) depicted on it; we are mysteriously brought face-to-face with Christ, his Mother, his friends the saints and angels—in short, with the heavenly kingdom. The icon makes them present to us, and us to them. There is a two-way traffic: The saints pass through the "window" of an icon to meet us, and vice versa.[3] The icon is a means of encounter, an entry into the presence of the holy. As the Fathers of the Seventh Ecumenical Council observed, "The more often we see such icons, the more we are led to recall with love the persons depicted."[4]

This chapter sets out to explain some of the ways in which Orthodoxy understands the significance of icons, reflecting on the validity and meaning of icons within the larger belief system. But first, what *is* an icon? Originally, the Greek word *eikon* simply meant an image of any kind, sacred or profane, and in any medium. Thus, in secular usage, it could be, for example, a landscape fresco, a miniature portrait, a panel painting of a still life. So to specify a religious work of art, the Fathers call them *holy images*. But in Late Antique/Medieval Greek usage, "holy icon" could still be any sort of sacred artwork (mural or panel painting, mosaic, incised gem or ivory, even textile) and on any scale, provided it followed established iconography, as approved by Church authority. It was the Russians who first used the word "icon" in the sense current in English, to mean a portable image, carved or painted, that expresses the content of Orthodox faith in an accepted form. But theologically, we must remember that all Orthodox art is iconic in the fullest sense, equally deserving of respect and veneration, and that is the sense in which I use the word "icon" here.

It is precisely because icons are believed to mediate something of the power and presence of what they depict, that "they may be honored with incense and candles, as is done with the emblem of the Cross and the Holy Gospels."[5] Protestants often find this veneration of icons difficult; indeed, the charge that the icon-cult was idolatrous was central to the attack of the eighth- and ninth-century iconoclasts, and of the more radical sixteenth-century reformers in the West. But believers do not *worship* a wooden panel; rather, *through* the icon, they are brought into contact with Christ and the saints.

"Through" is the proper preposition to be used with an icon in respect of its subject. The icon in itself is not worshiped, but it serves to *mediate* the heavenly world to us, and to convey our prayers to the holy person depicted. As such, together with other sacred objects, like the Cross,[6] the Gospels, the vessels of the Eucharist, it is treated with respect and veneration. (Iconodule theologians such as St. John Damascene take great care to distinguish between the *worship* due to God alone, and the *veneration* that may properly be paid in differing degrees to the saints, their icons, sacred symbols and liturgical objects, and indeed to each other, as living images of God.) Leontius and others trawl the text of the Old Testament to find examples of people venerating (prostrating before or kissing) holy persons or things (patriarchs, the ark of the covenant, the three-dimensional images in Solomon's temple), within a Jewish concept which forbade religious images. In the same way, the icon is not an idol, but an effective symbol and a point of encounter. It mediates a presence, and makes present the history of salvation. The Damascene remarks, "When we venerate icons, we do not offer veneration to matter; but by means of the icon, we venerate the person depicted. For, as St. Basil says, 'The honor given to the image passes to the prototype.'"[7] So in honoring the icon of Christ, we honor Christ himself. The icon fulfills a very basic human need for a visible, palpable, tangible point of contact with the holy. The danger comes only when the instrumental nature of the icon is forgotten, and the image is *identified* with its prototype. Among sacrament(al)s, only the consecrated

Eucharist can be metaphysically identical (consubstantial)[8] with what it signifies.

Bishop Kallistos Ware tells the story of a Russian abbess showing a party of Evangelicals around her church. They were shocked to see nuns bowing before the icons and kissing them. She remarked, "You honor the Bible, do you not? Not the ink and paper, but the word of God that speaks to you though the Bible. We honor the living God who meets us through the icon."

It's not a question of either/or, but of both word *and* image. The icon *is* the gospel in line and color, just as the sacred Scriptures communicate the same truth in words. Both equally affirm the reality of salvation, both equally are modes of revelation. St. John of Damascus writes, "What the written word is to those who know letters, the icon is to the unlettered; what speech is to the ear, the icon is to the eye."[9] But "all of us alike, whether learned or uneducated, benefit from what is painted in the icons. What the written word proclaims through letters, iconography proclaims and represents through colors."[10]

This is why the Church permits icons of events in the life of Christ, and of the Virgin and other saints. These have a clear teaching function—not so much because they tell us stories (most of which we already know); rather, they remind us (in the strongest sense) by making the events depicted present to us, releasing their power in our lives here and now. This realization of sacred history in and through the icons is strictly comparable to the dramatic re-presentation of the same saving events through the celebration of the Liturgy: It makes the crucial historical moments present as existential experiences. Thus, the Church sings, "Today Christ is born," "Today Christ is risen from the dead." Through the Liturgy and the icons, what happened then (the inbreaking into time of the eternal now) becomes for us a spiritual reality today, cutting across the parameters of time and space.

In a mysterious way, the icon is believed to make present what it represents; it can communicate the presence and something of the spiritual nature of the holy person depicted (Christ, the Virgin, or some other saint). As such it is a means of grace, something approaching a sacrament. This is why the icon is an object of veneration: Lights and incense are burned before it, people bow before it and kiss it.

Of course, the icon is not sacramental in the same sense as the Eucharist, which is not just an image of the Christ but is his true Body and Blood, something to be worshiped. None-the-less, on a different level, Christ is also present in his icon. Its matter (the wood, paint, etc.) is a channel of spiritual grace, as is the water of Baptism or the oil of Chrismation.[11] St. Theodore the Studite writes, "We should believe that divine grace is present in the icon of Christ, and that it communicates sanctification to those who draw near with faith."[12]

How can Christ's invisible and ineffable divine nature be shown in an icon? If only the human nature can be shown, does this not involve a heretical division of the two natures, or conversely, an unacceptable merging of the two into one? These difficult questions led to further debate about, and refinement of, Christology (reflections on the relation of the two natures in Christ).

For the first generation of icon defenders, the issue was less complex: It had to do with the question of idolatry, of the limits of the sacred, and of the implications of the archdogma of orthodox Christianity, the Incarnation, for religious art. For St. John of Damascus, the icon of Christ is essentially a celebration of the Incarnation, it displays the human face of God. Under the Old Dispensation (B.C.), to attempt to depict God would indeed have been idolatrous; but since God has deigned to take on a body and a face for our salvation, that face can (and indeed should) be shown in art.

John writes,

> It is impossible to make an icon of God the incorporeal, the invisible, the immaterial, the uncircumscribed, who has no form and is beyond comprehension: for how can that which is invisible be depicted? But while no one has ever seen God, yet the only-begotten Son, who is in the bosom of the Father, has made this unseen God manifest (John 1:18).[13]

This then is the essence of the theology of the icon: It is the concrete actuality, the materiality, the permanent reality of the Incarnation that validates the icon of Christ. Of course, the transcendent Godhead is by its very nature undepictable; but since God deigned to become fully human in Christ, assuming a real face and body, the icon can and must show forth that human face of God. If someone naïvely asks what God looks like, we should show him the icon of Christ, "God with us."[14]

What follows from this? Nothing less than a re-creation of matter itself as something potentially sacramental and spirit-bearing, and thus as something to be valued and deeply respected. "I shall not cease to venerate matter, for it was through matter that salvation came to pass."[15] In this way, all the sacraments can be seen as extensions of the Incarnation; in these "mysteries," simple, basic created things—wheat, grapes, oil, water—are received from their Creator, refined or transformed by man, and become for us channels of grace and modes of revelation. The same is true of the icon. Here, too, the God-given raw materials are creatively refashioned and combined by us, so that through the use of wood, plaster, minerals, eggs, and so forth, the glory and presence of God can be made present to us through a material artifact. As a result of the Incarnation, matter is no longer inert and warped, but capable of mediating the immanent energies and uncreated light of the Creator.

Because man is "God's crowned image," participating through his senses in the visible world and through his mind or soul in the world of spirit, he can "mould and manipulate the material, and render it articulate—the bricks in a Church, the cubes in a mosaic are matter made articulate in the divine praise."[16] Here, in a special sense, man the artist acts as priest of creation: He alone can re-form and transform the material world in such a way as to make it articulate and give it meaning. Although the creation may indeed (simply by existing) "praise God in musical silence,"[17] man the cosmic mediator is needed to express that praise. Leontius of Cyprus states, "The creation does not venerate the Maker directly and by itself; but through me the heavens declare the glory of God, through me the moon worships God, through me the stars . . . and all creation venerate God and give him glory."[18]

We have here the seeds of a rich theology of art, insufficiently developed by later Byzantine writers. The iconographer is a creator after the image of God the Creator. In making an icon, he glorifies God by cooperating in the sanctification of matter, reveals God in a new way, and gives creation a voice in praise of its Maker. St. Theodore the Studite sums it up thus: "Because man is made in the image and likeness of God, there is something divine about the act of painting an icon."[19] Because the human person is the divine image par excellence, we can be subcreators, in the image of God the primordial Artist. By expressing our creative gifts as human beings, and consecrating them to God, we can make manifest the divine glory or beauty hidden in the world.[20]

God is truth and beauty, the ultimate good; it is the aspect of God as beauty that the icon maker must aspire to express. Icons reveal the attractiveness of God which draws us to itself, invites us.[21] To respond is not to turn our backs on a suffering world, but to receive the strength and inspiration to bring a word of hope and joy to our world, a glimpse of beauty, that is part of divine salvation, a foretaste of the age to come.

Leonid Ouspensky boldly affirms, "Sacred art is a visible expression of the dogma of the Transfiguration—not only of Christ, but potentially of us all, as an objective reality."[22] Ouspensky tells us, too, "What the icon shows is precisely the body of a *holy* man," that is, a body already liberated from corruption, and participating to some extent in the life and light of the Ages to Come. Thus, the icon attempts to disclose to us, not just the natural features of the saint, but "his glorified state, his transfigured and eternal countenance."[23]

It is the same uncreated light or energy manifest in the saint that provides the inner vitality and dynamic of a true icon. This explains not only the tendency toward dematerialization of form in icons (which is much more than a stylistic mannerism); it is also the clue to the striving after an inner luminosity in the painting, as if the figure or scene depicted had its own internal source of light. The icon, in short, strives to be not a transcription of natural appearances, but an art of transfiguration.

This is why the art of icon painting is not a naturalistic art in the Western, post-Renaissance sense. If we understand the "weight" an effective icon must bear as the focus of prayer and revealer of the divine, we will also understand the expressionistic conventions often used by painters: the lack of shadows, the conscious distortions of form, the inversion or denial of perspective; similarly, the frontal, hieratic presentation of individual saints (or Christ alone) with the exaggerated staring eyes and pale features. The aim is to communicate the impinging of the divine world upon the human one: to depict persons already in the process of deification or transfiguration, and history as the sphere of divine intervention—"the intersection of the timeless moment." The icon reflects the life, historical experience, and belief system of Eastern Christianity in all its complexity and depth; as an integral part of that life, it aspires to offer a "window," a vision (however imperfect) of a transfigured world and humanity, which points forward to the final revelation of glory in the Age to Come.[24]

Where Do You Go from Here?
Icon Collections Worldwide

Examples of icons and of Byzantine, Russian, and East European art appear in galleries and art museums as well as churches and monasteries around the world. The following is a list of some of the largest, or key, collections. If you are making a special trip, it is wise to check first. Galleries, museums, churches, and monasteries have specific hours and may be closed to the public for certain holidays. The following is a short, initial list of icon collections worldwide:

BALKANS:
Serbia/Macedonia
Ochrid: St. Clement's Church
Skopje: Archaeological Museum
Belgrade: Archaeological Museum
Ecclesiastical Museum
Decani: Monastery Church
Bulgaria
Sophia: National Gallery; Archaeological
Museum
Rila Monastery: Treasury and Church
Backovo Monastery: Church and Refectory
Rumania
Bucharest: National Gallery, Archaeological
Museum
Plovdiv: Museum

ENGLAND, LONDON:
> *National collections*
>> British Museum
>> Victoria and Albert Museum
>
> *Private collections: by appointment only*
>> Royal Collection, Society of Antiquaries
>
> *Commercial Galleries*
>> Temple Gallery
>> Mark Gallery
>> Richardson Gallery
>> Axia Gallery

ENGLAND, OXFORD:
>> Ashmolean Museum
>> Christ Church Picture Gallery (catalogued by
>> Dr. N. Gendle)

ENGLAND, LIVERPOOL:
>> Blackburn Museum
>> Walker Gallery (ivories)
>> University Gallery (icons)

GERMANY, RECKLINGSHAUSEN:
>> Ikonenmuseen

GREECE, ATHENS:
>> Byzantine Museum
>> Benaki Museum

GREECE, THESSALONIKI (SALONICA):
>> Archaeological Museum

GREECE, MT. ATHOS *(MEN ONLY)*:
>> Great Lavra
>> Vatopedi Monastery
>> Stavronikita Monastery
>> Dionysiou Monastery
>> Xenophontos Monastery
>> Chilandar Monastery (also library)

IRELAND, DUBLIN:
   National Gallery
NEAR EAST:
   Egypt, Sinai
      St. Catherine's Monastery (church and museum)
   Israel, Jerusalem
      Greek Orthodox Patriarchate
NETHERLANDS, AMSTERDAM:
   Public Collections
      Rijksmuseum
      Joods Historisch Museum
      Stadhoudeskade
   Commercial Dealers
      Morsinck Ikonen Gallery, Kaisersgracht
      Jonas Daniel, Meijerplan
NETHERLANDS, UTRECHT:
   Museum Catherijneconvent
RUSSIA, MOSCOW:
      Cathedrals of Annunciation, Dormition,
         St. Michael, and St. Basil (Russian icons)
      Tretiakov Gallery
      Pushkin Museum (Byzantine icons)
      Kremlin Armory
      Rublev Museum
RUSSIA, ST. PETERSBURG:
      Russian Museum
      Hermitage
RUSSIA, NOVGOROD:
      St. Sophia Cathedral
      Cathedral Museum (in Kremlin)

RUSSIA, PROVINCIAL:
>   Museums and Cathedrals of Vladimir
>   Suzdal
>   Gt. Rostov
>   Pskov
>   Yaroslavl

SWEDEN, STOCKHOLM:
>   National Museum

TURKEY, ISTANBUL:
>   Greek Orthodox Patriarchate (Cathedral of St.
>   George)

UNITED STATES, BOSTON:
>   Isabella Stewart Gardner Museum

UNITED STATES, NEW YORK:
>   Metropolitan Museum (including Cloisters)

UNITED STATES, WASHINGTON, DC:
>   Dumbarton Oaks
>   (Harvard Byzantine Institute)

UNITED STATES, AUSTIN, TEXAS:
>   Menil Gallery

NOTES

CHAPTER 2

1 A label of convenience: The Angeli dynasty took over from the Comneni in 1185.

CHAPTER 7

1 Pendentives are inverted sphericl triangles that rise over the crossing of a cruciform church and form the circular base of the cupola.

2 It is often assumed that St. Sophia is a particular female saint: In fact, it is primarily a christological title (like *Pantocrator*)—though later legend invented a matron St. Sophia and her three daughters, Faith, Hope, and Charity!

CHAPTER 8

1 One case only supports this view, St. Sophia, Salonica, ninth century, but it seems very plausible.

CHAPTER 12

1 V. Lossky and L. Ouspensky, *The Meaning of Icons* (Olten, 1952), p.33.

2 Ibid.

3 This is the meaning of the famous remark of a martyr of the iconoclast crisis, St. Stephen the Younger (ob.c.764): "The icon is a door." (Migne, P.G. 100, 113A).

4 This is the last of the general (or "universal") councils of the whole Church. It met in 787 to define the true nature of the icon and to condemn iconoclasm (though the controversy dragged on till 843— "the Triumph of Orthodoxy"— when icons were finally restored to official use).

5 Dogmatic Decree, Seventh Ecumenical Council, Nicaea II, Mansi, *Concilia*, XIII, 377 B.E.

6 The Cross was the one primordial Christian image accepted by the Byzantine iconoclasts, though of course, without a figure of Christ on the Cross. Leontius of Cyprus points out (pg. 93, 1273D, 1384D) that the psychospiritual mechanism is the same as with an icon: When we venerate the Cross, we are "venerating the crucified Christ, not the wood" in itself. If the arms of the cross get separated from each other, they are then mere pieces of wood, "to be thrown away or burned."

7 *On Icons*, III.4, (ed. Kotter, p. 143), citing Basil, *On the Holy Spirit*, XVIII.45. Basil is talking about honoring the Father through the Son, but his remark is constantly cited in defense of the icon by later Fathers.

8 The iconoclasts made the basic philosophical error of claiming a true image must be of "one substance" with its prototype, but the very word "image" suggests difference as well as similaritiy.

9 *On Icons* I.17, ed. Kotter, p. 93.

10 Council of Constantinople (869–70), Canon 3. (H. Denzinger, *Enchiridion Symbolorum*, Barcelona, 1957), 337, pp. 164–165.

11 Used both in Confirmation (in Orthodoxy, part of baptismal initiation) and for the anointing of the sick and dying.

12 *Letter on the Cult of the Holy Images*, pg. 100, 505B (so, decree of Nicaea II; Mansi *Concilia XIII*, 269E). "If the person depicted is full of grace, the material object (the icon) shares in that grace to an appropriate extent" (St. John of Damascus, *On Icons* I.36). Cf. The Nicene Decree: "When we honor and venerate an icon, we receive sanctification" (Mansi, *Concilia XIII*, 269 E).

13 *On Icons*, II.8, I.4, ed. Kotter, pp. 74, 77–78.

14 Citations from original patristic sources (the Greek Fathers) are quoted from Migne's magisterial *Patrologia Graeca*, except where a modern scholarly edition exists. A most useful selection of these (and some modern) texts is provided by

Bishop K. Ware in "The Theology of the Icon: A Short Anthology" (*Eastern Christian Review VIII.1*, pp. 3–10), on which I have drawn heavily.

15 *On Icons*, I.16, ed. Kotter, pp. 89, 90, 92.

16 Gervase Mathew, *Byzantine Aesthetics*, (London, 1963), pp. 23–24.

17 A phrase of St. Gregory Nazianzen.

18 Pg. 93, 1604 AB.

19 *Antirrheticos* III.ii5, pg. 94, 420A.

20 This of course is equally true of the Christian poet, writer, musician or, architect.

21 Some patristic writers link the Greek words *kalos* (beautiful) and *kalein* (to call)—the etymology is fanciful, but the insight authentic.

22 *Theologie de l'icone*, (Paris, 1960), p. 215.

23 Lossky and Ouspensky, op. cit., p. 209.

24 For those wishing to read further about the theology of the icon, the best book for beginners is probably still the Lossky-Ouspensky, *Meaning of Icons* (1952). On the Byzantine theology of the icon, see P. Alexander, *The Patriarch Nicephorus of* Constantinople (Oxford, 1958), especially pp. 22–54, and 189–214; and C. von Schonborn, *L'icone du Christ: fondements théologiques (*Eribourg, 1976); (he takes the story up to Nicaea II, A.D. 787). One might also mention L. Ouspensky's *La Theologie de l'Icone dans l'Eglise Orthodoxe*, (Paris, 1960), now translated into English; and especially the admirable work by J. Pelikan, *Image Dei: The Byzantine Apology for Icons* (Yale University Press, 1990); and his *Spirit of Eastern Christendom*, ch. 3: "Images of the Invisible" (Chicago University Press, 1974). H. Belting's *Likeness and Presence* ("a history of the image before the era of Art") skillfully links history, theology, and artworks (Chicago University Press, 1994).

BIBLIOGRAPHY

These are the books that I have consulted.
Books and publications that I recommend are marked*.
Those suitable for beginners are marked #.

BYZANTINE ART AND ARCHITECTURE

#Beckwith, J. *The Art of Constantinople*. Oxford: Phaidon, 1981.

———. *Early Christian and Byzantine Art*. Harmondsworth: Penguin, 1970.

Bryer, A., and J. Herrin. *Iconoclasm*. Birmingham: Centre for Byzantine Studies, 1977.

Bunim, M.S. *Space in Medieval Painting and the Forerunners of Perspective*. New York, 1940.

Delehaye, H. *Synaxaires Byzantins, Menologues, Typica*. London: Variorum Reprint, 1977.

Demus, O. *Byzantine Art and the West*. London: Weidenfeld and Nicolson, 1970.

#*Dionysius of Fourna. *The Painter's Manual*. Trans. Paul Hetherington. Harmondsworth: Pelican, 1982.

*# du Bourguet, P. *Early Christian Art*. London: Weidenfeld and Nicolson, 1972.

Ebersholt, J. *La Miniature Byzantine*. Paris and Brussels: Vanoest, 1926.

#Gough, M. *The Origins of Christian Art*. London: Thames and Hudson, 1973.

Grabar, A. *The Beginnings of Christian Art*. London: Thames and Hudson, 1967.

———. *Byzantium: Byzantine Art in the Middle Ages*. London: Methuen, 1966.

———. *L'Empereur dans l'art byzantin*. London: Variorum Reprint, 1971.

———. *Sculptures byzantines de Constantinople*. Paris, 1963.

#Hutter, I. *Early Christian and Byzantine*. Herbert History of Art and Architecture. Herbert Press, 1988.

Katzenstein, R., and E. Savage-Smith. *The Leiden Aratea*. New York: J.P. Getty Museum, 1988.

*Kitzinger, E. *The Art of Byzantium and the Medieval West*. Bloomington, Indiana, 1976.

*———. *Byzantine Art in the Making*. London: Faber, 1977.

Kitzinger, E., and Kitzinger, E. Sr. *Portraits of Christ*. Harmondsworth: Penguin, 1940.

Krautheimer, R. *Early Christian and Byzantine Architecture*. London: Pelican History of Art, 1975.

#Loverance, R. *Byzantium*. London: British Museum Publications, 1988.

#Lowden, J. *Early Christian and Byzantium Art*. London: Phaidon, 1997.

Mango, C. *Byzantine Architecture*. London/Milan: Faber/Electra, 1978.

Mathew, G. *Byzantine Aesthetics*. London: John Murray, 1963.

Millet, G. *Recherches sur l'Iconographie de l'Evangile, d'apres les monuments de Mistra, de Macédoine et du Mont-Athos*. Paris, 1916.

#Runciman, S. *Byzantine Style and Civilization*. Harmondsworth: Penguin, 1975.

#Talbot-Rice, D. *The Appreciation of Byzantine Art*. Oxford: Oxford University Press, 1972.

———. *Art of the Byzantine Era*. London: Thames and Hudson, 1963.

———. *The Byzantine Element in Late Saxon Art*. Oxford: Oxford University Press, 1947.

———. *Byzantine Painting, the Last Phase*. London: Weidenfeld and Nicolson, 1968.

Van der Meer, F. *Early Christian Art*. London: Faber, 1967.

Weitzmann, K. *Art of the Medieval West and its Contacts with Byzantium*. London: Variorum, 1982.

ICONS

#Alpatov, M. *Color in Early Russian Icon Painting*. Moscow: Iskusstvo, 1974.

———. *Early Russian Icon Painting*. Moscow: Iskusstvo, 1978.

#Baggley, J. *Doors of Perception: Icons and their Spiritual Significance*. London: Mowbrays, 1987.

Brenske, H. *Icons, Windows to Eternity*. Brussels: Berghous Verlag, 1990.

#Chatzidakis, M. *Icons of Patmos*. Athens: National Bank of Greece, English edit., 1985.

Cormack, R. *Writing in Gold: Byzantine Society and its Icons*. London: George Philip, 1985.

Evdokimo, P. *L'art de l'Icone: Theologie de la Beauté*. Brussels: Desclée de Bruwer, 1970.

#Gerhard, H.P. *The World of Icons*. London: John Murray, 1971.

Grabar, A. *L'iconoclasme byzantin*. Paris, 1957.

———. *Christian Iconography*. New Jersey: Princeton University Press, 1968.

*Holden, T. *How to Read Icons*. Stylite Publishing Ltd., 1985.

John of Damascus. *On the Divine Images*. (Trans. D. Anderson), New York: St.Vladimir, 1980.

*Kalavrezou-Maxeiner, I. *Byzantine Icons in Steatite*. Vienna, 1985.

#Laurina, V., and V. Pushkariov. *Novgorod Icons, Twelfth to Seventeenth Century*.

Introduction to Russian Icons from the Twelfth to the Fifteenth Century. New York: Mentor-Unesco Art Book, 1962.

Lazarev, V. *Novgorodian Icon-Painting*. Moscow: Iskusstvo Publishers, 1976.

#———. *Moscow School of Icon Painting*. Moscow: Iskusstro, 1980.

———. *Old Russian Murals and Mosaics*. London: Phaidon, 1966.

#————. *Russian Icon Painting.* 6 volumes. Moscow: Iskusstro, 1983 (in Russian).

Limouris, G., ed. *Icons: Windows on Eternity.* Geneva: WCC Publications, 1990.

#Manafis, K.A., ed. *Sinai: Treasures of the Monastery of St. Catherine.* Athens: Ekdotike Athenon, 1990.

*Mango, C., ed. *Art of the Byzantine Empire, Sources and Documents.* New Jersey: Jansen, 1972.

Martin, E.J. *History of the Iconoclastic Controversy.* London: SPCK, 1949.

#Maslenitsyn, St.J. *Jaroslavian Icon-Painting.* Moscow: Iskusstro, 1973.

#Mathew, G. *Byzantine Aesthetics.* London: John Murray, 1963.

McGuire, Henry. *The Icons of Their Bodies: Saints and Their Images in Byzantium.* Princeton, New Jersey: Princeton University Press, 1996.

Millet, G. *Researches sur l'Iconographic de l'Evangile.* Paris, 1916.

Ouspensky, L. *Theology of the Icon.* New York: St. Vladimir's Press, 1978.

#————, and V. Lossky. *The Meaning of Icons.* New York: St.Vladimir's Press, 1982.

#Papageorgiou, A. *Icons of Cyprus.* London: Barrie and Jenkins, 1969.

Pelikan, J. *Imago Dei: The Byzantine Apologia for Icons.* New Haven/London: Yale University Press, 1990.

————. *The Spirit of Eastern Christendom, 600-1700. The Christian Tradition,* Vol. II. Chicago: University of Chicago Press, 1974.

#*Ramos-Poquim, G. *The Technique of Icon Painting.* London: Burns and Oates, 1990.

Salko, N. *Early Russian Painting, Eleventh to Thirteenth Centuries.* Leningrad: Khudozhink, 1982.

Schonborn, C. von. *L'icone du Christ: fondements theologique.* Fribourg, 1976.

\#*Smirnova, E. *Moscow Icons, Fourteenth to Seventeenth Centuries.* Oxford: Phaidon, 1989.

\#——. *Moscow Icons.* Oxford: Phaidon, 1986.

\#Sophocleous, S. *Cyprus: Icons Through the Ages.* Nicosia: A.G. Leventis Foundation, 2000.

\#*Sorokin, Inna. *Byzantine Art in the Collections of Soviet Museums.* (Trans. A.V. Bank.), Leningrad, 1977.

Stuart, J. *Ikons.* London: Faber, 1975.

Talbot-Rice, D. and Talbot-Rice, T. *Icons and their Dating.* London: Thames and Hudson, 1974.

*Talbot-Rice, T. *Icons, Art and Devotion.* London: Bracken Books, 1993.

Taverner, J., and Mother Thekla. *Ikons, Meditation in Words and Music.* London: Fount, 1994.

\#*Taylor, J. *Icon Painting.* Oxford: Phaidon Press, 1979.

*Trubetskoi, E.N. *Icons: Theology in Color.* New York, 1973.

Underwood, P.A., ed. *The Kariye Djami.* 3 vols., London: Routledge and Kegan Paul, 1975.

Ware, K. "The Theology of the Icon: A Short Anthology," *Eastern Churches Review.* Vol. XIII. Oxford, 1976.

\#Weitzmann, K. *Icons from Southeast Europe and Sinai.* London: Thames and Hudson, 1966.

\#——. *The Icon, Holy Images Sixth to Fourteenth Centuries.* London: Chatto and Windus, 1978.

——. *The Monastery of St.Catherine at Mount Sinai: The Icons.* Princeton University Press, 1976.

Weitzmann, K., et. al. *The Icon.* London: Bracken Books, 1982

\#Yevseyeva, L.M., et. al. *Early Tver Painting.* Moscow: Iskusstvo, 1983.

Mosaics and Wall Paintings

Demus, O. *Byzantine Mosaic Decoration*. London: R.K.P., 1976.

#Fischer, P. *Mosaic, History and Technique*. London: Thames and Hudson, 1971.

King, R. *Roman Painting*. Cambridge: Cambridge University Press, 1991.

Mathew, G. *Byzantine Aesthetics*. London, 1963.

Meyer, Peter. *Byzantine Mosaics*. London: Batsford, 1952.

Ravenna Mosaics. London: Arts Council, n.d.

Rice, D.T. *Byzantine Frescoes from Yugoslavian Churches*. London: Fontana Unesco, 1962.

Painting

*Alberti, L.B. *On Painting*. Trans. John R. Spenser. New Haven: Yale University Press, 1956.

*Ayres, J. *The Artist's Craft, a history of Tools, Techniques and Materials*. London: Phaidon, 1985.

*Baxendall, M. *Painting and Experience in Fifteenth Century Italy*. Oxford: Oxford University Press, 1972.

*Binski, P. *Medieval Craftsmen: Painters*. London: British Museum Press, 1991.

*Cennino, C. *The Craftsman's Handbook*. Trans. Daniel V. Thompson, Jr. London: Dover, 1954.

Paint and Painting. London: Tate Gallery Publications Dept., 1982.

*Thompson, D.V. *Materials and Techniques of Medieval Painting*. New York: Dover, 1956.

*Waldon, S. *The Ravished Image*. London: Weidenfeld and Nicolson, 1985.

Wehlte, K. *The Materials and Techniques of Painting*. Trans. U. Dix. New York: Van Norstrand, 1982.

Enamel, Gems and Jewels, Glass, Metalwork

#Cherry, J. *Medieval Craftsmen: Goldsmiths*. London: British Museum Publications, 1992.

De Mely, F., and C.E. Ruelle. *Les Lapidaires de l'Antiquité et du Moyen Age*. Vol. 3. Paris: Leroux, 1902.

*Evans, Joan. *Magical Jewels of the Middle Ages and the Renaissance*. Oxford: Clarendon, 1922.

Halleux, R., and J. Schamp. *Les Lapidaires grecs*. Paris: Societé des Belles Lettres, 1985.

Kunz, G.F. *The Curious Lore of Precious Stones*. New York: Dover, 1941.

London Gemstones, Geological Museum Publication. Before 1986.

#*Maryon, J. *Metalwork and Enamelling*. New York: Dover, rev.ed. 1971.

Strosahl, J.P. *A Manual of Cloisonné and Champlevé Enamelling*. London: Thames and Hudson, 1982.

*Theophilus. *On Divers Arts*. New York: Dover, 1979.

*Vose, R.H. *The Antique Collector's Guides: Glass*. London: Ebury Press, 1975.

*Wessel, K. *Byzantine Enamels from the Fifth to the Thirteenth Centuries*. Trans. Irene R. Gibbons. Dublin: Irish University Press, 1969.

Textiles

*Baines, P. *Spinning Wheels, Spinners and Spinning*. London: B.T. Batsford, 1989.

*Christie, A.H. *English Medieval Embroidery,* Oxford, 1938.

Sandberg, G. *Indigo Textiles, Technique and History*. London: A. and C. Black, 1989.

Studley, V. *Making Artist's Tools*. New York: Van Norstrand, 1979.

*Thomas, A.W. *Colors from the Earth*. New York: Van Norstrand, 1980.

Thurston, V. *The Use of Vegetable Dyes*. Dryad Press, 1977.

TECHNOLOGY

Blair, and Ramsey. *English Medieval Industries*. Hambledon
Press, 1991.

Singer, Holmyard, Hall, and Williams, eds. *A History of
Technology*. Oxford, 1956.

*White, L., Jr. *Medieval Technology and Social Change*.
Oxford: Clarendon Press, 1962.

*———. *Medieval Religion and Technology, Collected Essays*.
Berkeley: University of California Press, 1978.

HISTORY

#Baynes and Moss. *Byzantium, an Introduction*. Oxford:
Clarendon Press, 1962.

Byron. *The Byzantine Achievement*. London: RKP, 1987. pp.
330-1453.

Clucas, L. *The Byzantine Legacy in Eastern Europe*. New
York: Eastern European Monographs, 1988.

Coldsteam, N. *Masons and Sculptors*. London: British Museum
Publications, 1991.

Davis, R.H.C. *History of Medieval Europe from Constantine
to Saint Louis*. London: Longman, 1957.

Dawson, C. *Religion and the Rise of Western Culture*. New
York: Sheed and Ward, 1950.

Fox, R.L. *Pagans and Christians*. New York: Harper and Row,
1986.

*Haskins, C.H. *The Renaissance of the Twelfth Century*.
Cambridge: Harvard University Press, 1955.

Haussig, H.W. *Byzantine Civilization*. London: Thames and
Hudson, 1971.

*Huitzenga, J. *The Waning of the Middle Ages*.
Harmondsworth: Penguin, 1972.

Hussey, J.M. *The Byzantine World*. London: Hutchinson,
1970.

———. *The Orthodox Church in the Byzantine Empire*.
Oxford: Clarendon Press, 1986.

Kidson, P. *The Medieval World*. London: Hamlyn, 1967.

Lauritzen. *Venice*. London: Weidenfeld and Nicolson, 1978.

Mango, C. *Byzantium, The Empire of New Rome*. London: Weidenfeld and Nicolson, 1980.

C. McEvedy, ed. *The Penguin Atlas of Medieval History*. Harmondsworth: Penguin, 1961.

Phillippides, M., trans. *The Fall of the Byzantine Empire, a Chronicle by George Sphrantzes*. Amherst: University of Massachusetts Press, 1980.

Norwich, J.J. *Byzantium: The Apogee*. London: Viking, 1991.

———. *Byzantium: The Early Centuries*. Vol. 1 and 2. London: Viking, 1980.

Southern, R.W. *The Making of the Middle Ages*. London: Hutchinson, 1953.

#Talbot-Rice, D. *The Byzantines*. London: Thames-Hudson, 1962.

#Talbot-Rice, T. *Everyday Life in Byzantium*. London: Batsford, 1967.

#Whitting, P. *Byzantium: An Introduction*. Oxford: Blackwell, 1971.

EASTERN ORTHODOX CHRISTIANITY

Bur, J. *How to Understand the Virgin Mary*. London: S.C.M., 1992.

Cabasilas, N. *Life in Christ*. Margeret Lisney, ed. London: Churchman Publishing, 1989.

#Every, G. *Understanding Eastern Christianity*. London: S.C.M., 1978.

Mantzaridis, G.I. *The Deification of Man*. Trans. L. Sherrard. New York: St.Vladimir's Press, 1984.

Meyendorff, J. *Byzantine Legacy in the Orthodox Church*. New York: Crestwood, 1982.

———. *Christ in Eastern Christian Thought*. New York: St. Vladimir's Press, 1975.

Meyendorff, J., and N. Gendle. *Gregory Palamas, The Triads*. London: SPCK, 1983.

Neale, J.M., trans. *Hymns of the Eastern Church*. London: 1862.

———. *General Introduction to the History of the Holy Eastern Church*. Oxford: Oxford University Press, 1850.

Schmemann. *A Historical Road of Eastern Orthodoxy*. New York: St.Vladimir's Press, 1963.

Walter, C. *Art and Ritual of the Byzantine Church*. London: Variorum, 1982.

#Ware, T. *Orthodoxy*. Harmondsworth: Penguin Books, 1964.

#———. *The Orthodox Way*. London: Mowbray and Company, 1979.

Wellesz, E. *Byzantine Music and Hymnography*. Oxford: Clarendon Press, 1961.

Zernov, N. *The Church of the East Christians*. London: S.P.C.K.,1942.

RUSSIA

#*Billington J. *The Icon and the Axe, an Interpretive History of Russian Culture*. New York: 1966.

Dukes, P.A. *History of Russia,* 2nd ed. London: Macmillan, 1990.

*Duncan, D.D. *Great Treasures of the Kremlin*. New York: Abbeville Press, 1979.

Florovsky, G. *Ways of Russian Theology*. Trans. R. Nichols. Belmont Nordland, 1979.

Guliayev, V. *The Fine Art of Russian Lacquered Miniatures*. Moscow: Aurora Art Publishers, 1993.

Hamilton, G.H. *Art and Architecture of Russia*. Harmondsworth: Pelican History of Art, 1975.

Headlam, A.G. *The Teaching of the Russian Church*. London, 1897.

Kornilovitch, K. *Arts of Russia from the Origins to the End of the Sixteenth Century*. Trans. J. Hogarth. Geneva: Nagel Publishers, 1967.

*Lazarev, V. *Old Russian Murals and Mosaics, Eleventh to Sixteenth Centuries*. Oxford: Phaidon, 1966.

Meyendorff, J. *Byzantium and the Rise of Russia.* Cambridge, 1981.

Ovsianikov, Y. *Invitation to Russia.* London: Conran Octopus, 1989.

Salko, N.B. *Early Russian Painting, Eleventh to Early Thirteenth Centuries.* Leningrad, 1982.

Zernov, N. *Moscow, the Third Rome.* London: S.P.C.K., 1937.
———. *The Russians and Their Church.* London: S.P.C.K., 1944.

MISCELLANEOUS

Bucknell, P.A. *Entertainment and Ritual.* London: Stainer and Bell, 1979.

Cameron, R., ed. *The Other Gospels.* London: Lutterworth, 1985.

*Cole, A. *Perspective.* National Gallery. London: Dorling Kindersley, 1992.

Dengerink, A. *Reflections on the Arts.* Unpublished paper, Institute of Christian Studies, 1987.

Evo, U. *Beauty in the Middle Ages.* New Haven: Yale University Press, 1986.

*Fox, Sir D.S. *St. George, The Saint with Three Faces.* London: The Kensal Press, 1983.

#Gombrich, E.H. *The Story of Art*, 13th ed. Oxford: Phaidon, 1978.

*Grabar, O. *The Formation of Islamic Art.* New Haven: Yale University Press, 1973.

Harvey, J. *The Medieval Architect.* London: Wayland Publishers, 1972.
———. *Medieval Craftsmen.* London: Batsford, 1975.

Hopper, V.S. *Medieval Number Symbolism.* New York: Cooper Square Publishers, Inc., 1969.

Ivins, W.M. *On the Rationalization of Sight.* New York, 1938.

LeGoff, J. *Time, Work and Culture in the Middle Ages.* Chicago: University of Chicago Press, 1980.

Magnus, A. *Book of Minerals.* Trans. D. Wyckoff. Oxford: Clarendon Press, 1967.

McGinn, B., J. Meyendorff, and J. Leclerq. *Christian Spirituality, Origins to the Twelfth Century.* London: S.C.M, 1985.

McPartlan, P. *One in 2000?* London: St. Paul's Press, 1993.

Shelby, L.R. *Gothic Design Techniques.* Carbondale, 1977.

Whitlock, R. *Here Be Dragons.* London: Allen and Unwin, 1983.

Wilson I. *The Turin Shroud.* New York: Penguin, 1979.

Wood, J. *The Nativity, Themes in Art.* Geneva: Scala Books, 1991.

#Woodford, S. *The Cambridge Introduction to Art. Greece and Rome.* Cambridge: Cambridge University Press, 1982.

Young, K. *The Drama of the Medieval Church.* Oxford: Clarendon Press, 1933.

Zarnecki. *The Herbert History of Art and Architecture. Romanesque.* London: Herbert Press, 1971.

EXHIBITION CATALOGUES

#*Bomford, Dunkerton, Gordon, and Roy. *Art in the Making: Italian Art before 1400.* London: National Gallery Publications, 1989.

#*Buckman, David. *Byzantium, Treasures of Byzantine Art and Culture.* London: British Museum Publications, 1995.

Byzantijnse Kunst uit Roemeni Museum. Catalogue printed only in Dutch. Utrecht: Catherijneconvent, 1994–1995.

#Cormack, R., and D. Gaze, eds. *The Art of Holy Russia: Icons from Moscow.* London: Royal Academy, 1998.

#*Acheimastou-Potamianou, M., ed. *From Byzantium to El Greco: Greek Frescoes and Icons.* London: Royal Academy of Arts, 1987.

#*Roderick Grierson, ed. *Gates of Mystery, the Art of Holy Russia.* London: Vanda Museum, 1994.

#*The George R. Hann Collection.* Part I. New York: Christie's, 1980.

*Gendle, Nicholas. *Icons in Oxford.* Oxford: Christ Church, 1980.

#Temple, Richard. *Icons, a Sacred Art: 30th Anniversary Catalogue.* London: Temple Gallery, 1989.

*Ahlborn, R.E., and E. Ahlborn. *Russian Copper Icons and Crosses from the Kunz Collection.* Washington, D.C.: Smithsonian Institute, 1991.

#Piatnitsky, Y. et. al., eds. *Sinai, Byzantium, Russia.* London: St. Catherine Foundation, 2000.

#Vassuaki, M., ed. *Mother of God: Representations of the Virgin in Byzantine Art.* Milan: Skira, 2000.

#Weitzmann, K., ed. *Age of Spirituality.* New York: Metropolitan Museum of Art, 1979.

LIBRARIES AND RESEARCH FACILITIES CONSULTED BY LINETTE MARTIN

Centre of Economic Botany, Kew

Dumbarton Oaks Research Library, Washington D.C.

Oxford Libraries: Ashmolean, Art History Department, Bodleian, Central, History Faculty, Museum of Science, House of St. Gregory and St. Macrina, Pusey House, Rewley House

Wellcome Institute, London

BIOGRAPHY

LINETTE MARTIN, an Anglican, was a professional dancer who appeared in Guildford Repertory Theatre, with the Glyndebourne Opera Ballet, at the Edinburgh Festival, and in Pantomime and Variety around England. She worked for a number of years in the L'Abri Fellowship in Switzerland, then in Princeton while her husband attended seminary, and for many years in London. At different times she worked as a waitress, artist's model, theatrical costumière, and children's tutor. As a freelance journalist, she wrote for religious and secular publications in the United Kingdom, Ireland, the United States, and New Zealand. Her books include *Hans Rookmaaker: A Biography* and *Practical Praying*. In 1984 she was commissioned to write the biography of Cecil Jackson-Cole, the founder of Oxfam. After their son and daughter were grown, she lived for thirteen years with her husband in an Oxfordshire village, where she spent seven years researching and building the largest late-medieval garden in the UK. For six years she studied art history, including Byzantine art in Rewley House, Oxford University Department of Continuing Education (now Kellogg College). She died in 1998.